YOU, DISRUPTED

YOU, DISRUPTED

SEIZING THE LIFE YOU WANT
BY SHAKING, BREAKING, AND
CHALLENGING EVERYTHING

TODD MITCHEM

Prometheus Books

59 John Glenn Drive
Amherst, New York 14228

Published 2017 by Prometheus Books

Cover design by Liz Mills
Cover design © Prometheus Books

Inquiries should be addressed to
Prometheus Books
59 John Glenn Drive
Amherst, New York 14228
VOICE: 716–691–0133
FAX: 716–691–0137
WWW.PROMETHEUSBOOKS.COM

21 20 19 18 17   5 4 3 2 1
Library of Congress Cataloging-in-Publication Data Pending

ISBN 978–1–63388–295–9 (pbk)
ISBN 978–1–63388–296–6 (ebook)

Printed in the United States of America

For Diana, my love, who always believes in me
and who made this all possible with her unwavering support.
For my family, who never stops seeing the best in me.
For my best friend, Michael, who was there for me from the beginning.
For Tyler, Kariana, and Roby, who inspire me to be better every day.
This book is me, all of me, for you.

CONTENTS

FOREWORD

Deb Mitchem

One of my more vivid memories of Todd as a young teen took place about a year after his father, Doug, and I married. Todd was thirteen, already nearly my height, and he thought he was a really cool dude. Actually, he was really cool; it just wasn't a good idea to let him know quite how cool he was—he didn't need much encouragement!

We were shopping and, all of a sudden, I realized he wasn't next to the cart I was pushing. I turned around and noticed this big crowd in the aisle behind me, circling someone I couldn't see. I rushed back, thinking Todd had somehow fallen and hurt himself. What met my eyes was this really cool teen, in his red parachute pants (hey, it was the '80s), breakdancing in the aisle to the Michael Jackson song on the store's sound system. The crowd of people had gathered to watch, because Todd just decided to start dancing in the aisle—and because he was good. They applauded when he finished and went on with their shopping. As a new mom (since I didn't have kids of my own), I wasn't quite sure what I should say. So, I said the first thing that popped into my head: "Next time, put your hat on the floor so they'll tip you for your entertainment."

That was over thirty-two years ago, and it is only one of many stories I have about Todd and his "Disruptor" mentality—not worrying about what people think if his instinct tells him to do something. His entertainment skills, his zest for living, his tenacity, his ability to see a large obstacle as no more than a small speed bump if he's heading toward something he wants—all those things are part of his personality. After having watched him for years, I have come to know that some of this is an innate part of him—something he was born with or developed unconsciously. He has taken those personality traits, however, and honed them, perfected them, and shared them with others. That's what he's doing in this book—sharing his skills with others. He truly wants people to live life as he knows it can—and should—be lived: with gusto, excitement, challenge, and positive results!

The achievements in his life, to this point, amaze even his father and me. Watching him take some of the risks he's taken has been difficult, because he meets life head-on; we have somewhat more cautious personalities by nature. We know by now, though, he will succeed at whatever he sets his mind to do. It might take him longer than he wants (always), it might be more challenging than he expected (usually), but, in the end, he will get to his goal. And then he'll start all over again with his next goal.

It has been, and continues to be, a wild ride watching this son we love grow, mature, succeed, and prosper. I hope you enjoy just a little bit of the journey—and then set out on your own.

INTRODUCTION

What do we all really want in life? Is it more money, sex, fun, love, satisfying work, or a combination of all and more? This book is about getting all of that, but, more important, it is about teaching you how to disrupt your own life in the positive, without all the excuses and fears we tend to put in our path to a life fulfilled. I have taught countless leaders, companies, industries, and people like you these lessons and, in the end, the one thing that I have found that stops everyone from truly living up to their potential can be summed up as a lack of understanding of how to take a risk. When you read this book, you will see that we, as individuals, are in control of something very critical as we embark on a paradigm shift around risk. Disruptors love risk because, as you will learn, they have discovered how to take beautiful ones, learn from any mishaps, and maintain a powerful positive attitude along the way. That sums up my journey in this life as well.

When I was born, I weighed in at a whopping eleven and a half pounds! Clearly, I was meant to be a Disruptor from the first day. I wish I could tell you that I was some sort of visionary and, from an early age, had it all figured out. But I didn't. I was born in a small town in West Virginia and lived in a trailer at the bottom of my grandparents' property until I was five. So, yes, just like most of the population, I had a life filled with challenges, but they certainly didn't end there. My sister was born and was permanently mentally disabled by the second day of her life. This unexpected circumstance caused a ripple effect through my parents' marriage, my sister's life, and me, changing the path of my life forever.

Eventually, due to the added struggles of having a disabled child as well as personal differences, my parents divorced and my life was ripped apart. I would go from my mother's house to my father's house, and I felt lost for a very long time. There was no stability in my life and I struggled to fit in—all the way from elementary school through high school—mainly because I was viewed as a rebellious and "weird" child. But, through all this time, I was only trying to find myself. As time passed, my life didn't get easier: my mother was stricken with cancer, twice; I was nearly killed in a car accident at the highest point of my corporate career, when I was the top leadership advisor in my company and was speaking to companies all over the world. However, despite the rough patches, I managed to find the best in my journey through life. I worked as an entertainer, traveled the globe, took huge risks, worked as a consultant with some of the top companies in the world, and ultimately took the biggest risk of my life: changing my career path completely to take on the emerging marijuana industry as a leader, founder, and government-affairs consultant. Whew! It has been a bumpy journey, to say the least.

Along the way, I have achieved some amazing successes and, of course, some amazing failures. This book details some of those successes and failures, coupled with new concepts and learning activities to impart some knowledge I have gained, in order that you, too, can have what you want to have and be where you want to be. As I write this, I have never been happier in my life. All of my challenges, falls, and fails have led me to this place, where I am able to articulate a new way of disrupting the most important person in your life: YOU.

I figured out how to take life by the tail and deal with risk by shaking, breaking, and forcing myself to challenge everything. I experienced life on my own terms by overcoming great obstacles without excuses—and that's what I want to teach you. As I looked back on my life and all of my experiences as I was writing this book, I had a realization: I have accomplished more than even I had believed I would. In addition to the great experiences I get to share with you

throughout this book, I also reflect on all of the amazing relationships I have with my select friends, kids, fiancée, sister, mother, stepfather, father, and stepmom. To say the least, I had to go through
all of the ups and downs, figuring everything out along the way, to
become the leader I am today, to stand for what I believe in, and to
disrupt everything.

I must admit, I have read a ton of self-help books, but one thing
that always frustrated me about them was that they would give me
great information, stories, and hints about becoming a better me and
reaching success, but then they would leave the most important part
for me to figure out: the HOW. I would read a book and then say to
myself, "But, I don't live on a mountaintop in solitude. I live in the
real world and I'm struggling" or "I have done everything possible
to put together a plan for my future, but I have fear of taking a risk
and failing. How do I get rid of that?" I wanted these books, ideas,
and authors to articulate the learning as real examples I could use.
So when I started down the path of writing *You, Disrupted*, I wanted
it to be everything other books had missed. The REAL examples
pertaining to an average person who is struggling in many areas of
his or her life, but who wants to do work on him- or herself to get
better. So, I decided to write that book, where I let the reader join
me and experience parts of my journey, and to understand firsthand
how the lessons I discuss in this book are 100 percent applicable to
your life. NOW.

If you observe the world as I do, you, too, feel that our society is in a
crisis of epic proportions. That is why I feel this book is timed perfectly.
To tap into this knowledge, at this moment in history, is more critical
than anything we have ever experienced. Mostly, because we are surrounded by such a high level of overstimulation pervading our lives on
a consistent and daily basis. Instead of using all of our daily activities
to become disruptive, we are slowly destroying our happiness in an
outwardly directed, insatiable need to do more, yet we accomplish less,

while destroying everyone around us if they get in our way. We are terrified of taking real risks such as learning, growing as people, and working toward common goals for greatness. Meanwhile, we broadcast an appearance of happiness on every social media outlet we can, while hiding the unlived dreams and desires inside our little shells. You have to realize that there is never really a perfect time to take a risk, but when you do stop being afraid of the unknown, you will see that all of those goals inside of you are waiting to be disrupted into being.

With prescription-medication addiction at an all-time high, in a society that's on the verge of legalized marijuana, with kids becoming more and more addicted to technology, with depression penetrating all levels of society, and where there are employees changing jobs every two to five years, we have entered a period in which books like *You, Disrupted* are becoming an essential tool to help guide us into a more fulfilled life that starts to have real meaning and purpose, as opposed to a made-up life online.

You, Disrupted also conquers the concept that our work lives and personal lives are no longer split. Today, we are connected twenty-four hours a day; we are always living in both worlds, and sometimes we can't even distinguish if some things are personal or work-related. Therefore, to finally draw the line and integrate these two worlds, I felt that we needed a book encompassing both business and personal success to create our path toward a more fulfilling and distinguishable future.

As you take this journey into harnessing your Disruptor and Disruptive Influencer, I will be there with you at every step. After all, I lived each and every story, having absolutely no idea in what direction I would be heading or how some of the events were going to end. The stories in this book are real. While I changed the names of some people, to protect them, I told the real, factual story each time. This book is not about meditating your way through life, nor is it filled with psychobabble jargon; that may work for some, but this book is not about that and, frankly, we don't have time for that. I am a real person who found a path that you, too, can travel as you apply the learning from this book. It can help you design a blueprint for how to truly change some or all parts of your life. I will share deeply personal parts of my story as an entertainer, business leader, corporate executive, and, eventually, entrepreneur in the marijuana industry. It will be a wild ride, but the point is that you will see that anything and everything can be conquered—you just have to trust yourself.

Before you read on, you need to make a promise to yourself. You need to promise yourself that you will do the work, apply the lessons, and start to think of your limited time on Earth as a challenge to get as much done as possible. It's the only way you can accomplish everything you want to do and live the life you've always wanted. But, all of that rests on you and only you. If you do the work that needs to be done—not just on the outside, but, more importantly, on the inside—you will have an easier and faster way of reaching your goals. You need to understand that every person on this planet is vital to a new, positive future filled with disruptive thinking that leads to fulfilled lives. So, you need to ask yourself if this is for you—a life lived fully. Ask yourself if you are ready to change what's not working and work hard for what will. You must promise yourself that you will start to take a hard look at your relationships, your job, your desires, your family, and the way you are currently existing in the world. The life lessons I'm sharing in *You, Disrupted* will change you as they did me, but only if you do the work. This is the biggest risk of all—growing. This growth that I keep mentioning is a new perspective, a new thought process for dealing with stressful situations, becoming a better you, seeing the opportunities, overcoming obstacles, and, most of all, kicking the fear out of your way, so that you can reach your visions and goals. This book will help you start a journey to a life that is the epic world you have dreamed it could be. I have learned that you can't do epic stuff with simple people. You can only do epic stuff as a smart risk taker who becomes a disruptive force. So, get ready. Let's begin.

CHAPTER 1

DISRUPTION IS NOT DESTRUCTION (NO MORE INNOVATION; START DISRUPTING)

disrupt: to cause (something) to change, to be unable to continue in the same way

TIME TO BREAK STUFF AND HUSTLE

Aday in November 2013. 9:15 a.m. Denver.

My hands are sweating. Sweating. That has never happened to me before. I have never been so excited and terrified at the same time. As I look around the O.penVAPE office, I feel as if I am in a dream. A thousand thoughts run through my head, but the ones that stand out the most are: *Is this real? Is this actually happening? What have I done? What am I about to do?* For the first time in my life, I feel afraid. *What if I make a mistake? What if I say something that will ruin me for life?* I am freaking out inside. At the end of the hallway, I see my fellow leaders trickling into the office. *Keep your head on, Todd, and don't let them know you are freaking out about this.* As I twitch nervously, I look down at my phone to check the time, but instead I focus on another text from a former client that just flashed on my screen. This time it's from a prominent beer-making company, the third such message today, and all of them from past clients. The message reads, "We can never work with you again." *Wow. Really? It's that bad? Okay . . . breathe, here they come, followed by the camera crew. . . .*

A man introduces himself to me, his dark hair and clean-cut look emanating a powerful and intelligent reporter style. As we start to talk about what we are about to put on global news for the first time, I am, on the surface, calm, strong, and confident. On the inside, I am just trying not to screw up any words or talking points, which could cause a real mess for the company. *What have I done? Oh yeah . . . something huge . . . something disruptive.*

I show the reporter and his camera crew around the office so that they can get the best shots and pick and choose what areas they would like to use for this interview. After a short debrief, the time for the on-camera interview nears; I collect myself and look at the microphone logo—this is seriously something I have only seen on TV: CNN. Everyone takes their places, the camera light goes on, and Miguel Marquez of CNN asks, "Todd, so, this is the new world?" My only coherent response was, unbeknownst to me, about to launch the company to top brand status in an instant. "Well Miguel, this IS the future; we are more like a tech company. I guess you could say we are the Google of cannabis, and we grew by over 1,600 percent this year alone." I could see his surprise at the data I had just spit out, but the strongest feeling in that moment was me realizing that I had just fully left the corporate world to take a huge risk in a new industry with the new and growing company. That company was O.penVAPE, a small brand that, at the time, was manufacturing and selling cannabis-filled devices that vaporized marijuana on inhalation. This turning point of my career began a three-year journey in a totally different direction and disrupted my life completely. How? By literally breaking my career completely and jumping headfirst into a new industry that was in its infancy. In one moment of disruption, I set on a dangerous mission of changing the direction of my career. This abrupt change in direction allowed me to be a part of the most rapid-moving, stigmatized, complex, and talked-about industry in history thus far. I didn't just want to be a part of it, I wanted to disrupt it completely, help create standards that protect the consumer, and establish a relationship between the government and the cannabis operators. The experience of a new and wildly different industry was like living through two life-times. It was terrifying, thrilling, life-altering—but every single step got me where I am today.

BOOM!

"Boom!" is something I say a ton. I use this word because it signifies the breakthroughs in my life that happen through disruption. The great news is that you, too, have the power of the "Boom!" Unfortunately, you either were never told that you had the power to emerge above your current circumstances, or you were so busy going through the motions of everyday routines that you forgot. Did you ever have a vision for your life that was different than it is today? Even if you are wildly successful in a career, do you ever feel a pull to do something more? Or even a burning desire to do something completely different with your life? I once knew an entertainer who was one of the most talented comedians and acting performers I had ever met. He was also a dear friend of mine, and for years I would work day in and day out to motivate him to reach for his full potential. When I say that he was talented, I mean that he could read a script the first time and it sounded like he was the character that the producer had imagined for the part. He was absolute acting perfection. He would walk on a stage to perform comedy and in an instant the audience loved him. His presence on stage was mind-blowing, and he could have become one of the most successful performers of all time. Sad news: he never did. He settled for a life that was a fraction of what he could have become. This was not because he never had a chance but because he was afraid of success. Whenever he was about to attain recognition that would guarantee him fame, he did something to self-sabotage the opportunity. That is not disruption, that is certainly destruction. I wish I could tell you that he finally disrupted this mental block and became a famous entertainer, but unfortunately he ran out of time. He died of cancer at a very early age, and all his potential died with him. My friend's death impacted me greatly on many levels. The first one being the devastation of losing a dear friend much too soon, and the second one being anger. Anger that he wasted his time and talent thinking that he always had more time. Anger at him for not doing what he could each day, to let his inner Disruptor emerge.

So, as we begin the book, I want you to take an inventory of your life. What are you not doing that you need to go after now, like your life depends on it? The harsh truth is that your life DOES depend on it, or at least a life of thriving does. Humans, at least as far as I can see, were not meant to eke through life, tracking receipts, checking social media, and overall wasting hours a day only to then perish with great disruptive stuff still bottled up inside of them. Throughout my years of speaking and meeting thousands of people from all walks of life and all over the world, I came to realize that there are two types of people. The first is someone who lets the fear of success or anything new control every decision, just to self-sabotage in the end. The second is a person who has not found a talent or a power that they can be disruptive with in order to reach maddening heights of success.

So ask yourself this, are you a Disruptor? In other words, have you been bold in your recent choices and decisions? If not, I have one goal on this journey that we will be taking together throughout the book, and that is to get you started on a new adventure. Remember, you can't get from here to there unless you are willing to take the step in the direction you want to go. And let me be clear, it's a *step* we are taking with this book, not a jump to the moon. Everyone needs to start somewhere, and the best part is—regardless of what you have done, not done, or wish you had done—you can start moving in a new direction again, but this time, *now*. If you are reading this, you are breathing. Your time is not up.

Disruption is inside all of us. To disrupt literally means "to change direction." That's exactly what happened to me on that November day. Less than a month before the interview, I was the senior vice president of Business Development for a prominent and respected company in corporate America when, almost overnight, I switched industries. I went from Corporate America to The Cannabis Industry. It was a huge leap, and it changed everything in my life. So why would any sane person leave a stable, rewarding career that was simultaneously filled with professional challenges? Let me ask you first, what would it take you to get out of the rut? We all get stuck at some points in our lives. Where are you stuck now? What would you like to change about your job, life, relationship, or any other space of your life? Write it down and be honest with your answer. If you are satisfied with everything, then write down what you would like to improve on.

Throughout my life I have felt stuck many times, especially in my career path. I saw that I wasn't being as disruptive as I could be, and I could feel inside me that this was my chance to disrupt what wasn't working. I wanted to disrupt a major aspect of my life; to do that, I had to become my own catalyst and get myself out of the rut I was in at that time. After all, I was not getting any younger, there weren't many more prospects to advance within my current company, and I always pushed my kids to take risks to improve their situation or go in a more fitting direction that worked better for them. So the last thing I ever want to demonstrate to my children is cowardice when life gets stuck. The only thing I could do was leave the corporate world and head in a new direction to expand my skill set and make a small, but positive, difference in the world to help people like my mother have at least a few extra days of life.

WHY THIS BOOK AND WHY NOW?

What I realized, and what you need to realize, is that we are all racing headfirst to our eventual death. The biggest risk we all take is to head toward that inevitable future having never tried to reach our goals. It's insanity. While that sounds morbid and not very motivational, it is a reality we have forgotten. Therefore, this book is a call to action to make the most of the time we have left. To take risks, to challenge ourselves, and to fully live the life we were meant to live. I know if I take my life by the horns and refuse to be slowed down by fear of challenge and change, I bet, on my deathbed, I will NOT say, "Oh no, I did too much!" Now is a great time to wake up and go get what we have always wanted out of life, because we have already mastered the part of life called procrastination, and it's killing our progress.

This fact remains constant: we will all die. And yet with limited time, instead of living a fulfilling and powerful life, we are a very depressed society. Depression has become an epidemic to the point that opiate prescription and drug addiction are on the rise at a staggering pace. In 2015, the results of a study by *JAMA: The Journal of the American Medical Association* reported that, from 1999 to 2012, the percentage of Americans on antidepressants increased from 6.8 percent to 13 percent, and that number continues to grow annually.[1] I surmise that the real reason for our depression as a society lies in the fact most of us do not live, not truly. We keep our heads down and our mouths shut (except on social media), and we have lost the skills necessary to make authentic connections, relationships, and real-life changes. I also think we, as a society, are looking for satisfaction in "things" instead of making "mental" changes that would truly impact our fulfillment.

You may be wondering, "So where do I start?" Well, the first stage of becoming the fulfilled Disruptor is to realize that, you, in fact, do want to shake up your life. I am not saying that you will want to shake it into destroying the things you love; what I mean is, shake it up enough to adopt some new ways of thinking and to change things that are not working. I hope after reading this far you have a new sense of urgency—not panic, but urgency—to start becoming a more thoughtful Disruptor. Now, you don't need to invent the next solar-powered airplane that also travels to Mars in order to become fulfilled, but to take action on the ideas you do have, on the solutions that could change your workplace or relationships, and on the positive influence others could utilize.

WHAT IS DISRUPTION?

Our entire civilization was founded on the concept of being disruptive. We have airplanes because two men (and their sister) decided to do some VERY disruptive experiments and proved people can fly. We have amazing smartphones because companies wanted to disrupt how we view our phones. Every invention, gadget, social change, and anything you currently watch on TV or video, is the direct result of a select few individuals who decided it was time to disrupt something they cared about and create a change in the world.

A great example of incredible disruption in business is the iPhone. The idea was to change the way you think about the phone. The phone had already been created, so that's no longer disruptive. What is disruptive is how the phone developers changed (and continue to change) the phone's features. Instead of accepting the phone as a little brick that makes calls and sends messages, innovators made the phone flatter and sleeker with a giant screen on it—that's disrupting the look and functionality of the common cell phone. Then they added a new format for storing and using phone numbers and answering calls—that's disrupting calling. I could go on about every feature, but I think you get the point. The idea does not have to be something new, but the aspects of the idea must be wildly different and thought-provoking.

But disruption is not only for those people who are building groundbreaking products, nor is it only reserved for the new innovator who has the foresight to develop the next popular gadget or company. People can disrupt their lives in huge ways and also in small ways that have impact. Buying a coffee for the person behind you in line is disruptive. Speaking up more at meetings and adding value at work is disruptive. Turning your phone off to really listen to your partner, kids, or friends is disruptive. The key is to have an awareness of what positive disruption looks and feels like at each moment of your day.

Disruption is the catalyst for change sitting inside all of us, just waiting for us to unlock our own potential. It manifests itself in both our mind-set and our actions. If you have a mind-set of disruption, you see the world filled with possibilities you can use to solve your challenges or take you to new heights. A Disruption Mind-set is vital to engage your brain and get it moving in the right direction toward a new way of existing in the world. In your own life, the difference between a Disruption Mind-set and your normal habitual way of living can be subtle and simple. For example, when I want to find a new solution for my executive coaching or corporate development clients, I do not ask myself what has happened in the past. Instead I engage a mind-set of determining what the clients need now. My perspective is based on fresh facts, fresh information, and a focus on new solutions. I always ask about the clients' history and how they have approached situations in the past, but my disruptive focus is centered on the situation at hand. If I want to start a new business or engage with startups to help them elevate their company, again, I look at the merits of the current parameters and seek to disrupt those in a positive and profitable way. For example, our social network, High There!, the world's first global social network for marijuana enthusiasts, worked so quickly and so well because I did not obsess over the details and numbers and how far ahead of us some of the "competitors" like the giants of Facebook, Tinder, or Twitter were, or what the past companies in the marijuana space had attempted to do, or even pay attention to the negative comments from people who voiced doubt about the potential success of High There! Because we were building something never before experienced in our industry, I stayed focused on the same lessons I have written in this book. Keep in mind that until this moment in time there had not been a main-stream app developed for cannabis-loving people to find friends or dates or to just talk about their medical needs for marijuana. I was taking a huge risk by introducing something never before accomplished. So my task to help develop the app could not be met with an internal negative dialogue brought on by listening to naysayers. Instead I had the mind-set that this app was disruptive and different and would make a significant impact to millions of people. I had eliminated any space for doubt. When you engage this mind-set, you will find your passion level increases dramatically. Why does this happen? Because you are now taking intentional actions toward your new vision. These elements are important as we tackle the first part of our journey into a new you, disrupted, where you will begin to realize that disruption is attainable for all of us—and it's not just for business—it applies to every aspect of everyone's life.

DISRUPT THIS . . . LET YOUR IDEAS BE BORN

Let's go back a bit now before High There!'s success, in fact, let's go way back before I even entered into the corporate world. It was 1992 and I had an idea, actually a series of them. At the time, I was out of college and desperately wanted to become a television host, comedian, or actor. At that stage of life, I had an extensive experience performing at nightclubs, bars, and weddings through my DJ company, and with some moderate levels of acting success in a few local commercials and one national commercial. I knew I had potential. All this time, seeds of change were being planted while a calling to entertain and my passion to be a performer were growing. There was no way I could possibly go down the same path as my peers. I can still feel the brief sting of thinking that my life was going to consist of simply getting a job, any job, and then sort of wandering my way through life in a "safe" fashion. When I say "safe," I mean that, at that time of my life, the path that we were told to focus on at school was graduating, going to college, and getting a job in which we make money doing work we cannot stand, just to sustain a life we cannot stand. I simply could not accept that this was supposed to be my future. I wanted to be happy; and in order to do that, I had to focus on my dreams. Something clicked inside me, and I felt that I had to go for it. I just knew that I wanted to be a memorable performer, and my Disruptor inside was pushing me.

My mind was swirling with so many different ideas for the entertainment world, but one of them was bigger than the rest. That idea was creating an interactive comedy show. At the time, I was working as an emcee for a karaoke bar and was already interacting with audiences, so I knew what it would take to pull this off. I knew that in order to achieve the success I wanted, I needed a large audience—which I wasn't going to find in my then hometown of St. Louis. Before I set off into the sunset, though, I began to plan my idea by searching for possible locations, coming up with skits, musical comedy sketches, and—to make the idea even more real in my mind—I started acting as if my ideas were already a reality. You may ask, why would you pretend your idea was working when, in reality, it wasn't? Well, you can call my pretending "a deeper level of planning." See, when I thought my idea was already working and I, of course, was facilitating the show, I would walk myself through every step of the process, notice what could be changed to make things better, how many people would be the ideal audience, and so on. It was my way of planning for a better success when I finally made it into reality.

The same should be true for you. If you allow an amazing idea to flow into your mind, you need to write it down, plan it, and find a way to make it a reality. Take the time to act as if it is working, and then go through all of the key parts; see if you can break your concept, and then figure out how to fix it. Make your idea bulletproof. By doing that, you will quickly find you have more thoughtful solutions inside you than you had dreamed. Let your ideas be born and honor them by giving them the attention they deserve. And there is no rule that says you need to tell others about your plans, so keep it to yourself unless you have supportive people in your life.

THE NAYSAYERS

So, there I was with my idea to create a unique and fully interactive concept for comedy. With limited resources, only $1,400 to my name, and my old car, I was not sure how I was going to make this work. Along with all these obstacles, I also had plenty of naysayers around me. My friends, some family members, and countless others were telling me several key "naysayer" phrases:

> *NO. Don't do it!*
> *It can't work!*
> *It won't work!*

I'm sure you have also heard these same types of comments before. Isn't it interesting how the biggest naysayers are often the people closest to you? While I was brimming with excitement about my idea of revolutionizing the entertainment business, I was surprised to be hit with a barrage of comments fitting into all of the categories of failure, lack of belief, and a need to stifle my hopes. They all apparently believed I would fail and that I should get a "real job" and fall in line like they had. Even after the hail of negativity, I simply could not just quit on my dream and settle for a regular life. My motivation was far too strong to be swayed.

It's important to understand how the outer dialogue and other people's comments begin to impact you. If you listen to the negativity long enough, you start to believe in it and then allow it to influence your decisions; and your ideas—no matter how large or small—they can be destroyed in an instant. That's almost what happened to me. The negative outer dialogue started to influence my positive inner self-talk, and I had fits of doubt and concern. At times, that inner negativity and self-talk was like a cold I could not shake. In fact, when I finally packed up my car and headed for Chicago, I was terrified. Still, with $1,400, my old car, and the constant battle of the loudmouth negative critic against my inner positive hope, I set out and drove to my exciting and uncertain future. What I learned from this experience is that there is a point in your life when you have to stop asking other people how to live your own life and go for it. Even if you face a difficult journey, you do not need the approval of others to succeed or even to embark. At some point in your life, you will need to stop worrying about everyone else's opinion, and only pay attention to yours because the risks you will need to take will be often ones you can't explain.

DOUBT FROZE ME

With all the zest for success, I wish I could tell you that it was easy and that I drove happily along with not a care in the world, passionately heading for my eventual fame; but the road was far more challenging.

About an hour after I left home, I was suddenly flooded with fear and anxiety; I pulled off the freeway and froze. There I was, sitting in my car, completely panicked. A flood of thought was storming through my mind: *What had I done? What was I doing?* I had never been to Chicago, didn't know anyone there, and had no idea how I was going to make it. *Was I making a mistake?* This was the voice of self-doubt, and it was getting louder and louder. After about an hour of panicking on the side of the road, I finally started to calm down. I remembered why I wanted to do this in the first place, and I realized that if I didn't make this move to Chicago, I would always regret the missed opportunity. While I just sat there in my 1987 Honda Accord, I started to reread my notes about my idea and my goals.

After reminding myself of the original plan that was drawn out in my notebook, I shifted my focus to my inner dialogue. Of course, my inner voice was negative and mean, but I knew I had to change it in order to find the courage to move on and figure it out in Chicago. Instead of allowing this negative dialogue to demolish my dreams, I slowly started to turn it into a positive inner dialogue. With a few tries, the voice that had been taunting me became positive, wildly positive, but most importantly, it further inspired and reignited my confidence. I started to say things out loud like, "You can do this!" "You are stronger than you know!" and, "Just go and see what you can do!" Once that dialogue changed, I pulled back on the highway and accelerated onto the road to the future. It wasn't a very long trip and, within a few hours, I made it to Chicago. As I saw the cityscape looming in the distance and then finally saw the city up close for the first time, it lit an intense fire for success and advancement in the entertainment business. I knew, no matter what happened from here on out, I had made it this far, and I wasn't going to stop here. I looked down at my plan and started to work on the next step.

I often wonder if perhaps the absence of various social media outlets was what made me stick to my idea. I could not check Facebook; it did not exist. I could not call my friends or family; we had no cellular phones. I had no way to check the Internet and see what other people had done before me (the Internet would not be popular for another five to six years). I was cut off from the opinions of others, and I had to rely on my own inner decision compass. Can you imagine what direction I would have gone if, in 1992, we had this explosion of social media and the addiction of asking others what we should do with our lives? I know I would most likely not be where I am today, because the opinions of others can be stronger than your best ideas if you are steadily hit from all directions with the comments of naysayers. Remember that we don't have unlimited time to waste on distractions and negativity; we are not characters in a video game in which you get do-overs accompanied by unlimited lives. We time out. Make your decisions count, and stop waiting on endless suggestions about what will work and not work in your life. What you do in your life is your choice. Everything is always your choice.

SQUASH THAT FAST

I hope this book will serve to help you to quiet your personal inner critic and silence the negative critic (there's always at least one!), and to seek out positive people who can always help you find motivation and inspiration in the darkest of times. The technique I used to reverse the negative inner dialogue as I sat on the side of the road was simple and effective. As I sat there, contemplating forgetting Chicago and my interactive show idea, I stopped myself and asked out loud, "Is this true?" "Is it true that my idea is stupid?" My answer was, *Absolutely not!* "Is it true that I am scared?" *Yes, but that's okay; fear is always here and I can manage it.* "Is it true that I have the power and potential to succeed?" *Yes, a thousand times, yes.* I realized in that moment that my success lies in my willpower and strength to keep moving forward. To this day, the simple question "Is it true?" helps me pull myself out of the worst situations. That day in the car, I told myself, "I can't do this," and then I followed it up with, "Is that true?" The answers showed me the way and dissipated the negative cloud of fear and self-doubt. In my mind, that was the turning point of my journey. Now, many years later, I look back and realize that the moment when I didn't give up, I beat my own fear, and I quieted my negative critic on the side of the road, was the time I showed myself that nothing is impossible. If you just believe in yourself and go for it, you will be unstoppable.

APPLY THE IDEA—AND KEEP GOING

When I arrived in Chicago, I was already far beyond the point of no return. The option to go home and quit on my original plan was no longer a plausible scenario. There was only one thing I could do: move forward. I never created a Plan B because that would have destroyed my motivation. What I always had was Plan A, and only Plan A. I want to make it clear, in this part of my story, that I am not encouraging you to simply toss your financial future aside, risk your kids' safety, or run into traffic in order to meet your goals. Instead, I am showing you that life is composed of many risks—we are just accustomed to the small ones and fearful of the big ones. Every plan has to be thought through, every choice has to be weighed, and you have to find whatever it is that turns up the fire on your motivation so that you can move forward with confidence.

Let me remind you of the obvious: risk is all around you. Any idea you want to see come to fruition will be wrapped in risk. It's just a part of life. Heck, just driving to your job is inherently risky. The Insurance Institute for Highway Safety reported that over thirty-five thousand people died in US automobile crashes in 2015 alone.[2] Every morning, you choose to either leave your home or to stay in your house and never attempt to drive anywhere due to fear of death. Then again, the Centers for Disease Control and Prevention (CDC) reports that annually there are nearly thirty-two thousand deaths from accidental falls in the United States.[3] Technically, you're not safe anywhere. The point here is that life is risky, so you might as well keep going after your ideas, dreams, and ambitions while you still have time.

After arriving in Chicago, the first task was to find a place to live, so I drove around looking for the right spot. I don't even think I could have described what the "right spot" was, but I knew that I would know it when I saw it. I arrived in Lincoln Park. There I found a studio apartment for rent; back then, it was $475 a month. In order to get a lease, I had to pay the security deposit and first month's rent. After I finally had a place to stay, I unloaded my car, bought my first round of groceries, and, having barely any cash left, set out on my next phase of the journey: finding the venue for my idea.

I had read about a club venue from one of the local Chicago papers; it sounded pretty good and, since I needed a job right away, it was the first place I went to see. The place was called the Excalibur Club. It was a massive venue of forty-five thousand square feet, sitting in the heart of Chicago. Oh, and I suppose I should mention that it was built to look like a castle. To me, this was the perfect place, and I didn't care what the outside looked like, I just needed a place that attracted crowds of people—and this was it. Inside the castle was a myriad of rooms, and every room featured a different genre of music. It had high energy and was brimming with tourists and Chicago locals. Since it was already late in the evening and I had just made a long trip, I decided to stay at the club, checking out the rooms, observing the people, mulling over my idea, and modifying it in my mind to fit Excalibur. That night, I knew this was it, this was the space where my idea would work. I was ready to present my idea to the management of the club. With every ounce of confidence I could muster, I walked up to the manager and asked who oversaw entertainment, because I had a revolutionary idea to change the way people enjoyed the club. He obliged by giving me the name of the entertainment director, a man named Tim Borden. Tim had already gone home that night, and I was told to come back the next day so I could speak to him in person. I couldn't believe my ears; I was going to talk to someone about my idea tomorrow. Excitement flooded my body; finally, I was going to live the vision I had planned.

Do you see how doors can open if you are determined to push forward and toward your goals and ideas? This is not complicated science. But to be in the flow of disrupting your life, you must remember that YOU are in charge of YOUR ideas coming to fruition. It's "you, disrupted," remember? No one else will care about your ideas as much as you do. If you have courage to take the initiative, you will get to your destination. It may take longer than you want, you may have to do it several times, or it just may require you to have confidence that you can do it. Leave your fear in your back pocket; there's no space for it next to you or in your head.

FIND A DISRUPTIVE LISTENER

The next day, around noon, I arrived at the empty Excalibur Club and asked for Tim Borden right away. The club wasn't going to get crowded until late that night, so I had the perfect setting for a very detailed meeting: it was quiet and all of the space was opened up so I could walk around and explain my idea without bumping into partying people and trying to yell over the music. I was lost in my daydreaming when the receptionist informed me that Tim had left just minutes before I arrived for his two-week vacation. WHAT!? Keep in mind that after finding a place, buying groceries, and filling my car with gas, I was almost out of money. To make my idea work, I had one shot. I needed this job at this club; it was just perfect for my idea. After I found out I wouldn't be talking to anyone for two weeks, it felt like my luck and confidence had hit rock bottom. For an instant, it felt like my only chance—a place where my idea could thrive—just slipped through my fingers. Quickly, I pulled myself together, took a deep breath, and stopped the negative inner critic. There must be another way, so I pressed on.

I looked at the receptionist and said, "Okay. How can I reach him?" Unfortunately, it was the era before cell phones, and she had no idea how he could be reached. Those were the days when you could go on vacation and leave work and everything else at home. Unlike today, we weren't uber-connected and hadn't blended our work and personal-life boundaries. By now, I was about to go into a full panic attack, but something told me to stay and tell her about my idea. So, for at least ten minutes, I explained my vision for the club and how an interactive comedy show would make Excalibur better. She was captivated with my concept. The more I shared my idea, the more I realized I was going to need to figure out a way to get by financially for two weeks and then come back here to talk to the entertainment director. With regained excitement and confidence in my idea and abilities, I was on my way out, headed to my apartment. In my mind, I was already adjusting and improving my plan, but this time I was even more excited than before. This was going to work!

As I neared the door of Excalibur, lost in my idea development and detail adjustment, I heard the receptionist yelling and pointing at a man who had just walked in. "That's Tim!" WHAT!? I turned around and said, "Tim ... Tim Borden?" THE Tim, the man I needed to talk to? It turned out that he had forgotten something in his office and had to come back to the club to grab it. He was in a rush to finally go on his vacation, but to my surprise, Tim actually stopped and said, "You have five minutes." What ensued could only be rivaled by the best *Shark Tank* pitch you have ever witnessed; I took the big risk of doing something that scares many people—I spoke up. It helped that Tim was an amazing listener. He added supporting questions, advice, and even laughed at my jokes. He was engaged in my idea; and even though Tim had to leave for vacation, he gave me the chance I was waiting for. He stopped and listened to my pitch of the interactive-comedy idea from start to finish. I am sure it was much more than five minutes long. While we were chatting about my idea, I came to realize that Tim was authentic and smart. I could tell right away he was a Disruptor like me. However, at this moment, he was the disruptive listener. When I was finished, Tim said, "You're hired. I want you to start immediately, but I will be gone for two weeks, so I need you to work at another one of our locations [the company owned twelve nightclubs and restaurants around Chicago] until I get back." Filled with adrenaline and excitement, I took the job! Tim finally left on his vacation, and I headed home to prepare for the next day in the other club, while I plotted how I would make the interactive-comedy idea work at the Excalibur location once Tim returned. I had two weeks to get it right.

My first day at the alternate location was full of meeting people who worked there and getting to know what kind of entertainment they had. Since I had acted as if I already had this job even before I left for Chicago and had run the first few skits through my mind for almost a month, I was ready to get on the stage that night and go for it. Because I had spent so much time envisioning what my show looked like, I was a success and the concept was a definite crowd pleaser. So, for two weeks, I treated the other nightclub location that was in Chicago as a practice place; I worked hard to come up with exciting material, and I went to work every night for those two weeks so I could master my vision in real life. Two weeks later, after Tim returned from his vacation and saw the show in action at the other location, he loved it. He loved it so much that he put me in charge of the entertainment team at the original Excalibur location. Let me repeat that: I, a young and inexperienced kid, was in charge of a senior team of six entertainers/DJs at the most popular Excalibur location. I realized I not only hit the target but won the lottery of a lifetime. From day one, I worked at my vision, making it better, adjusting it, and working with the team to bring entertainment to the masses. It was a lot of work, but it was what I wanted to do. I was happy and fulfilled for nearly five years at Excalibur. Then I decided to leave, because I had reached my goal, executed my vision to the fullest, and I was ready for a new adventure. While I was at Excalibur, I created a show we called *Comedy You Can Dance To*, and it kept going even after I left. Finally, after nearly twenty-two years from the time I created it, the show ended when the Excalibur Club took on a new name and became a different type of venue.

If it had not been for Tim and his desire to listen to my vision and to add to what I was saying by being the disruptive listener, I would not be telling this amazing story. If not for my desire to keep going and find a way to make my idea a reality, I would not be telling this story either. We all have a responsibility to each other to not only bring ideas forward but also to be active and disruptive listeners. Even the fact that I spent time talking to the receptionist and that she took the time to listen to me is important to my story. Without the extra time spent explaining my concept to the receptionist, I might not have met Tim as quickly as I did, he might not have given me the job, and my story might have been entirely different. If I had left Excalibur without talking to Tim, I may have even found a different job somewhere else, to make sure I could make enough money to buy food for the first two weeks of my new life in Chicago. To move forward in life and walk on the path of the most fulfilling life you can have, you have to connect with people, give them your time even if they seem unimportant, and be thoughtful about your responses. You never know what new inspiration you could be setting in motion, or what connections you might be making.

To allow the Disruptor inside you to break free in small and big ways, you—and you alone—control your mind-set. Pushing yourself to new heights, moving your ideas forward, and never giving up on yourself is a choice only you can make.

HOW TO APPLY IT

As I share my experiences, I want to make sure I leave you with the application tools that helped me get to where I am today, so you, too, can immediately start to build a new plan for your life. Below are three actions you can take now to begin to release your inner Disruptor.

1. *Set a disruptive intention for your day.* Every day, when I wake up, I spend ten minutes before getting out of bed just to set my daily intention for something disruptive. I say, "Today I will have three new ideas for my business" or "Today I will create a way to work more efficiently." It's almost like a mental list of things I want to accomplish. Every morning, I set an intention beyond "I hope I get through the day." If you don't think about what you want to get out of your day, or what you need in order to create a vision of what you want to live out in your life, then you will always be stuck where you are right now. It takes work to get off the ground and to figure out what you truly crave in your life. Sometimes I think the first steps are the hardest, but if you unleash your mind and start to think creatively and out of the box, you will figure it out in no time. It doesn't matter if you think about ideas that may not be possible today, or if you think your idea looks like a young child came up with it. Imagination has no limits, and you are full of ideas—you just might have locked them away while you were working and trying to fit into the space created by generations of hard workers who have stopped dreaming that things can be different. Break out of your everyday

monotony and go dreaming; let the ideas flow, even if you only have five minutes a day. All ideas and inventions start small; you just have to start. You have a choice each day to set a new intention for a new idea or figuring out your most fulfilling vision, so make it a choice to find a disruptive solution that will help you with work, family, or your personal dreams.

2. *Give birth to ideas.* Figure out your goal and then write down your ideas, no matter how big or small. It may help if I define the difference between a goal and an idea. A goal is an endpoint, like "I want to become an entertainer." An idea is an answer (or answers) to the question about how you can get to that endpoint; for example, "What can I do to become an entertainer?" When you write down your goal, you unintentionally start a cascade of more and more ideas that come together and expand. Sometimes we have a goal and then forget we need to create a path to reach the goal. I can tell you from experience that your ideas to reach your specific goal will change with time and circumstances. One day, you may think a certain idea will be the best route in order to reach your goal; but the next day, you may find a new opportunity that may take you on a different path but still help you arrive at the same, original goal. Don't get frustrated with changes, even if the change is as big as coming up with a new vision or a new goal. Nothing in life is constant, so why would you expect your dreams to be?

Please take time right now to write down your goal or vision. Be very detailed. For example: "I want to make $100 thousand in the next six months, while working as an entertainer in Chicago." You can even add more details than I have; essentially, you want to take your vision and write down everything about it. Fully flesh it out. After you have done that, underneath your vision or goal, write down ideas on how to get there. Will you need to save "X" amount of money? Will you need to move? Will you need to go to a different city (here is that first change in the details of your vision I talked about earlier)? Will you need to take classes for singing or learning to play some sort of an instrument? Just keep on writing until your ideas become a logical and actionable plan. Don't give up! Your visions and goals and ideas can change as many times as you want!

3. *Reverse the phrases.* Each day, with every idea you have, whether seemingly small or large, you will encounter naysayers and negative influencers. They will say things like:

> *NO. Don't do it!*
> *It can't work!*
> *It won't work!*

It is your job to reverse these statements in your head so that your negative inner critic does not sabotage your vision. When I taught innovation in a corporate training program, we would tell people to confront naysayers (in a friendly way). Over time, I realized that to live as a Disruptor, I had to transcend the need to confront other people who may be saying I will fail. Instead, like me, you only need to confront your own inner critic. Below are some suggestions of how you can, to yourself, articulate new thoughts about your ideas and reverse the common negative comments.

When someone on your team, someone at work, or your partner in life says: "NO. Don't do it," "It can't work," or "It won't work," ask yourself "Is this statement true?" You will always face naysayers, negative people, and people who will want to extinguish your fire. Maybe even ask yourself, "I wonder why they're afraid of my idea?" Remember, these most common negative phrases are only words. They have no power unless you give power to them. Most of the time, others are scared that you will succeed; they are angry because they didn't come up with the idea themselves; or they are just trying to limit you. Whatever their reason for being a negative influence toward your ideas, remember that you have no control over their thoughts. The only thing you *do* have control over is yourself; you are the one who has the vision, you are the one who has ideas about how to accomplish it, and you are the one who must be motivated to do all the work. You are the only Disruptor of your own life, and it's your thoughts that matter most.

Remember, this section is about getting rid of your negative self-talk. When you accomplish that, you will be more equipped to work as a team player in a professional or personal setting. To inspire those around you to disrupt with you, talk about the idea, paint the picture of how it fits in the grand plan, how it will improve the original plan, and what the result will look like. You need to make sure you communicate clearly and explain the idea thoroughly. Also, you must fully believe in the idea yourself before you can convince anyone else to believe in it too. And always beware of negative people—they're everywhere. Just stay motivated and never let anyone discourage you. If someone points out something that won't work, and it really won't work, then thank that person; he just saved you time and perhaps money. Adjust the idea and keep on moving toward your vision or goal.

CHAPTER 2

BEING A DISRUPTIVE INFLUENCER: THE ART OF PAYING ATTENTION

Disruptive Influencer: a person who regularly adds valuable input having a profound effect on the outcome of any idea

WE'RE ALL IN IT TOGETHER

It was a normal Wednesday morning when I walked into the office; well, as normal as those days were. On my way to my office, I picked up a copy of our local *Denver Post* and, since no one reads papers anymore, I was going to drop it in the waiting room. But, for some reason that day, the newspaper captured my attention and I stood in my office, reading it. I scanned the paper for any breaking news around the world and, of course, I looked for any cannabis-themed articles, since that was my new industry. As I was browsing through the articles, an idea leaped out at me. Right in front of me on one of the pages was an advertisement for a Home Depot job fair in Denver. This was not breaking news or cannabis related but because my mind-set was always centered on disruption, it triggered some interesting thoughts. *Hmmm*, I thought to myself, *a job fair . . . we need to hire people . . . a job fair for our company in marijuana . . . wait! A job fair for people who love cannabis!* The idea hit me hard and fast but, most importantly, this idea could really work. To make sure I hadn't stumbled upon an idea that was previously established and the city already had a job fair for the marijuana industry, I ran to my computer and started researching marijuana job fairs. I found nothing of any significance pertaining to both a job fair and the cannabis industry. Since the full legalization of cannabis in Colorado, no one had done a job fair for cannabis-loving people—in Colorado, or anywhere in the United States. I was a little surprised, since this was a new and up-and-coming industry. Companies were popping up everywhere, and they all needed employees, so why wasn't there a job fair? As I thought more and more about this idea, it seemed better and better. Finally, I walked up to the whiteboard in my office and, in big capital letters, wrote, "Job Fair," and the vision was created.

Even though the idea was great, I had one problem: I had never organized a job fair for any industry. I had no clue what needed to be done in order to have a job fair, one centered on cannabis jobs. Even with no experience in creating job fairs, I felt that the idea had two benefits: it would get us a great deal of media attention and we would find our new employees. These two reasons were enough to motivate me to learn about how to put together an event. I was brimming with excitement, so I called a team meeting to discuss the idea. Convincing the team a marijuana job fair was a good idea was the easy part. However, actually getting us to organize the first marijuana-industry job fair in Denver was going to take more motivation. When the team and I discussed the benefits of the job fair, everyone was very enthusiastic and had some great ideas. However, at the mention of the logistics required to plan this job fair, everyone looked a bit dazed. It didn't take me long to realize that none of them had organized a job fair either, and we were outside everyone's comfort zone. After further and deeper discussion about the idea and what it would mean for the company, our office manager spoke up, "It's basically just a cool event, and the fun of this is: you are trying to get hired. Let's just make it a fun event!" The comment may seem very simple and a great way to approach the job-fair planning, but even the simplicity and enthusiasm of one person opened the flood-gate of ideas, add-on comments, and valuable input. Since everything in the cannabis industry moves at light speed, we realized that we had to successfully execute this job fair within the next few weeks. So, after some planning and basic logistics, we came up with a plan and were on the road to preparing a great event. We came up with a name, a location for the event, the date this event would take place, and volunteers who would help run the job fair. To make sure that it had a wide variety of jobs to offer the attendees, we invited fifteen other cannabis companies to join us in finding talent at our job fair. And that's how CannaSearch was born. The next and final step was marketing it on social media to attract a variety of people from different backgrounds with diverse skill sets, and who wanted a job in this up-and-coming industry.

Are you paying attention yet?

Now, imagine that you were me in that moment. What would you have done? Would you have called a meeting only for the VPs of the company? Would you have even allowed the office manager to be in the room, let alone add valuable input? Do you build an environment around you, in both your personal life and work, in which people feel comfortable sharing their ideas, feedback, and input or do you constantly live in your hyper social media customized bubble of views that coincide only with your own?

The challenge that we face as a culture, and I believe it to be a dire situation, is that we are customized to a level that almost completely shuts out the world. Have you ever commented or viewed a comment on your friend's Facebook feed that was in opposition to your view? Did you observe other people or even yourself attacking the person who posted the comment, simply because they had a different opinion? Over time, we have been systematically and gradually tricked into believing that our opinions are useless, unless they align with the person that we are talking to. Because of social media, rapid-fire text communication, and lack of real connection to others, we oftentimes live or interact in an environment where our opinions are not valued. We have all become the "boiling frog." This is a theory that you can actually boil a live frog if you simply drop it in warm and comfortable water, then slowly turn up the heat until the water boils. Because the temperature change is so gradual, the poor frog never realizes that it is being boiled alive, and it eventually dies. Are you like this frog that has been bathing in over-customized environments void of real conversations and meaningful relationships? Are you being slowly customized more and more by your "likes" and company marketing strategies? Have you lost all sense of reality and only believe in one that is stuffed with confused and mislabeled emotions and feelings about different issues? Is all of this destroying your personal sense of contribution and self-growth?

If you think about my idea to hold the job fair, you will realize that I was trying to collaborate with as many Disruptive Influencers as I could. I did this by creating an environment in the meeting so that different people from different levels of management could participate in the brainstorming and creation of the event, while adding their own ideas and thoughts. All I wanted was for all of those people in the room to help me figure out a solution, even if it meant that the meeting would take longer. Why? Because in any environment, what I want are disruptive solutions that help us reach a successful outcome. As a leader who had to be truly disruptive in that moment, I had to pay attention to everyone and all of the opinions—no matter how silly at first they may seem. You have to take everyone's suggestions, and before shooting them down, you have to think about them. Maybe it can be tweaked there and changed here to make it work. You can't judge the book by its cover, and only when you are paying attention can you hope to leverage each person's disruptive ability.

Did it work? Was it disruptive? Well, a few days before the actual event, I was watching *The Late Late Show with Craig Ferguson* when

I heard him joke, "A marijuana job fair in Denver—people who want to hire stoners and stoners who want to work—I don't think anyone is going."[1] Of course, his audience erupted in laughter; after all, this was the funny part of the late-night show. However, that statement wasn't just a joke about the company and about me; this was like a shout-out to the media to come and cover the first cannabis-industry job fair in Denver. On the day of the actual job fair, social media and relentless marketing attracted coverage from every news outlet in America, and even from a few in other countries. The day of the event, we were offering just over one hundred jobs from fifteen companies in Denver. We had everything and more a job fair needed: food, coffee, professional people, and jobs waiting for the right candidate. We expected only a few people to attend the event. So you can imagine our surprise when people just kept showing up one after another to drop off their resumes. Instead of a small turnout, we had over twelve hundred people who lined up around the block just to get in and submit their applications. At that moment, our company reached a new level: now, we were seen not just as the largest brand in cannabis but also as a job creator. If it had not been for my openness to new ideas that were outside the box, always being a bold Disruptor, and the Disruptive Influencers around me, the job fair would never have happened. It wasn't just people coming together with a common goal; it was the fact that all members of the team became Disruptive Influencers. They added to the idea, challenged the ways we should advertise, and created a new opportunity for people in the cannabis industry. Oh, and we held the CannaSearch job fair on the same day as the Home Depot job fair. Of course, ours was better.

WHO IS THE DISRUPTIVE INFLUENCER?
HINT: IT'S POTENTIALLY ALL OF US.

After reading the last chapter, I'm sure you're thinking, "But, Todd, what if I am just not the outgoing Disruptor who wants to shake it up? What value is there for me to keep reading this book? Should I just put this book down right now since I'm not comfortable with stepping out of my comfort zone?" The short answer to all of these questions is, "If you want a truly brilliant fulfilled life, then stop trying to hide behind your fear." You have a huge value, and I'm not asking you to run out of your safety zone right into something dangerous, but at least start to push yourself a little toward where you want to be. The important step at this point is to wake yourself up and start to pay attention to the world around you in a more intentional way. Everyone is at a different level of being a Disruptor and a Disruptive Influencer. That's why some people may go crazy and shake up every single thing in their lives and some may take small steps. Some may have to start with disrupting their drive home, perhaps by taking a slightly different route. Or some may have to start reading a different genre of books. The possibilities are limitless and the pressure is completely off, because we don't all need to be innovative Disruptors at every turn of a day to be fulfilled. Being disruptive can simply mean you are activating your skills of paying attention so you can add tremendous value at the right time. The power we ALL have is the power of becoming a Disruptive Influencer. To be a Disruptive Influencer powerhouse, all you have to do is listen, allow your ideas to come forward, speak up, and voice your valuable input at a meeting or at home in order to solve a problem or come up with new ideas as a solution. Remember, small steps in the right direction are always better than giant leaps with constant backtracking to start over. If you don't add your valuable input and ideas now, when will you have time to come back and do it?

If you are a Disruptor as I outlined in the last chapter, that's a great start; but having this skill is only a part of the equation. In fact, Disruptors without a support team of other like-minded people, called Disruptive Influencers, will often find themselves in a figurative tornado of ideas with nowhere to touch down and create tangible results. Disruptors MUST be surrounded by a group of positive Disruptive Influencers who can help bring the ideas to life. As I mentioned earlier, everyone is different. We all add value at the right time and in the right context, but only if we are paying attention. In fact, we are all, at times, Disruptors, and, at other times, we are Disruptive Influencers. The two cannot thrive unless you are allowing them to flow fluidly inside you. They are two key factors in the equation of success.

Our world is full of people with different backgrounds and talents who, when they pay attention and collaborate disruptively, can be an unstoppable force. This comes in handy when you are assembling a group of people who need to solve a complex problem or come up with a new concept, and it is especially useful when hiring for a certain position. Many times, I assembled a team of people who individually had many different ways of thinking and problem solving, so we could have more choices and different input to make an idea extraordinary. Those teams had every single level of Disruptor and Disruptive Influencer, because everyone has a unique perspective and that's what is needed in order to solve any problem or realize any idea at hand. You may not know it yet, but you already are a Disruptor and a Disruptive Influencer—you just may not have explored those roles yet, or you haven't realized your own potential. Unfortunately, this happens to countless people who work in a typical company culture. Most people who are not the trailblazers or leaders often feel left out and see themselves as less valuable or feel that they don't have beneficial ideas that will add to a company's overall vision. The result is a less engaged and fulfilled workforce.

WHAT IT MEANS TO PAY ATTENTION

Finding and becoming a Disruptive Influencer is very rewarding. For example, when I am working with an executive coaching client and the goal is to help him or her truly gain more value from his or her team, I first need to teach the client to pay attention. I know that paying attention seems very rudimentary, but here is an example to illustrate exactly what I mean. Think for a moment about your day so far as you are reading this book. Can you remember what the last three people you encountered looked like? What they were wearing? Can you remember the entire conversation between you and the second person you interacted with? It's difficult, is it not, to remember the details of your day this way? Do you still think that your paying-attention skills are sharp?

Now let's take this another step further. Let's take your work for a moment. Think about the three people with whom you work most closely. Do you know with certainty how they see the world? Ask yourself if you know how these people view you. Can you list three personal and not well-known things about them that paint how they interact with the world?

If these exercises were difficult, don't be alarmed. Every executive leader I work with struggles with this, because they have also been conditioned to tune out the world. They can tell me about some useless Internet meme they saw three days ago on Twitter, but they cannot tell me one thing about how the individuals of his or her team can add value to finding a solution. That's a tragedy of human connection. Because we are not paying attention to others, we are missing the opportunity to allow their Disruptive Influencer ideas to beautifully color our lives. I am here to challenge you to begin to remember that you are in a world with many other people who, if you will simply pay attention, can use your input and, in return, can add valuable insight to your new disrupted life.

I AM STRONG, BUT TOGETHER WE ARE UNSTOPPABLE.

You really can't do it alone. Take, for example, a small-business owner. He or she may have a truly wonderful idea, product, or service, but he or she can't do all of the work all of the time. Plus, as the business expands, he or she will need more input, suggestions, and ideas from a strong group of positive thinkers. Don't believe me? Imagine that you were the engineer who had the idea for the first cellular phone. You drew it, made a concept in your mind, and then . . . what? You would need to consult with an army of other people who would add to the idea, push its concept to the technological edge, and work together to bring the concept to fruition. Those people, in that moment, are Disruptive Influencers. They listen to your idea or plan, take a look at it, and then help you to build on it. They ask questions that can shake the whole concept to the core. They matter to the big picture of accomplishing the goal of the new device. And they do it together.

The good news is, while not everyone may want to be a Disruptor by driving new ideas and outcomes, EVERYONE is a Disruptive Influencer at some point. This is true regardless of a person's job function, company, family, or nationality. We are all, at some point, presented with an opportunity to support ideas or the people who bring them forward.

Realizing that, at times, you need to become a Disruptive Influencer is powerful, because of the value the shared ideas have on the overall success of any innovation. This can also be applied at home when we think about relationships and interactions. You have a partner, friends, spouse, or significant other who provides you with constant opportunities to work on being the Disruptive Influencer and assist in shaping their ideas into a reality. Check yourself and see if you lean more toward support or are quick to criticize a person close to you who offers solutions and ideas. Often we forget the right suggestion to ANY of our fellow humans at the right time could be just the message they need.

THE DISRUPTIVE INFLUENCER HELPED US ALL FLY

We all have tremendous value, ideas, and roles to play. No one is less than anyone else. Some of the most important ideas and solutions on Earth came from someone on the team other than the leader. You may not have noticed earlier in this book when I mentioned the sister of the Wright brothers to whom we owe the gift of flight. That was no accident. I wanted you to understand that she had a huge role as a Disruptive Influencer, which sparked the next phase of her brothers' adventure and ultimately gave us the ability to fly. Many people are aware of the exploits and experiments of the Wright brothers. They worked tirelessly at Kitty Hawk to attempt winged flight. What you may not know is, like most entrepreneurs, their first experiments did not yield the results they had desired. They returned home to Dayton, Ohio, defeated and feeling like all hope was lost.[2]

Just after the brothers returned home, Wilbur received a letter from Octave Chanute, president of the Western Engineering Society, asking if he would speak at a meeting of the First Flight Society. Below is an excerpt of what happened next, from Dr. Richard Stimson, a member of that society.

> A discouraged Wilbur intended to refuse the invitation after the poor results at Kitty Hawk. But Katharine intervened and talked him into accepting the invitation. She thought it was a great opportunity to expose the relatively unknown Wilbur to the *aeronautical* community. She even helped Wilbur prepare for the speech.
>
> She made sure that Wilbur's appearance would make a good impression. She substituted Wilbur's baggy suit with one of Orville's. Orville, unlike Wilbur, had a reputation as a sharp dresser.
>
> The speech was well received and served to bring Wilbur out of his

funk. Reenergized, Wilbur and Orville decided to find out why the glider didn't behave as predicted by published engineering data. This led them to design and build a wind tunnel in which they tested some 200 wing configurations. Their test results enabled them to correctly calculate lift and drag, leading to the design of an efficient wing. All of this was made possible because of Katharine's intervention.[3]

You see, the Disruptor is only one person and, without the power of a Disruptive Influencer, the Disruptor cannot keep the engine running. Sometimes all he or she needs is a little spark from the Disruptive Influencer. We all have a role to play—you just have to decide which one fits the situation at hand.

WHAT A DISRUPTIVE INFLUENCER IS NOT

As I mentioned before, many people confuse disruption with destruction. In this chapter, I want to take it a step further and help you to understand that destruction is taking action out of anger or frustration and then destroying people or ideas around us. Destroying people or ideas in the form of gossip, hostile words, and judgment is a fruitless effort for people who truly want to live a full life. If you have an idea that is a solution to a problem, you can use the principles of disruption to take charge and constructively solve the problem at hand without causing harm. We don't need more destruction, bullying behaviors, and overall angst. What we do need is disruption, connection, and true problem solving brought about through cooperation.

You can see the impact of destructive behavior or disruption in our society. I once observed a company led by very passionate, yet often destructive, founders. While these founders felt like trailblazers, renegades, and pioneers who were disrupting their industry, they were actually the opposite; they were very destructive in the ways that they treated the industry, and especially their employees. They could have fostered an environment in which the cannabis culture and business merged and created a respectful environment, where the team could be allowed to bring ideas forward, take action on those ideas, and ultimately feel empowered to enjoy their own solutions. Unfortunately, this was not the case. The consequences of a stifled culture and ideas were painful to watch. Many employees would either walk out of a meeting in tears or simply quit. Regardless of the excitement of this start-up's success, the agony of rude leaders who were not at all thoughtful about their approach to running a team stifled creativity, discouraged new ideas, and stagnated everyone's potential success. While this company has survived, barely, it is wrought with negativity to this day. The sad part is that the people running an organization like this may find commercial success and, sadly, we often only use commercial success as a metric. But commercial success is only one part of a company; the best companies that build longevity are filled with happy, fulfilled team members.

You need to remember this lesson when you begin to engage in a more disruptive way of thinking. You must be respectful and kind to those around you. Disruption becomes destruction only if the Disruptor acts out, argues, and fights, instead of simply sharing or helping to implement ideas.

DISRUPTIVE INFLUENCERS ARE IMPORTANT IN BOTH BUSINESS AND PERSONAL LIFE

Let's say you are in a meeting and working to solve a complex problem. Each person around the table has a different and unique background, education, and current life situation. The problem being presented is urgent and needs to be solved right away. Here and there, some ideas are being discussed, but nothing impressive comes up. The rest of the group members at the table just sit—and wait. They wait for someone else to be the Disruptor. Perhaps this is you. Perhaps you have a great idea. Unfortunately, you talk yourself out of it, thinking it may be too out-there, or you're not sure how it would fit in. This happens to everyone, but the Disruptors break out of that mind-set and share their thoughts; they work with the group to find a solution. Sometimes the solution is a combination of the original idea and something far-fetched that has been modified to fit or leverage the solution. Without you speaking up, you will never know if your idea is great, and you will never break out of your silent mind-set.

If you are a leader and you don't have a Disruptor in every meeting, you should look long and hard at your goals. Ask yourself if you want to sit in a meeting that will not end with a creative solution or if you want to find a creative solution to the problem at hand. Bottom line, you need a Disruptor in the room to spark the fire of creation. This is where I want you to consider the power of the Disruptive Influencer.

The same is true at home. Your spouse, partner, or friend may be dealing with some powerful challenge and need your input. He starts to articulate his challenge and his idea for a solution, and it is at this critical moment that things can dramatically change for the worse. If you are like most people, you will wait for a moment when he pauses to catch a breath. Then you will interrupt with all of the reasons why you think he is wrong, or how he should play it safe. Instead of adding value, we (perhaps unintentionally) tend to pull other people down or, if their idea threatens us in some way, we try hard to steer them away from it. Becoming a Disruptive Influencer in your personal life is equally as critical as being a Disruptive Influencer at work. As my fiancée Diana and I were preparing for our wedding, she was struggling with the one thing a new bride often faces, selecting the wedding dress. After three months and trying on over forty dresses, Diana was finally feeling defeated. Let's just say that it was getting beyond frustrating for Diana to keep trying on dresses that were missing something to complete the look. I had been paying attention the entire three months and adding as much value as I could to the discussion, but we were attempting to keep with tradition in that I would not be seeing the wedding dresses or attending the fittings. Finally, after seeing and hearing the defeat coming from her, I suggested something disruptive. Because Diana and I are a great team, I knew I could take a sensitive topic and add value that she would appreciate, because we listen to each other, debate beautifully, and in the end find breakthrough results faster than anyone I know. I am inspired each day by how well we click personally as well as in our business. So, I harnessed my Disruptive Influencer and suggested that we stop messing around with this dress problem, we break from the tradition, and I join her for a dress fitting.

She gladly accepted, and off we went. I was playing the role of the Disruptive Influencer, and as we walked into the first dress shop, I walked by Diana's side, commenting on the dresses that I thought were amazing, all the while asking what she liked and disliked about the dress. The best part of the experience came when Diana began to try on the dresses. They were all very different, representing a different look and feel at our future wedding. This time she didn't try on ten or fifteen dresses, Diana only tried on three. After the third dress, we discussed the attributes of each and both decided that the first one was the one that she has been searching for. Just like that, in thirty minutes, we completed the one part of our wedding that was completely overwhelming to her. That is the power of the Disruptive Influencer and how fast you can find amazing solutions if you are paying attention. This learning is universal, at home and at work.

Also, kids need adults to teach them how to become a Disruptor in their own lives. They need us to help them understand what it means to push through adversity, push through pain, and find a way to be fulfilled when no way is presented. When life hits our kids with a challenge, a parent can either attempt to solve all the challenges for them, or he or she can teach the child to rise to the top of the challenge and eat it for breakfast. We have a responsibility not only to ourselves but also to our family members, children, friends, co-workers, and, in general, our fellow humans, to become positive Disruptive Influencers.

My best relationships with my friends, partner, business associates, and even family members, all work beautifully when I look at their situations as an opportunity to support their thinking and help them see the best or something new in a situation. That is when real positive change occurs and our relationship strengthens.

THE DIFFERENCE BETWEEN
DISRUPTIVE SUGGESTIONS AND CRITICISM

At first it may seem confusing to think about the difference between these two concepts, but the fine line between suggestions and criticism lies within your intention. To illustrate the difference, here is an example: you are in a meeting at work and your boss is attempting to solve a complex challenge. Some of the suggestions a Disruptor in the room is offering as solutions may mean more work for you. So you speak up and (unwittingly) offer only criticism. You are offended that the Disruptor would even think about piling more work on your plate. Thus, in your mind, the idea must be stupid. Instead of criticizing the person who came up with the idea, and aggressively pointing out this person just created twice as much work for you, you ought to become a Disruptive Influencer and find a way in which everyone can benefit without you doing twice the work. Being a Disruptive Influencer in this situation doesn't mean you just have to sit there and have all the work piled on your desk. What it means is that you have an opportunity to come up with a new process, find a faster way to get all of the work done, or suggest that a team be created to help you carry out the needed steps to get everything sorted away. In addition to challenging the problem at hand, you just solved the logistics of the problem and perhaps set in motion a new and better way of working as a team.

We are programmed to ease our own personal pain, so sometimes it feels as if we have the right to criticize others. Our first instinct is to attack and then to assess the situation afterward. If you do this, later, when your review comes up, don't be surprised if your leader says that you don't go with the flow or offer valuable ideas. You may not even realize that your comments are coming off as stifling criticism instead of as a positive, disruptive spin on the ideas being discussed. If that is the problem, then the key to actually giving positive, influencing, disruptive suggestions is this: just before you give the suggestion, put yourself in the right frame of mind by asking yourself, "How can I help?" I personally write this question in my notebook before every meeting so that it becomes second nature to me. When I enter the meeting, I am always asking that same question, so my mind is focused on solving the problem and not shifting blame around the table. Does this mean I agree with everything Disruptors are saying? NO! It means my mind is focused on the big picture, while assisting in achieving the goal, giving advice, or simply steering the meeting in a better direction. Taking the time to ask yourself "How can I help?" pushes you to put away the defensiveness while directing you to support the search for a solution.

HOW YOU HIRE, WHOM YOU HIRE, AND HOW YOU GET HIRED—THE POWER AND THE TEST

When I co-founded High There!, the world's first social connectivity app for marijuana enthusiasts to date and make new connections, I admit that it was a challenge. From finding new ways to secure users of the app, to hiring the right team to help me execute the day-to-day operations, we definitely faced some obstacles. Since this was an app start-up, we needed to attract consumers to the app to become what we called, "Our Users." We defined "Users" as any person using the app. User engagement, user population, and even user interaction became critical metrics. In fact, that was one measure of our success. We had to come up with disruptive ideas to attract people to this app. In order to achieve great marketing and content, and to generate disruptive ideas, we needed a team with certain skills. Over the years, I have developed a hiring process that, when implemented, works every time. Some of the best team members I have ever hired were successful because this hiring philosophy put them in the right job from the start: a job in which their talents matched the requirements to get the task accomplished in the right way. They were comfortable expressing their ideas and working to add real value to the organization. Frankly, it's so simple, and the results are so incredible, that I am often surprised by anyone who resists it.

One great example of my hiring philosophy is when I had to hire a social media person to manage and increase our social media presence at High There! I posted a job description and its requirements on LinkedIn, Craigslist, and other social media outlets, asking for someone who could get the job done and who wanted to be part of something truly groundbreaking. Out of the dozens of submissions, I pulled only five possible candidates who I thought had the experience needed to achieve our desired results. In the initial meetings with these five hopefuls, I was purposely pushing each one of them to see if they demonstrated the characteristics needed to be a Disruptive Influencer in our company. In a start-up, you don't have time or money for what I call "seat warmers," or those who are satisfied sitting all day and achieving minimum results while collecting a paycheck. You need people who actually produce results. So my level of scrutiny was . . . high.

I held initial meetings with these five potentials. At the meetings, I interviewed them and then, as I always do, asked them to "work" for a couple of hours to complete a selected task without pay. They had to pretend that they already had the job, and this was one of the tasks assigned to them. This means they, on their own time, would have access to our system in order to demonstrate their ability to produce real, valuable input. This is my test. It seems easy, right? Why wouldn't anyone with the right set of skills jump on that? The point of the test is to see what they will actually accomplish with little to no direction from me after the initial instructions were given. They were tested to see how dedicated to the job they would be and how seriously they would be in taking on every task. Out of the five possible candidates, only two agreed to complete the test. The other three simply refused, throwing out excuses such as, "I need to get to know the company better," "I don't have time," or "I don't work without pay." Excuses have been a very large part of our society, and I believe it is the core reason we have a society so out of touch with real work, sacrifice, or achievement. We have started to believe and act as if everything should be handed to us without any effort on our part or that we deserve something even though we have done nothing to earn it. If you don't take the time to demonstrate how good you are, either by articulation of your track record or by actual work as in the test, then you most likely won't be able to add value to the organization for which you are working. I wonder if the people who wouldn't participate in my test, and those like them, realize that their biggest issue with success, with becoming a Disruptor, and, overall, with not achieving a fulfilled life, is their own excuses.

THE TEST YIELDS RESULTS . . . AND A DISRUPTIVE INFLUENCER

One of the applicants took the test very seriously. In fact, in one day, she lit up our social media and in an instant was generating accolades from my other business partners and our users; all the while, she was adding much-needed attention to our social media. The test could not have gone better. As a second part of the test, I briefly talked to her about how she could add input and have confidence in sharing her ideas with the team. I wanted to see not only how she took direction but, more importantly, how she would add disruptive ideas to the work. Again, she answered the call and demonstrated to us all that we had a Disruptive Influencer in our midst. She was hired!

Her hiring story is just one example of how you can begin to rethink your life and the power of being a disruptive force. We are all asking how we can be more competitive in the workplace, better partners, and better lovers, but rarely do we ask the hard questions to ourselves about how dedicated we truly are to making it happen. I would highly recommend this test for every employer so he or she can test every possible candidate before hiring or promoting. If we adopted this thinking, our society would instantly become more innovative and adept at problem solving, as well as having pride in their jobs and their accomplishments. I have never witnessed more dedicated people than the ones who go through this test.

Regardless of your reasons for becoming a Disruptor or Disruptive Influencer, remember this new hire's story when you opt to passively get through that next interview or advancement. Remember how dedicated she was. By the way, after being hired, she demonstrated her worth on the job repeatedly by speaking up and adding a powerful level of value. She was doing her best not just during the test, but, most importantly, she was doing her best at work every day.

PUTTING IT TO WORK

When you decide to engage and add to the discussion by building on ideas, pushing the envelope, and taking risks—that is when true positive change can occur. To illustrate this better, here is another example with the same new hire. While we were designing the app High There! we were trying to come up with a new way for app users to reject people. The whole team was tired of the usual "red x." It felt like such a snub. I knew we needed something different—bold, but still playful. We had a team meeting that lasted for hours, trying to find a different way to reject people. After some discussions and throwing some ideas around, the ultimate Disruptive Influencer, the new hire, simply said, "High There! Bye There!" She went on to explain, "Sure, let's use High There! to say we like you, just like we do one-on-one in life, and then let's make a button that says, "Bye There!," which is a friendly and nice way to say bye if you were face-to-face." This is the power of the Disruptive Influencer. She did not need to come up with all of the concepts, the ideas, or even the philosophy for rejecting people on the app. She just spoke up confidently at the right time and added a very disruptive concept to the discussion. The result was a beautiful solution users loved.

Disruptive Influencers can also flourish at home. Because you are not usually paying much attention, it may seem that your partner, spouse, or kids could not have great ideas that bring about solutions, but that's where you are completely wrong. If you approached your spouse or partner, asked for her ideas on a specific topic, and then actually listened, you may be surprised. She may not have great ideas all the time, but how will you know if you don't ask and give her a chance to express her ideas? Sometimes a seemingly stupid, simple, or far-fetched idea can spark a truly creative one that may be just the solution you have been looking for. To find more creativity, look for ideas from your kids—creativity flows constantly through their minds. So the next time you want to brush off an idea someone at home is telling you about, instead you should listen, try to apply the concept, and see if the results solve a problem or can be a solution for some totally unrelated topic. Most of the time, it takes more than one person to light the creativity fire.

IT TRULY MATTERS WHO IS AROUND YOU

Just like hiring the right employee or becoming the right employee who views disruption as a necessary part of living a fulfilled life, the people you choose to allow in your life outside of work are also critical. Have you ever known someone at work who loved life, loved their peers, and seemed to enjoy every aspect of their existence, only to discover later that they had a miserable home life? This is often because outside of work this person had surrounded him- or herself with negative individuals—friends who only sought to bring him or her down. Conversely, have you known people who surround themselves with amazingly positive friends, and then constantly complain about their work?

Being a positive Disruptor has one important distinction that you must realize in order to move forward. You may want to get rid of some people in your life who are weighing you down. Am I saying that you never speak to them? No. I am saying that you will start to gravitate toward the people in your life or new people coming into your life, who are positive, are supportive, and believe in your potential. With only so much time in your day, this means you will start to shift away from the people who steal your energy and your passions with their constant barrage of negativity. These are the people who can destroy your visions and your goals very fast if you let them into your mind. Along my journey, I have had to let many people go, because their negativity simply exhausted me. Sometimes I moved away from people because my passions and ambition took me away. Then, after their negativity had been eliminated in my life, I realized that moving away from them was the best thing for me. One of the businesses I helped elevate to great success had several leaders and founders. We were all very passionate about our goals, but often there were several founders who pulled the team into despair and could be said to have a unique style of destroying everything and everyone around them. We all tolerated these people because they were founders, but their vitriol was a destructive force. When I left that company to move into other levels of my career, I was at first deeply saddened, because the team at that company had become sort of like my family. However, it was not long after our parting that I realized how unhealthy some of the founders were—not just to the team, but also to my own well-being. I remember, for example, waking up one morning about a week after I left, and I had this overwhelming sense of peace. There was no one in my day who was going to cause a ruckus, yell at staff, or create an environment of fear. I was free, and it felt great. This freedom allowed me to springboard to new career heights. Sometimes you make the choice to move away from negative people, and sometimes your aspirations, dreams, and vision for your own life moves you.

Whom you choose to be your friends and partner will have a massive impact on your life, your connections, your happiness, and the amazing things you can do. If you get a horrible job and you hate it even before you get hired, that job will impact your fulfillment. This concept can also be applied to every other aspect of your life. While you cannot choose your family (parents and siblings), you can certainly pick your friends, spouse, work situation, and so on. You have the power to become a Disruptive Influencer; to become the best you can be, you need to surround yourself with positive and supportive people.

BURN A BRIDGE

Sometimes you need to burn a bridge. Most commonly, that bridge is between you and the negative people who are not adding anything positive to your life. It's fitting to end this chapter on a note of empowerment, so you start to take control of your life and, more importantly, you begin to ask how you can disrupt your way to fulfillment. If you truly want to be a Disruptor or Disruptive Influencer, you will need to learn the art of burning a bridge. I am not talking about ignoring a good friend's phone calls for a week or walking out on your job. What I am talking about is this: you need to identify those people in your life who are having the most negative influence on you, and then remove them from your life.

If you were on a boat, lost at sea with all of the closest people in your life, and the boat started to sink, which ones would immediately begin to complain, whine, and talk about how you can't make it to shore if you swim? If the only way to survive was for everyone to jump in the water, tether each other to a rope, and then swim to the shore together, who would do it? Who would support you in this approach to safety and help you get to the shore? And which of your closest friends or family members would be the ones screaming at the top of their lungs as you all started to swim, "We won't make it! You can't lead us! We will die!" Who would pull you down with them? And who would refuse to leave the seeming safety of the sinking boat?

Burning a bridge means you sever toxic relationships that are taking you down. Those friends who constantly take up your time by complaining and never making changes ... they've got to go! That person who always tells you how stupid you are for speaking up ... gotta go! Those family members who can't wait to insult your dreams and desires ... gotta ... well, limit your time spent with them and ignore their negativity as much as possible. Family is difficult to get rid of entirely, but burning a bridge between you and toxic family members will certainly make it more difficult for them to yell at you across the canyon. I know it's hard to rid yourself of negative people, because they're so close to you and you have let them be there for so long. Just remember, you can't do epic shit with basic people. And you can't swim to the shore of your best life if you are dragging those negative, complaining people behind you. People who are drowning your dreams and keeping you from a brighter and better future. Unfortunately, if you don't burn a bridge between you and those toxic people, they will cause you to drown.

HOW TO APPLY IT

Add value, not just opinion. When engaging in your work or personal life, remember to reset your frame of mind by asking, "How can I help?" This simple question will pivot you away from the negative, self-serving mind-set and toward helping the idea or solution come to fruition. When you hear an idea, do you think the idea is actually stupid, or are you mad because someone else spoke up and offered an idea? Before you jump in and offer your input about someone else's thoughts, ask yourself, "Am I just criticizing them, or am I truly adding value and input to the idea to make it better?" The latter will gain you the respect and support you need to truly grow, while giving you control over the one person you can control . . . you.

Challenge for the positive. To be an effective Disruptive Influencer, you will need to start asking better questions internally instead of letting your negative inner naysayer come out. The naysayer inside you serves no value. Instead, when you're about to speak up and share your influence, first internally ask yourself, "What can go right?" This puts you in a hyper-positive mode. Whatever people around you are saying and doing, this one internal question can rev up your disruptive power in a way you never imagined.

Burn a bridge. Remember, burning a bridge means you sever toxic relationships that are taking you down. As hard as this is to do, you need to begin to look around at the people who hold the most influence in your life. If you have any negative people around you, these people must be carefully removed from your life (as much as humanly possible). When I say *negative*, what I mean is if their most common response to ideas of your disruptive thinking is negative, and if they hold an overall adverse opinion of the world around them, then these are the people who are pulling you down. If you need to destroy a bridge between you and them, then do so. Set it ablaze so that they won't cross over to your side, carrying bags filled with negativity. Remember, as a metaphor, you should never attempt to save a boatload of negative people who are drowning, because they will pull you down with them into the abyss of negativity, self-criticism, and death of your ideas. You can't pull them to the shore while they complain either, because that will make your ideas and their execution impossible due to second-guessing yourself, your capabilities, and your limits. In the end, everyone drowns—because they will pull you down with them, and you will drown before you have a chance to make any difference in your life.

"But, Todd, how do we do this? It's hard to cut people loose." you might be thinking to yourself. Yes, while I agree that it may be difficult to pull yourself away from certain negative people, like close family members or longtime friends, you need to ask yourself what your life—your new, fulfilled life—needs to have in order to be successful. Sometimes what it needs is less of the negative people. When you master the lesson of burning a bridge, you will be equipped to manage any type of person in your life, and you will realize that the negative people around you serve only to spin you into a reactive mode of fear. One of the most effective strategies to find out who is a negative influence on you and your ideas is to simply and ONLY speak positively about your ideas in front of your family, friends, and other people who influence your life. If any of them starts to spew negativity about your ideas (that is, to criticize rather than to make suggestions), you should stay positive. If this person keeps on being a naysayer and a negative influence, saying things like, "But you could fail at that business" or "You will never have a better life, so you just need to deal with it," then you need to see that this person is a negative influence and a destroyer of your hopes to become a Disruptor in your own life. Cut those people out of your life; they're not providing value or support. You don't owe negative people an explanation for why they need to go. They just need to go. However you choose to eliminate the negative people in your life, very carefully and intelligently burn your bridges, never forgetting that they often must be burnt completely in order for these energy drainers to get out of your way so you can become a Disruptor in your own life.

HOW TO IDENTIFY A DISRUPTIVE INFLUENCER

So, how do you know if you have a Disruptive Influencer in your life or if you are one? Below are some of the attributes of a Disruptive Influencer in action:

- Inquisitive about the problem: A Disruptive Influencer wants to solve the problem but needs to know all of the details and what did not work previously before they dive into new and unique ways of looking at all of the possible solutions. They are inquisitive about the parameters, expectations, and end goals, so that they know they're going in the right direction.
- Paying attention and listening to people and ideas around them: People who are the Disruptive Influencers are the ones who pay attention to those around them and their ideas. Almost every meeting has a wide variety of people with dif-

ferent backgrounds, life experiences, and ways of analyzing and solving problems. A Disruptive Influencer has to get to know the people in the room and have a face-to-face interaction. After getting to know the details of the problem and the other people's skill sets, a solution can finally start to be formed.

- Focused on the solution rather than just giving their opinion: A Disruptive Influencer's focus is always on the solution rather than irrelevant chatter and voicing an opinion just to be heard and to feel that he or she contributed in the meeting. When a Disruptive Influencer speaks, it is because he or she is moving toward a solution and new thinking, in collaboration with the other team members in the room.

- Collaborative in nature: This type of contributor is collaborative in nature because they know that they cannot solve a complex problem on their own if they don't have the skills or knowledge in certain areas. The Disruptive Influencer always seeks to link with other people who have expertise in different areas. This is hard to do for some people because if they don't come up with most or all of the solution on their own, they feel inadequate and see no value in further contribution. The ego has to be minimized in these situations to make sure that a collaborative environment is established.

- Speak up to introduce new ideas: A Disruptive Influencer offers new ideas or ways of thinking when they see that the process of figuring out a solution has stalled or is going in a direction that may not work. This person offers little tweaks to make a plan work or gently presents new ideas that will help solve the problem in a different way. Don't be afraid to speak up if you have an idea, the other team members can collaborate to determine if your idea is feasible or suggest a few minor changes to make it work.

- Leaves cynicism at home and thinks creatively: A person who thinks and acts creatively rather than cynically and attempts to add value in solving a problem is a Disruptive Influencer. Some solutions require a more creative and out-of-the-box way of thinking.

- Willing to take feedback while giving feedback: Teachability or a willingness to take feedback is an indication of being a Disruptive Influencer. These people are not afraid to accept feedback that they can evaluate to see if anything about the way the problem is being solved or the approach can be changed based on those comments. They also give feedback freely to others.

So as you take an inventory of the people around you and their ideas, use the list above and pay attention to these people to see if they are Disruptive Influencers. That co-worker who is always attempting to add new ideas, no matter how bizarre they may seem, could simply be a positive Disruptive Influencer who is not afraid to speak up, because they are focused on solving the problem. Some ideas may come off as stupid, but don't be quick to dismiss them because of your judgments. Rather, expand your thinking and find out why that person thought it would work. Seek to understand rather than to judge. Mistakes and misunderstandings happen, of course, but pay attention to all of the ideas. Instead of judging your teammates for their behavior, your homework is to observe them in the next meeting and determine if they have some or all of attributes in the list above. I promise you that if you want to positively disrupt your own life, you must begin to rethink the way you see the people and things around you. We were not put here to live behind the computer and our devices. We were put here to interact, thrive, and experience full living. Exploring your inner Disruptive Influencer and finding others in your life will be fun. Who knows, you may even learn something about your ability to pay attention to something other than yourself.

CHAPTER 3

YOUR "WHY": GIVING UP IS NOT AN OPTION

Habitual Why: doing something constantly or as a habit

Intentional Why: doing something on purpose, deliberately, or for a reason

I walked down the long hallway that seemed to last forever. At the end of it stood giant double doors carved from heavy chunks of wood, opening into the room where I was about to speak. As I listened to the echo of my shoes against the freshly polished floor, I was lost in thought, my hands tightly clenched around my presentation outline. I realized, for the first time in my life, I was actually terrified. This feeling had to happen sooner or later, but why today? I had spoken in front of thousands of people. I had opened for Britney Spears, Ziggy Marley, Jimmy Buffett, and countless other acts. I had spoken to thousands of business professionals and leaders. In my coaching, I worked with some of the world's top companies and gave almost three thousand presentations. The stage was my home and speeches just rolled off my tongue—so why was I terrified now? As I approached the double doors, I tried to clear my head while I slowly reached for the handle, pushed the door, and entered the room. What lay behind the intimidating doors was a packed ballroom. I stepped into the room; everyone was facing front and carrying on light conversations as they sat in a U-shaped table arrangement. Of course, my seat was all the way at the top of the "U." I was about to face top officials from almost all fifty American states. As I was walking to my seat, my mind was racing about a thousand miles a second. My most important moment was upon me, and all of the years of work, trials, failures, acquired knowledge, and information in my head were about to come together for what I would consider the presentation of my life. After all, it was not every day that I spoke about the need for a higher level of standards in a new industry. And not just in any industry, but in the marijuana industry. I was about to launch into a speech and Q&A about the cannabis industry to nearly forty attorneys general and a room full of their staffers. Me. I was actually about to do this. A heavy realization crushed me under its mere weight; my words could either build or destroy the entire industry. As I stood, about to begin, in front of the officials, it hit me . . . not fear . . . but my "Why." Many people have talked about having a reason for taking on goals in life, but no one really helps you figure out how to find your own reason. Frankly, no positive disruption can happen in your life unless you are willing to take a risk, and no risk is very smart unless it is driven by an intentional reason for doing it. The risks people take in haste, without real reason or thought, seldom work out. You need to find your Intentional Why if you want to break through the fear of taking a positive risk.

My "Why" in life and for everything I do was so big, it made me forget about all of the fears and replaced all of the negative feelings with energy and excitement. I faced the attendees, greeted everyone, and thanked them for being there. Then I reached down deep into my Intentional Why. That thing that was bigger than my fear and petty insecurity. I used that intentional reason for being as a fuel to push past my trepidation and began to speak.

You see, we have been programmed and, for the most part we live, to make decisions or more importantly, habitually act in a certain way. The technology we all love was supposed to add value to our lives, yet, more often, it creates a reactivity inside of us, making us less and less intentional each day. Instead of data being assimilated into our lives and being utilized effectively, it has become a source of constant entertainment and a very large part of life where we live and die by countless shares and likes. This is why it's not surprising that we fail to live a fulfilled life, or to take a simple risk at work or in our personal lives. Our "Why" for doing what we do each day is clouded and often replaced by sound bites of data, false information, or shared content that serves to distract us without really being useful. In order for us to truly move into a new disrupted reality of fulfilled living, we must break away from that Habitual Why type of thinking and instead move into a very tuned-in Intentional Why. There are some things that should be left habitual, such as brushing your teeth, taking a shower, or breathing. But when it comes to taking a risk at work, speaking out, starting a business, or the vast array of ways you can become a Disruptor, your Intentional Why will be paramount to finding the strength to push through adversity.

THE BIRTH OF MY FIRST "WHY"

When my sister, Holli, was born, she was normal for just one day; it was only for twenty-four hours that my parents could have the highest hopes and dreams for their healthy newborn daughter and could see a bright future for their now well-rounded family of two kids. As all parents do, my parents envisioned a life with two amazing kids growing up together and living a blessed life. Our family was complete.

On Holli's second day of life, something went terribly wrong. Holli stopped breathing. Her oxygen loss was so severe that, when she was discovered by a nurse, her skin was a dark-blue color. After baby Holli was revived, she was never going to be the same. This massive oxygen loss left my sister with permanent scar tissue in her brain and left her mentally disabled. Tragedy had struck our young family. The brain scarring created more than enough health issues. The biggest issue was epileptic seizures that, for years to come, would often send her to the hospital in the middle of the night, causing near-death experiences and incredible stress for our family. For many years, I can remember countless nights when my dad would rush Holli to the hospital because she was having a severe seizure. Many of Holli's seizures were life-threatening, and we never knew how much time Holli had left in this world. My parents and I would stay by her side through the night, making sure she was going to see another day.

I was only five years old when newborn baby Holli came home. As I looked at her sweet little face, I had no idea that both of our lives were forever altered. What I would learn years later was that my sister's disability would send my life in a direction I could never have envisioned. It is these moments in life—these powerful, life-altering situations—that define us. They define us in one of two ways: we become strong or we become weak. I have found over the years that situations like this, often in childhood, have very different lifelong impacts on each person. For some, these moments of stress and strain destroy them, while others use the same or similar situations as positive fuel to build a strong and fulfilled life. What I have also learned is that each of us has control over only one person—ourselves. The only things out of our control are outside circumstances, such as where we are born, how, and to whom. But as we grow, mature, and learn about life, we have the power to control how we interpret and perceive the situations we experience throughout our lives. At one point or another, each of us has a choice to make in life: filling their lives with either Habitual or Intentional Whys and then owning the experiences resulting from their choices. Everything we decide to do and not to do is our choice. Regardless of circumstances or age, we all can make new choices or alter those choices that no longer benefit our current lives. The best part is that continuing to let a Habitual Why drive your life or thoughtfully choosing an Intentional Why to propel your life from now on is completely up to you.

HABITUAL VS. INTENTIONAL WHY

I bet you know some people who are either very unhappy or very happy in their lives. These two total opposites of living are examples of the very same choices presented to you every day. Some people begin a long life rooted in a victim story. It's not really anyone's fault, because a story of "life's hard" and "nothing good ever happens to me" can begin very easily, creating a downward spiral of negative self-talk and emotional struggle. Most of these negative associations with emotion begin during childhood and young adulthood. These experiences can negatively impact us and latch on for the long haul of life. Once the negative experiences are converted into memories, or, actually, stories we tell ourselves every day about our lives and our worth, they are imprinted in our memory. That story of our perception becomes our everyday reality, which turns into what I call the "Habitual Why." The Habitual Whys tend to be negative and, more often than not, they are the reasons you are hindered, lead with fear, and generally live life in the safely of your comfort zone. These reasons are born from past experiences in your life that you view as negative. They are the reason for doing what you do every day. The Habitual Whys are so rooted in your subconscious mind that you most likely don't even know where they came from or who put them there, let alone how to overcome them. For example, if you had parents who always put you down and called you stupid, you will most likely have low self-esteem and personal-value issues. So every time you speak up in a meeting at work and your idea gets shut down, you immediately feel as if you are stupid and punish yourself for even thinking you had a great idea. Unfortunately, you have become accustomed to using these stories—*I am stupid, I am not worthy*, and so on—to define yourself in comparison to everyone else and to assign yourself a place on life's totem pole based on your inner feelings about yourself. When you are caught in a habitually reactive trap, it leaves you feeling as if life is against you or you are always at a disadvantage. To make things worse, these stories don't just stay in your head, they actually spill over and manifest as anger, irritation, and jealousy at work, home, or throughout the countless interactions you have with other people every day.

It is necessary that you have a clear view of what your Habitual Whys look and feel like and realize when they are leaking negativity into your personal life and business life. Let's start with a business example. You are at work and your boss critiques you in front of the team, and then you get a pile of work dumped in your lap, which seems impossible to achieve before the deadline. If you are like most people, when this happens, you start telling the story that defines your perception of life. The story is that you are unlucky, always have the most work to do, are ignored, and are never going to be promoted to a better position at work. Everyone just uses you and you never get the recognition you deserve. This story may be told over and over again, silently or under your breath, to your attentive audience of one. Unfortunately, since you are so used to this story, you completely believe what it says about you and the world you see. Most people go through their lives not even realizing that they have such stories. Why? Mainly, because they are so used to the way they see the world that they don't even know they are doing it. The story plays like a carefully written song of despair uttered uncontrollably, and it begins a negative spin that leaves you feeling like a kite in a hurricane— blown all over life, out of control and a victim of the circumstance. So you finally start to chip away at the heap of work that was tossed on your desk, complaining the entire time and never feeling any sense of satisfaction—not just from finally completing the huge list of tasks that you have been assigned but also from your job in general. Maybe you don't get any satisfaction from your life until you get home, open a bottle of wine, and start your complaining session with the next person who will listen. Now your Habitual Why has traveled with you from the office to your home or to some other place where you will feel the need to unleash it onto your family, friends, or, sometimes, strangers. You are not alone in this dilemma. In fact, most of us have at least a few Habitual Whys that we need to overcome. And from my personal experience, most Habitual Whys are steeped in negative mud surrounding a person's life, like a deep moat of despair. As long as you keep the Habitual Whys and never change them, no matter where you step in life, you step into the muck.

Another business example is from coaching leaders. I will often test leaders right away. One of the most important tests I give is an evaluation of their reaction to tardiness. Before you get excited about thinking that I teach them how not to be late, I should explain the test. In the first or second coaching session, I will schedule a one-on-one coaching meeting, and I will arrive at least twenty minutes late, on purpose. The reason for my tardiness is twofold. First, I want to see how that specific person reacts to me being late. Do they become agitated? Are they passive-aggressive about it? Do they demand an excuse or simply say, "No worries"? Either way, their reaction tells me a great deal about their temperament and patience level. The second reason for this test is to learn about some of the Habitual Whys they have developed over time that might come out due to my tardiness. Essentially, I want to understand what triggers their core destructive behaviors. Mostly because nothing triggers a leader to be anxious, irritated, and passive-aggressive better than tardiness does. This one concept, lateness, is such a significant trigger that it works in both business and personal situations.

Let's talk about your personal life for just a second. Where does a Habitual Why rear its ugly head? A common issue in relationships arises when you and your life partner start arguing, let's say, about tardiness. In this example, one of you is late, which triggers an argument starting something like this, "You don't respect my time!" or "You are always on time for work but not our dinner!" and on and on. You two argue for so long that the dinner gets cold and both of you feel completely drained after the fight. This is not an ideal end to a night that could have been spectacular and filled with affection. I surmise that arguing, anger, and all of the resulting emotions that are stirred up during these circumstances are wasted energy as well as wasted time. I know what you're thinking, "But, Todd, I've heard that arguing can be good and even healthy for a relationship" or "Why should I let someone else walk all over me and disrespect me?" This may sound counterintuitive, but people who have not yet figured out how to eliminate arguing altogether use those questions and justifications just for the sake of continuing with their destructive actions, in this case, arguing. Arguing creates stress, stress leads to illness, illness leads to more stress, and so on. Destructive behaviors, no matter how small, in a relationship or in other aspects of life, are just extra stressors and a sign that you are not personally accountable for your own actions. However, when issues arise between people at home or at work, I do believe that discussion, negotiation, and solving key issues are critical and powerful tools to living a fulfilled life. If you and the person in question are seeking to understand all of your Habitual Whys that are creating conflict, and then turning them into Intentional Whys, then discussion (not argument) can be a very powerful tool. Figuring out what is causing one or both people to overreact is a powerful way to remove roadblocks and have a less stressful relationship and work environment.

Let's continue with the personal example of tardiness in a relationship that started a fight between two people who are supposed to be in harmony. Let's say, your partner planned a dinner out. With both of your hectic work schedules, finding quality time lately has been difficult. Unfortunately, on the evening of the romantic dinner, you have been pulled into a meeting at the end of the workday. The meeting lasted only minutes, but it has made you late to the dinner by at least twenty minutes. With so many last-minute things going on, you forget to call your partner and let her know that you are running late. She sits at the restaurant, and waits and texts and calls and sits, while her anger and frustration rise at an exponential rate with every passing minute. Suffice it to say, by the time you arrive, she is livid, and feeling unimportant, since you apparently have more regard for your work than for her. It's also clear that this critically important evening as a couple took second place. What ensues next is the argument. I would guess the actual "fight" took off from either a lack of understanding or a total disregard for actually solving the challenge at hand because you were tired and just wanted to take the pent-up anger out on someone. Instead of stopping to think and taking a deep breath to candidly look at your Habitual Why and the reasons for your behaviors, you both decide to dig in and argue. Your partner complains about your work obsession, your lack of respect for her time, and your general lack of concern for her well-being, since you didn't even bother to call or text. You then become agitated because she doesn't understand the importance of your job, and that you simply forgot to call or text because you were so stressed with a variety of last-minute issues with work. From your perspective, your tardiness should be okay, if she only understood the complexity and pressure of your work. But, instead of having a real conversation and coming to a much-needed resolution, you are both steeped in the muck of arguing.

Pause here for a moment. Reflect on the situation above. Can you see the habitual reasons for each person "digging in" to the argument and their deep agitation with the situation? The Habitual Why is usually not obvious, because you are experiencing only this small snippet of the couple's current situation. Perhaps your partner was raised in a house where the father or mother was *never* on time. This agitated your partner as a child, who felt discarded by the tardy parent. This trigger, which has been implanted into your partner by someone else at a very young age, is the reason she is mad at you for being tardy. However, not experiencing what she had lived through as a child gives you no perspective on the reason for her unconscious fits about tardiness. You, on the other hand, had a very understanding mother who never complained about your father being late. In fact, your mother would often say, "Dad's work provides a great life for us, so we must always be understanding." So, when you and your partner enter the tardiness argument, you are each coming from two different circumstances that paint your current view of tardiness; thus, you begin an argument in which both of you feel that you have a good reason to be angry and that the other person is at fault. So, instead of having a lovely dinner, both of you bring a basket of mud to throw at each other in this ridiculously silly argument. The irony is that you did not put the mud in the basket. Your parents did. Still, you are quick to throw it at the person you are claiming to love the most. We all fall victim to this type of thinking at some point, but I am here to tell you that it is useless. As you keep reading, start to analyze your behaviors and ask yourself where they originate and what, in your past, may have created your views that have turned into triggers. When you do this, you will eventually discover that preventing yourself from falling into the muck next time takes less effort and awareness than you might think.

THE OPPOSITE OF MUCK

Those who take adversity, painful situations, and even failure, and use those circumstances to find energy, passion, and unwavering faith, can create the "Intentional Why." Intentional Whys are your internal fuel that keep you going and improving yourself in every possible way. When you discover a Why that is intentional, it's usually connected to some inner drive that's almost inexplicable to others and sometimes even yourself. It's a feeling rather than a thing. It's a feeling that exhilarates and energizes you to keep on pushing through the bad, until you get to the good. It's the force giving you strength and a reason to get up every morning and push through your day with a positive attitude. If you have this feeling about anything, then you are living with an Intentional Why as your key motivator for that specific goal. The Intentional Why is what it sounds like: it's intentional, because you have chosen to represent something in your life in a positive way when you face adversity in life.

No matter where your Intentional Why originates, you will find the most powerful ones, the ones that get you through the tough times, are the things you hold dear to your heart. I have worked with leaders all over the world, and the one thing the leaders with the most amazing results have in common is that they *always* have an abundance of Intentional Whys motivating them and pushing them to excellence. When I joined the emerging marijuana industry, it was apparent to me that the entire industry was filled with people who had a bevy of intentional reasons for being there. If you are not familiar with this industry, you have no concept of the passion needed to motivate you to participate in an industry that can help people while still being federally illegal. The leaders in this industry, the ones still existing, are completely focused on their Intentional Why, because it gives them the reason and strength for them to continue. A massive misperception from the world outside of cannabis is that it is a huge group of potheads who got together to create a marijuana movement and simply want to get people high. Most people outside the industry do not understand the passion associated with helping people manage pain with marijuana or helping that next soldier with PTSD feel better. The reason you have witnessed the cannabis industry grow to huge heights so quickly is because the majority of these leaders know that staying focused on their Intentional Why is the key to success.

Habitual Whys and Intentional Whys are choices. Regardless of how each situation comes to pass, at the end we have a choice to either create a Habitual Why and sink in the muck of despair, or to create an Intentional Why and make it our driving force in life. You can have dozens of each Why, and some may rank first in importance and impact; the more Intentional Whys you have, the more in control you are of your life. Choose wisely, even the smallest of the choices determines the outcome and direction of your life.

My sister's situation, at such an early stage of my life, started as a Habitual Why that luckily for me turned into an Intentional Why as I grew older. I realized early on that life presents many disruptive moments that may be perceived as negative, but it's all in the perspective. It would have been easy as a kid for me to feel that Holli's situation was negatively impacting my life; and I could have taken the perfectly paved road to victimhood and lived my life from that vantage point. Certainly, the repeated trips to the emergency room with her ailments were taxing on our family. The constant attention she needed could have jaded me as a child and then as an adult. However, I leveraged all of the situations to make my life more fulfilling. I took her issues and disability, and I used them to make myself better, to improve our relationship, and to build a strong sense of self.

Thankfully, as I grew older, I made a choice to live in a way that took the challenges my family faced and used them as vital fuel. I used them to propel my career, experiences, and overall mind-set into the stratosphere of amazing experiences. Holli became my Intentional Why in life. She is the reason I never give up in life and, no matter how hard the situations seem to be, I keep pushing onward. When I am feeling scared, stressed, or hopeless, I reach for the memories of my sister. She knows only the life she has, so I intentionally strive to become more, be more, and do more, so that she can vicariously live a life she could only dream of. There is no room for fear—only focus—and moving forward.

WHAT DO YOU DO WHEN LIFE DISRUPTS YOU?

Let's return to the day I delivered a presentation to the attorneys general officials for the first time in my career. It was a critical risk that I had to take, because, if I was successful, I would gain a huge amount of credibility in my career as well as within the cannabis industry. Since the topic was very controversial, I put myself in the fire of criticism even before I started my presentation. However, it was a profound experience for several reasons. First, in order to prepare and re-center myself, I had to reach into the deepest parts of my motivation and leverage that very first Intentional Why in my life to overcome my fear: Holli. Second, I had a chance to be the spokesperson for an entire industry at the highest levels of government. This was a time to make an impact in the world of cannabis, to bring about better standards and to help create a safe and long-lasting industry. My government-affairs team and I needed to convey clear messages about consumer safety, consumer protection, and how we would help the government work with a set of quality standards to protect all consumers and workers, and to follow the rule of law. It was not enough to simply speak in broad terms. I needed to work every aspect of the presentation with completely crafted intentionality. This was the highest-pressure presentation of my career for those very same reasons. In the end, I was helping millions of people who need cannabis as medicine and, at the same time, I was living a fearless life, in my mind, for both Holli and myself. Every risk I take always has an Intentional Why fueling it to drive me forward and do the work needed to be successful.

WHICH VERSION OF "WHY" ARE YOU CARRYING?

To figure out if your life is filled with Intentional or Habitual Whys, you have to ask yourself, "How do I react when I am faced with situations in my life—risks I need to take—that scare me, that make me doubt myself, and my strength?" In other words, do you tell a victim story about your difficult childhood, your abusive parents, your horrible siblings, your adoption, or then as an adult, your failed marriage, the boss who oppresses you, lack of opportunities, or anger at the "system"? Do you still complain that life is "unfair," "unjust," and "unkind," in a habitual triad of negative self-talk? If that sounds like you, your life is filled with Habitual Whys. Am I saying you should never complain? Well, yes. You are damn right I am. For you to truly move into a disrupted and powerful life situation, you need to drop the need to complain and get more specific about the truth of a situation. The truth is that you may be scared, frustrated, or upset, but, as you will find out later in the book, you have tools to control those emotions and feelings. What you need to remove from your life are the repetitive complaints you file every day with those around you, on social media, and with family. In the end, your complaining is only the endless list of habitual reasons to justify the way you act today, the reasons you have been cultivating your entire life.

Maybe you are not a complainer, maybe you do gather all your strength and stand tall in the face of adversity. You already see the importance of having a fulfilled and happy life, and because of that, you ask far bigger questions, inadvertently (or on purpose) changing your negative self-talk into positive self-talk. When encountering a challenge, people working with the power of the Intentional Why under their feet say "What can go right?" and "How can I make this work?" They tend to make powerful statements that turn them toward a new direction and help them say, "I will make this work," or "I am better than this situation." Regardless of their circumstance, they have trained their mind to find new ways of living and thinking. Make no mistake, it's a choice to have Intentional Whys. It takes work, sometimes harder work than you have realized, to fill your life with Intentional Whys. If you are this person, keep on reading anyway—there's always more to learn. If you have already learned it, then read on and master it.

HOW TO MAKE A NEW CHOICE

Take a moment and pause. I want you to think of a situation where you were so negative that your behaviors defaulted to anger, hostility, or even lashing out at a co-worker, spouse, or friend. Do you have a memory in your mind? Now picture how you could have acted with a more intentionally positive sense of direction. What if you could go back and re-participate in the situation? How would you react today? Take your time and think about it. The rest can wait.

One key element of becoming an Intentional Disruptor or Disruptive Influencer is harnessing your many Intentional Whys and getting rid of the Habitual Whys, fast. If your life is overrun with Habitual Whys, you need to start looking at your life in a way that gives you motivation while you stop waiting for someone else to inspire you. You are the only one who can change your life and create a life worth living.

HERE'S HOW YOU CAN CREATE
MORE INTENTIONAL WHYS IN YOUR LIFE

Take a closer look at the people in your life. The people you are closest to are the ones you have brought into your life for a variety of reasons (family can be the exception). Are they negative? Or do they uplift you with encouraging, success-driven words? In order to have a positive life and positive experiences, you need to surround yourself with positive people as often as you can. Don't be afraid to burn a bridge between you and someone negative. If you are impacted by the negative people in your life, it will be hard to find Intentional Whys. This is mostly because the naysayers and negative critics will always find something wrong with your ideas and provide good reasons for you to be negative and unhappy (just like they are).

Reverse the negative. When you hear yourself utter a word of negativity, regardless of the situation, immediately turn the statement around. For example, if I say, "My work is stressful and over-whelming," I would immediately turn it around to say, "I work at this job because it provides me with the lifestyle I want." If you are truly unhappy after that statement, then take it one step further and ask yourself, "What job would make me happy AND give me the lifestyle I want? How can I get there and what is my Intentional Why for switching a job and finding a new one?" By reversing the negative Habitual Why (complaining about your job and doing absolutely nothing to change it), you turn your focus to something more positive. You equip yourself with the power to shift this into an Intentional Why to lead you to the positive results you want, by either finding a new job or figuring out what is making you unhappy.

When you hear yourself utter a negative habitual comment, ask why. Often we are so caught up in the habitual world that we fail to ask ourselves where these negative comments and thoughts originate. When you say something like, "Nothing good ever happens to me," stop yourself and ask, "Wait, where did that come from? Who told me that in my life? Is this true?" This awareness, especially when you are being negative, will begin to refocus you in the direction of more positive outcomes, while simultaneously pushing you to tease apart your negative habits (Habitual Whys), figure out what triggers them, and, most important, determine why you have them.

WHY I CHOSE MY INTENTIONAL WHY: HOLLI

As I mentioned earlier, as I was growing up, I was imbued with the feeling that I had to do things differently than other people because my sister could not do many things and experience everything I could. Instead of moping around, feeling sad and defeated, I chose to soak up life like a sponge for both of us. Holli became the Intentional Why daring me to take huge risks, go for my dreams, and fight fearlessly to accomplish things that would scare most normal people. With more experiences and passing time, I created more and more Intentional Whys to get me to different parts of my life. Some of them became so big and so deeply rooted in my sense of purpose that, to this day, they are still unshakable.

My Disruption Mind-set was always based in the grounding of "Do it for Holli," in a way that caused me to go further, explore more, and dream larger. Her disability has also taught me valuable lessons in unconditional love, and how to find joy in *any* situation. Holli's unwavering love for our family and me warms my heart and has motivated me to do greater things than I had ever dreamed of doing. Not only that, but if I tell her that I am doing something new or challenging in my life, she will relentlessly call me just to ask, "How are you doing?!"

Every situation brings out different Intentional Whys. Find as many of your own as you can, so that you can conquer the roadblocks in your life and realize that life has more to give to us than we have ever thought possible.

DID MY VIEW WORK?

By 2005, I had more accomplishments than most anyone I knew who was the same age as me. To name just a few of those achievements,

85

I had built an entertainment concept that would last in Chicago for twenty-one years, performed on stage as a-warm up interactive comedian in front of tens of thousands of people, traveled all around the world while speaking and inspiring audiences, studied at the famed Second City improv theater, become an actor, built a successful entertainment business, and moved into the corporate world as a leader, speaker, and expert in corporate change management.

In 2006, my career took an even bigger turn for the better, when my team and I built a four-day learning curriculum for twenty-five hundred Pizza Hut managers that taught them a variety of leadership skills. In fact, I was so on my game at this time that I disrupted the conference even further. After four days of accelerated learning, everyone was wiped out, and we needed a big push to end the conference. So, against the advice of the rest of the team, in an impromptu last hurrah to make sure that those twenty-five hundred people got every ounce of inspiration we could muster, I went on stage dressed as a male cheerleader. Drawing on my Excalibur experiences, in true nightclub entertainment style, I electrified and rattled the exhausted audience into a burst of energy. I brought the crowd the energy to take the "right now" and give it all they had. Everyone was excited—some people were dancing on their chairs, and some were singing and clapping to the rhythm of "Rock and Roll Part 2." The most special part of that day was sharing the moment of complete exhilaration with one another after working so hard for four days. At the end of the presentation, our team received a standing ovation. To this day, people still e-mail me about that event, telling me how much the learning impacted their lives. My motivation had caused a positive and impactful disruption, not just in my own life and career, but in other people's lives and careers as well.

All you have to do is look for a positive motivator—an Intentional Why—your personal drive, and fire in your own life. Then leverage all that to do amazing and fulfilling things. All it takes is an undying desire to live a better and happier life. Once you stop complaining, you will need to replace those Habitual Whys that make you a complainer and a victim, and change them to Intentional Whys that drive you to unimaginable heights of success and happiness.

A LEADER EMERGES AND TURNS HIS
HABITUAL WHY INTO AN INTENTIONAL WHY

A few years ago, I was coaching over two hundred leaders for a company based in Denver. Each week, I would meet their leaders face-to-face or via phone and discuss all the improvements they wanted to make within themselves and within their team. One of my favorite leaders, who made the most improvement, was a man we will call Thomas (this is not his real name). Thomas had some serious anger issues, and it would bleed out in meetings or stressful situations. In fact, while this leader achieved amazing results, those results were often overshadowed by his hostile and abrasive manner. So I spent each week working with him in one-on-one sessions. I wanted to truly understand what was driving his decision making and temperament, because this one personal issue was holding back his entire career.

Finally, after months of work and lots of powerful debate and discussion, we had a breakthrough. I found out Thomas, as a young boy, had a slight learning disability. That's when his hostile Habitual Why was born. Thomas was dyslexic and had difficulty reading. As a kid, growing up with dyslexia was hard; it was something his peers, siblings, and even his parents didn't fully understand. Instead of being supportive and encouraging, they were harsh, pointing out every mistake he ever made, and calling him stupid. The pressure to perform and not be seen as stupid created a huge insecurity that Thomas would carry well into his adult life. The anger at work and in his personal life was triggered by his insecurity, unleashing rage and frustration onto the closest person. But what was causing the trigger?

To find out the real cause of the trigger, I asked him to take a huge risk that would require more work, so in the one-on-one meetings, we started playing out real scenarios in his work world. Ultimately, what we discovered was that when Thomas would come up with an idea or a suggestion in a meeting and someone did not like the idea, he would get triggered and revert back to being that small boy with dyslexia who felt that people were calling him stupid. He took the greatest risk imaginable, which was telling me about his childhood pains. He shared his story so he could grow, improve, and overcome his challenge. This negative Habitual Why was the reason for all his inappropriate aggressive behavior. It was time to replace it with a more positive Intentional Why.

Now, imagine if Thomas had decided he did not want to be disrupted, because of the fear of facing his Habitual Why. He would have continued down a deeply volatile and negative path. You must understand the importance of courage when facing your reasons for acting the way you do. You may not like the finger being pointed back at you and your habitual choices as you discover what really makes you behave the way you do. It was difficult for Thomas, but he wanted to excel, grow, and disrupt himself far more than he wanted to remain living in that Habitual Why. He was motivated to solve his issue so that each moment from that point forward would become intentional. For the majority of the population, perhaps even for you, the feeling of being "good enough" stops us from truly pushing forward into the world of becoming disrupted on purpose. Safety is a powerful weapon of the bored soul that convinces you to remain out of harm's way of past hurt rather than face emotional pain, struggles, or issues from your early life. I would argue that the most powerful Habitual Why you are operating under most frequently is the one based on the Play It Safe model. Imagine again if Thomas continued to live by that model. It would have not been a disrupting or very happy ending for sure. Thomas would have lost his job as a corporate leader, and his life would have been thrown into a new direction. Maybe he would have found a better job, but how long would that have lasted had his behavior stayed the same? My guess—not long. And what happened next for him certainly would have never occurred.

REINVENT CONSTANTLY AND DON'T LET ANYTHING DESTROY YOU. EVERYTHING IS GROWTH.

Thomas and I finally devised a new "Why" that was positive, was beneficial to him, and subdued his trigger. We accomplished this by finding his personal "Why"—a reason that drives and motivates him every day. A reason to keep living a life he loves. For him, the Why was his need to have a happy and wonderful marriage and to become a better leader. These two factors came together to build an Intentional Why, which was deeply personal and motivating. He became focused on his now pleasant leadership skills and improving his new marriage by thoughtfully acting, instead of simply reacting to life. When Thomas was hit with a triggering moment that made him feel stupid, he would ask himself, "Is that true? Are they really saying I am stupid? Is that person just rejecting the idea itself, or rejecting me as a leader?" After a few questions like that, he would quickly divert his thinking over to his positive Intentional Why, avoiding altogether the trigger that used to spark conflict. This change helped him to build a better business team and a better personal relationship. And, in just a few months, he had jumped from one of the lowest leader assessment scores to one of the highest assessment scores, based on feedback from his team. Those scores measured communication, conduct, and building a team of people who felt valued.

Thomas was promoted from vice president to senior vice president and, to this day, he remains one of the most valuable leaders in his organization. That is the power of "Why." *Your* personal "Why." Your Intentional Why. When you put this to work as a daily practice, you will start to feel better and better about taking a more calculated risk like speaking up, starting a business, or finding a new partner. The point is that breakthrough: risk-taking. Disruptors are deeply connected to their Intentional Why.

A SHORT EXERCISE IN PERSONAL INTENTIONAL WHY

What motivates you? I am pausing here so that you can begin to look at your work, your life, and your reasons for living the way you do. Take notes or simply mentally log your thoughts as I take you through this exercise. In my workshops, we work to devise each person's Intentional Why for every aspect of his or her life. Then we share those individual Intentional Whys with each other and discuss the importance of those Whys to their life. Now I want you to acquire a new, positive purpose for your work, your family, and even your trivial daily decisions. Remember, all actions and thoughts, Habitual or Intentional, lead to your life going in certain directions. In order for you to begin to make changes, disruptive ones, that will move your life in the direction you want, I want you to do the same exercise now. Make a mental note or write down the top four to five most important areas in your life.

For me, my top four (in no particular order) are:

Work
Family
Time to myself
Goals for my life

Next, look at each one and ask yourself what would be the ideal Intentional Why for that category. It should be something to give you the feeling of thriving or a sense of total fulfillment. You must be clear and honest and truly feel a connection to the Why that you create. If you do not, the Intentional Why will not be powerful enough to push you forward when you face many risks on the way to success. You could even ask yourself what would make you feel like you actually made it to a new level in these areas.

Here is how mine look:

Work. My Intentional Why for cultivating a career in speaking and helping others achieve their desired results is rooted in my belief that we all must live up to our potential talent and need for fulfillment. I also believe we are all connected and that strengthening our support of each other is our human responsibility. Therefore, each day, I work to bring these two parts of my Intentional Why to life in my work. So my Why for my work is motivating others to become the best they can be.

Family. Growing up, I did not always have a stable family life. Therefore, my Intentional Why for my family is stability. I seek to build a safe, stable environment for my kids, my partner, my parents, and the many other family members who come in and out of our lives. I feel a strong sense of purpose in building a stable, loving family environment since I know what life is like without that stability. I use my past as a tool, an intentional reason for my decisions, my actions, and my thinking.

Time to myself. I am motivated by the feeling of taking care of myself. I know I am only good for others when I am good to myself. My own sense of well-being and knowing I am better for the others in my life are my Why for taking time for myself.

Goals for my life. I go for my dreams and goals and take life on full-force because people like my sister cannot do these things. I do them a disservice when I fail to take risks and live a full life. Holli is my Why for conquering fear as I reach my life goals.

You will notice that my Intentional Why framework starts with what I am doing and follows up with the reason why I am doing it. These are the critical elements of Intentional Why building, and you *must* be 100 percent authentic with yourself. If, for some reason, you find one or more of the categories difficult, that is normal. This process takes time. Keep coming back to it each day until you find your Why. Trust me, you need to know your Whys, because it will be easier to get out of the muck of despair when things get tough or when life throws you a curveball when you have strong motivation.

LIGHTS-OUT

December 7, 2007, started as any normal, laid-back Sunday in the mountains of Colorado. I woke up, had my coffee, played with the kids, and then had to run an errand down the mountain in Denver. When I left the house, I had no clue what was about to happen. As I was heading to Denver, my music was playing, the sun was shining, and all was good in my world. I was booked to travel to Europe the following week to give a series of talks to Monster.com, and it was my daughter's second birthday. I had reached a level of business success where I was traveling, speaking, and inspiring thousands of people each year.

At 9:00 a.m., I stopped at a red light in our small town and just sat there, listening to the music. I reached down, took a sip of my coffee, put the mug back in the holder, and WHAM! Traveling at nearly 55 mph, a woman, in her massive Ford Expedition, slammed right into my car. She had been looking down at her phone, trying to dial a number, and she never saw the red light or my car stopped at the intersection. From a complete stop, my car was thrown over 126 feet through the intersection, then it rolled off the road and down a steep hill, where it came to a rest against a tree. I remember saying "Oh, God," when the car stopped moving, then I looked at my car's clock; it said 9:01 a.m. Lights-out.

When I regained consciousness, the clock said 9:08 a.m., and I was in a mental fog. I could not see well, everything was cloudy, and, to this day, I remember only flashes of images of the next six hours. It was as if I were watching a movie of my life, but I had no control of the events or time lapses. The doctor said I had a severe closed head injury, a massive concussion, and that I would be "off" for a long time. Being the resilient guy I am, I thought he was exaggerating. I called my parents and told them what had happened. Upon hearing about the accident, my stepmom rushed to my side and stayed until I was better and able to venture into public on my own. But my condition was more severe than I had thought. I didn't realize just how bad my injury was until my stepmom and I walked into a Wal-Mart for Christmas shopping a full two weeks after the accident.

For the first time in my life, I had a full-blown panic attack, caused only by the lights, the music, and the few people who were shopping at the store. I ran out of the building, huddled against a wall in the winter cold near the entrance, began shaking and crying, and ultimately nearly passed out. In that moment, life as a father and everything I had worked for in my career flashed before my eyes. I was panicked. Locked up. Then the self-talk started. *How would I provide for my kids? How would I live without the career I loved? What would I do? How would I function in society?* Had it not been for the patience and love of my stepmom, who was there to help my kids and me to go through the hardest part of my life, I don't think I would have made it off the ground that day. She took care of my kids while I recovered; but during this time I was falling into a secret depression, despair, and agony due to the massive trauma to my brain.

For nearly six months, I was in a spin. I could not go out in public, let alone speak to thousands. I could not see the future or any hope of regaining myself further than twenty-four hours into the future. The old Todd felt dead, and I was hopeless. I was in a circumstance that was, without me realizing it, creating a deeply negative and dangerous place where a Habitual Why was about to be formed. I was running blind, headed for the muck of victimhood, and my excuses for doing so were getting louder and more justifiable.

I know life is hard. Certainly, some life situations are tragic and hard to go through: a family member dies, your child is tragically injured, you lose the use of your legs in an accident, cancer strikes, or an even worse situation haunts your life. What I need you to realize is that the power to continue to live a full and happy life, regardless of current or past pain, is completely within you. No one can fix the troubles or make them go away; you are the only one who can make the choice and who has the willpower to rise above the circumstance and live a fulfilling life. Will it be easy? Definitely not. It will require a ton of work. But, after a while, you need to accept the reality, no matter how hard it may be, and remind yourself to get back on course. You will have to adapt and more than likely establish new goals. In the end, no matter how much pain you may be in, the world doesn't stop to wait for you to get better or accept the reality of your situation. Just like everyone else, you need to keep going. The key is not to beat yourself up for whatever happened but to save yourself from the muck of despair, anguish, and self-loathing by finding your Intentional Why for life.

The good news is that there are warning signs before you actually create a new Habitual Why. For example, if you are in a difficult situation and catch yourself complaining and justifying negative behavior, that is a sign. If you are at work and, for some reason, you are not succeeding at a project or a promotion, and you start to hear yourself blame others for your failures—that's another warning sign. Complaining, nagging, blaming others, and verbally beating yourself up are all huge warning signs that a Habitual Why is being formed, taking hold of your life, and ruining your future and new opportunities.

I have even more good news. During dark times, beacons of light show up in certain places and become your guideposts to help steer you back on course. These guideposts come in all shapes and sizes. Sometimes a song plays and wakes you up. Sometimes a friend or a family member will reach out to you with a reminder of who you really are. Another time, your fellow employee may ask for your opinion about an issue they have, which surprisingly awakens you to your forgotten or misplaced values. And sometimes your inner self can be the direction-turner you need. The key is, when a reminder comes into your life, you have to grab it and take life in that new direction.

MY REMINDERS

During my recovery from the head injury, I had a dream about my sister and me walking together down the driveway of the place where we grew up. I could see the trailer we lived in and feel the driveway rocks crunching under my feet. Everything in this dream seemed so familiar, but one thing was out of place. Holli was not disabled. In my dream, she was healthy and happy and all grown up. In my dream, we were adults, but we could see ourselves playing as kids in the small sandbox in front of us. As we walked down the driveway, Holli turned to me and said, "You are not me." I shot out of bed, startled. The dream felt so real. After settling down, I realized that

Dream Holli was right; I could get better, retrain my brain function, and at least make the attempt to push ahead. The dream made me realize that the disruption-minded guy inside me was still in there, and I just needed to wake him from his slumber.

Not too long after my dream, I was finally getting a grip on my life and remembering who I was. As I was following this guiding post, a call came from my mother that refocused me once again.

On the phone, my mother told me that she had cancer. This was her second bout of the disease. My mother had breast cancer in the '90s—she beat it with an unwavering will to live. She fought each day to survive and, after intense chemotherapy, my mother won the battle. This new call came to me with a painful memory of her suffering and doing everything she could to survive. It brought back memories of the pain I felt when she was sick the first time and I thought I was going to lose my mother forever. But this was also a reminder for me to pick myself up, refocus in the right direction, and get disruptive again. My mother and I talked about the power of will, the power of standing up and facing whatever life brings you. We talked about her first cancer diagnosis and planned how she could beat this one. My mother has always been strong, but that day she was even stronger than I had ever seen her before. As she stood tall and strong, even when faced with her second cancer diagnosis, the least I could do was get back to who I was. She told me, "If I could beat cancer, son, you can make your brain better, so stop complaining and do it." My mother's words resonate with me to this day, and they were the words that helped me to push myself to get better when I had my head injury. So I did. I beat my head injury and remembered who I was before the car crash. I was finding myself again and, after a few months, I took on a keynote presentation and got back on stage. No matter what, I was going to do it. And I did.

I won't lie to you. The first presentation after the accident was strange. I spoke for two hours using a script, and when I finished, the room stood in ovation. It worked, except for one small thing: I could not remember a word of the presentation. After the presentation, people from the audience came up and talked to me, shared their stories, and thanked me for my inspiration. I had no idea what they were referencing from my presentation. From the presentation I had *just* given! I blanked. Despite the fact that I had a memory lapse, I kept going. Eventually, after nearly two years of work, I regained my sense of stage, disruption, and the ability to entertain audiences without anxiety, fear, or panic. I overcame a devastating situation because I was reminded who I was, and I refused to let it end at that crash site. This was my choice.

Everything in my life—my sister's disability, my destructive car accident, my mother's cancer, my stepmother's support, my dad's words of wisdom—these things have shaped me into the Disruptive Influencer I am today. After my crash, I went on to be the top leader on our team, helped generate millions in revenue for the company, and ultimately reached levels of success even greater than prior to the accident. I used my experiences to grow and improve. I used my will to get better. I was on my game again in ways I had never expected.

This is how the Intentional Why can and will impact your life. When you set the Why into motion, there is no obstacle you can't overcome. I constantly reevaluate my Intentional Whys on a regular basis. Some days I need to review and adjust as a crisis or life situation arises, but this refocus constantly reminds me of what matters the most.

DO YOU OWN IT?

You can have all of your Intentional Whys in place and work extremely hard, but if you don't add the last piece of the puzzle to this picture, you will not see the outcome you desire. So here is the last piece. It's been in front of you all along . . . did you miss it? Have you ever watched a movie, only to find out at the end that you missed all the clues actually foretelling the surprise ending? You were so caught up in the action and the moment-to-moment excitement that you completely missed the little hints? It happens to all of us.

If you read this chapter again, and put your inquisitive eye on it, you will notice a common theme and thread running through it. I get asked all the time what it takes to be successful, happy, and fulfilled, and how to help people from all walks of life take more disruptive risks that lead to amazing results. People want to know what the secret equation is that works. The one trait many people tend to miss is the one most important to success—ownership. Have you ever witnessed the passion of a specific small-business owner about his products or services? He owns the business, and it's either a success or a failure; but when it fails or succeeds, he owns the outcome. The same is true in your life. If you fail, own it. If you succeed, own it. This one concept will obliterate all possibility for complaining and blaming others in an instant. Did I mean to be in a car accident? No. But how did I approach my recovery? I. Owned. It. Did Thomas keep blaming his co-workers for his issues? Yes, at first—but as soon as he started to own it, everything changed for him. The simple phrase I have taught literally tens of thousands of people in companies all over the world is "Own It." One of my clients loved this so much, the COO of the company plastered a sign all over elevator walls, "We Own It."

When you make a mistake, don't compound it with other excuses. Instead, own it. When you are applying this learning in your life: own it! I believe our society is missing this core element in day-to-day, moment-to-moment interactions. We fail to take owner-ship over our contribution to the collective society. We instead revert to a narcissistic point of view. That is no longer acceptable for you, because, starting today, you are going to begin taking more and more calculated risks, leading to a disrupted life that is fulfilling. Now you must adopt this learning by taking ownership over the person whom you have control of, YOU.

HOW TO APPLY IT—LET'S RECAP

At this point, these lessons are a great deal to take in. Your mind could certainly be racing right now with all of the habitual reasons you have for why you do what you do. So, for this section, let's apply it and review.

Risk

The Disruptor is a risk taker. He or she finds a powerful Intentional Why and uses that why to build toward taking calculated and smart risks, regardless of social status, walk of life, or job. If the thought of a risk locks up your ability to forge ahead, then your Intentional Why is not strong enough. I suggest that you get back to the drawing board and look again at what that Intentional Why is for you.

Remember the list of the top four to five most important areas in your life that I asked you to write down or mentally make note of? Well, here they are again, just as a reminder, so you can take your Intentional Whys and keep moving them forward with the following steps.

For me, my top four (in no particular order) are:

Work
Family
Time to myself
Goals for my life

Next write out your Intentional Why for each of these areas and why you want to change any of them.

List all the reasons (the Habitual Whys) that are part of your current behaviors or actions that are negative in each of the above categories (your categories). This exercise helps you to reveal all of the reasons you may not be aware of that lead you to act in a certain way that is counterproductive to your disruptive self. Write down all of the negative reactions you would like to change in your life. Some of the most common ones are: overreacting over small things/issues, getting quickly irritated with other people's actions (that are not done on purpose), getting upset because something is not happening fast enough, getting road rage because someone cut you off in traffic, getting upset with other people's behaviors because you don't have control over them, engaging your victim story when you feel that life isn't giving you everything you want, and reacting in a negative way to the stressful situations in everyday life you cannot control. Be honest with how you react to the outside stressors and write them down. After you have a few (or many) negative reactions to external issues you would like to change, picture in your mind how they make you feel (stupid, worthless, irritated, etc.). Then look back in your life and see how far you can go back, remembering an event or a circumstance that made you feel the same way you feel now. This will take some time; soul searching is not easy. After you discover the original trigger, slowly try to change it. The way you can do that is by changing your behavior and reaction to the external events that trigger anger, self-loathing, low self-esteem, and so on. If you don't get rid of the Habitual Whys and their triggers, these reactions and behaviors will create barriers to your growth.

Think of a situation in which you were so negative that your behaviors defaulted to anger, hostility, or even lashing out at a co-worker, spouse, or friend. What if you could go back and re-participate in the situation? How would you react to the same situation now? If your answer is "I would react the same," then you have not done your due diligence in digging up the Habitual Why that caused your blow-up.

You may need to return to the part of the chapter that explains why some Habitual Whys are hard to see and what can be done about them. However, if you did find your Habitual Why, and you would change the situation for the better in a positive way, then, please, keep going with the exercise.

HERE'S HOW YOU CAN CREATE MORE INTENTIONAL WHYS IN YOUR LIFE

Take a close look at the people in your life. The people you are closest to are the ones you have brought into your life for a variety of reasons (family can be the exception). Are they negative? Or do they uplift you with encouraging, success-driven words? In order to have a positive life and positive experiences, you need to surround yourself whenever possible with positive people. Don't be afraid to burn a bridge between you and someone negative.

Reverse the negative. When you hear yourself utter a word of negativity, regardless of the situation, immediately turn the statement around. For example, if I say, "My work is stressful and overwhelming," I would immediately turn it around to say, "I work at this job because it provides me with the lifestyle I want." If you are truly unhappy after that statement, then take it one step further and ask yourself "What job would make me happy AND give me the lifestyle I want? How can I get there and what is my Intentional Why for switching a job and finding a new one?" By reversing the negative Habitual Why (complaining about your job and doing absolutely nothing to change it), you turn your focus to something more positive.

CHAPTER 4

A BAG OR A BOX . . .
TIME IS TICKING

when: *at what time.*

YOUR "WHEN" IS NOW: A BAG . . . OR A BOX?

I looked up at the man standing in front of me in the airport TSA line. He looked like any ordinary man, simply dressed and cleanly shaven. I could see in his eyes that he was unsettled about something; I thought it could be nervousness about travel, or maybe he had an important meeting and was anxious to get it over. As I was mulling all of the situations that could make someone nervous at the airport, the mystery man pushed his plastic bin containing his belongings into the security scanner and got in line for the final body scan. Since he didn't present any immediate signs of hostility or danger, I ignored him and his restless agitation, returning my attention to placing my items into one of the plastic bins for scanning. I was about to enter the body scanner just as the man exited it on the other end. That's when everything changed. Suddenly, one of the TSA agents began barking directions to the man in front of me in a way I had not heard before, "Sir, I need you to remove the contents of that bag, NOW!" The TSA agent and some of the security guards who gathered around this man had terrified looks in their eyes; the man in front of me was unsettlingly calm but emotionally on edge. As directed by the agent, he gently reached into his large travel bag.

The man moved his hands carefully and, with utmost care, pulled something out of his bag that put more fear in everyone around him. It was the largest Ziploc bag I have ever seen, with contents known only to the lone traveler. No one behind me noticed the bag, chiefly because of the growing number of TSA agents, security personnel, and police gathering around at an alarming rate. But as the crowd of security grew, it was clear even to the most distracted traveler that something was wrong. And there I was, right next to this man and his mysterious bag.

This dark-haired man held up the cryptic bag in front of the TSA agent who had originally given him the orders. The contents of this special container were a mystery to anyone looking on; it looked like light-gray powder, and there was a lot of it. The man gently sat it on the counter. I noticed that the police officers standing next to me reflexively slid their hands up to the holsters of their side arms, as if planning a response to a possible attack. It was then that I asked myself, "How did I end up in this situation?" "Was I so distracted that I ignored all the signs indicating that this man might be a terrorist?" "Would I be shot in the cross fire?" I froze. Until, a few seconds later, I was asked by a police officer to step into one of the TSA check stations, right next to this bag-carrying individual. So I did. The line of people behind me was stopped, with a guard blocking the only possible entrance to the other side of security. I had never felt more vividly that I was in the wrong place at the wrong time. You could feel the fear of everyone rising, as no one could figure out what was in the bag and if it was causing harm to the people around it. What if the contents were already airborne? What if everyone was already sick from whatever was in the bag?! The TSA officer looked at the man and sternly said, "Explain." As the man started to explain what was in the bag, the mood of the crowd immediately surrounding him began to quickly change.

As it turned out, this man and his wife had been vacationing in Denver. They had been there for about two weeks when his wife suddenly died from some type of brain aneurism. While he was explaining the situation to the crowd of security, he was getting more and more distraught, with silent tears streaming down his face. He continued to explain that he wasn't able to afford any other means for transporting his wife's body home, and someone had convinced him that cremation was the best method. You could just feel a wave of relief and, at the same time, a wave of sadness blanket the entire area. No one said a word; no one moved; everyone continued to listen to the man and his heartbreaking story. He slowly reached into the open duffel bag still on the checking station and pulled out a much smaller Ziploc bag. This one was filled with personal belongings, which he dumped on the table. Out came a woman's watch, assorted keepsakes, a necklace, and a phone. The last things to fall out of the bag were her engagement and wedding rings. The man began to cry more as he talked about what had happened and that he did not mean to scare anyone. He was just trying to get his wife home.

I still choke up when I think about that moment, which I was so close to as a spectator. I wish I would have said something to this poor man, but I was in complete shock. The police and TSA instructed the man to repack his bag and told him he was free to go. This time there were no instructions that were rapidly and forcefully barked. Instead, everyone was quiet and no one knew what to say. There really wasn't much anyone could say. The mystery man took his belongings and quickly disappeared into a crowd of travelers heading for their gates. He was finally free to take his wife home.

Silence encapsulated the entire security area for a while, even after the man had walked away from the security line. I collected all of my belongings just coming out of the scanner. Half-dazed by the event that had taken place, I started to walk toward my gate—my mind forever altered, thoughts running through my head. Just minutes ago, the situation looked like a scene from a disaster action film, with feelings of danger lapping at everyone's heels. But everything changed so fast that no one even saw it coming. At the end of the day, no one was hurt. The onlookers may have stopped and felt sad for a few minutes; perhaps they called loved ones to tell them how much they loved them. Everyone just got back on their electronics and returned to whatever they were doing, as if nothing had happened. Of course, the most affected person was the man who will carry the pain of his dead wife in his heart for years, while, for everyone else at that security station, he was just a simple man carrying his beloved wife home in a bag.

THERE IS ONE FACT OF LIFE WE ALL IGNORE CONSTANTLY: LIFE WILL END

We will all end up in a bag or a box after our death. We have all heard this before, but we seem to forget just how fragile and short our lives truly are. And maybe we will not realize the importance of our lives until it's too late, when we are out of time, thinking back and realizing that we could have done more. The one important foundational lesson I hope you learn from this story is your "when"—to be, to do, and to have everything you want—is *now*. Let me repeat that: Your WHEN is NOW! All you have promised to do for yourself and for others—that moment to start doing them is *right now*. You have no guarantee you will have another moment after this one has passed.

The fundamental problem is that the majority of the population has been desensitized about death. To be more specific, we don't take seriously that one day we will die and be out of time to do everything we wanted to do. Everyone thinks dying is this horrible and awful thing we can avoid. It isn't. We all will end. If you look around your office or your apartment building, the people there probably range in age from twenty-five to seventy-five. The illusion is that if they're twenty-five, they have more time than that seventy-five-year-old. What we see can be deceiving, because twenty-five-year-olds die young sometimes. Everyone is made from the same building blocks; no one is made from permanent matter. That seventy-five-year-old just got lucky; he or she has been around longer and survived. The fact of the matter is that you don't know. There is no way to find out when you will die and then plan accordingly for all the things you want to accomplish. Thinking you have forever, or even another few years, is just an illusion. You could be dead wrong about how much time you have left, and then, you're just dead.

Before we go too far into a more detailed definition of your "When" and how to get a grip on it, let's take a moment to do this simple yet emotional exercise. Let's start out by remembering a person in your life who is gone; someone who meant a great deal to you. Let me point out that this exercise is not designed to create regret or stir negative emotions inside you, but rather to help you reflect on the time you have left on this earth. The goal of this exercise is for you to remember that life is short and, because we never accomplish everything we want to accomplish in life, we choose to have regrets—it's a *choice* we make. Regret comes only after we squander our powerful life moments or miss them completely. This exercise is meant to wake you up to the certainty of death, but only because we need that contrast to remember how to truly live and disrupt our own lives in amazing ways. While we still have time.

Do you have that person in your mind? Good. Now ask yourself, what conversation would you have right now with that person if he or she were sitting right next to you? What would you talk about? Would you complain about your work? Would you bitch and moan about your bank account? Would you complain about the government, your kids, your lack of achievement, or your failed business venture? NO! Hell NO! If you could have another conversation with this person, you would only talk about the present moment and positive things happening in your life, and you would just chat about how great it is to see this person again. You see, it is often AFTER we lose someone that we think, "Oh I wish I had not wasted so much time complaining when he was around," or "I wish I would have spent more time with her." You see, part of finding your "When" is getting your hindsight into the foreground, instead of waiting, regrettably, for it to come later. The point I make, again and again, when I speak to audiences is "Welcome, look around the room. Look at each other. What do you see?" I pause so the audience can take a good look around, and then I say, "I see dead people." While this sometimes gets a laugh or a groan of realization that our biggest enemy is time, that statement makes a very clear point: not one of us will survive this life experience. When you personally realize this fact, it's only then that you will begin to see life differently. Life will take on a new meaning for you. In other words, you will finally get it: you are going to end. This realization then causes you to begin to truly live. This exercise also helps you to remember that the people in your life who are still here matter. From simple interactions like the person you meet standing in line at the grocery store, to the more intimate ones like a co-worker who needs to talk, or your best friend who needs your advice, every moment is a big moment and every person is important, so treat each moment with care.

AN OPPORTUNITY . . . LOST

A very personal example of this recently happened to me. I was at lunch with one of my former clients, who told me that a man I had coached years ago to become a better leader and change the team dynamic at his company had taken his own life shortly after my time as a consultant with that company had ended. The reasons given for his action were based on very personal challenges he had faced. Still,

I could not help but be profoundly affected by the news. For nearly three years, I worked as his leadership coach, along with two hundred other leaders at the company. I knew these people, and he was one of the rising leadership stars among them. Since that lunch and the devastating news of his death, I have wondered what I would say to him if I had one more chance to talk to him—if I had the opportunity to help him one more time. I would tell him that he can handle anything. I would tell him that he can manage any and all of his life stressors; all he needs are tools. I would have reached further, below the surface of leadership coaching, and attempted to connect to the troubled man inside. Of course, it's too late now, and I deeply regret that I did not have this conversation when he was alive. Certainly, many would argue that his death is not on my hands, but I am the coach, the leader, and I could have done more. That is me owning the situation. He was a fellow human, and he is gone. Did I do enough to help? No. So when I did the exercise outlined above, where I talked to him as if he were still alive, I felt my own mortality talking back at me. One day I will be gone, and I will no longer have the ability to accomplish what I still want to do. To me, there is not a more humbling experience than to express yourself in this way and see your life from a different perspective. This exercise will provide you with a different angle on the same perspective you have now; it will show you that no one is immortal, and there is no magic pill (yet) to live forever—you *will* run out of time.

As a final note, this exercise is not designed to cause you to have anxiety or a panic attack because death is imminent. Instead, it should help you to refocus on the positive future you can keep creating and to reflect on your past mistakes so that you don't make them again and waste more time getting the same results—results that didn't help you move your life in a positive direction. We all talk about changing, doing things differently, and wishing we had done more in life, but that can only be accomplished when you stop your after-the-fact whining and blaming and finger pointing. That's when you can finally turn the needed focus on yourself and start to take powerful action forward.

You can change, we all can. The human mind is capable of amazing growth, change, and evolution. But real change occurs only after you have had this realization: you, everyone around you, and all the people on this planet will, at some point, be gone. This should be your fuel to stop your complaining and negative thinking and remember to do what you came here to do. To live . . . to truly live. You came here to take chances, seize the moment, and never apologize for actions moving you toward your fulfillment. You are here to become disrupted in positive ways and accomplish everything you ever wanted. This is the only way to thrive and not just exist.

DO YOU BELIEVE PEOPLE CAN CHANGE?

It's a cold morning in Seattle, and I am standing at the door of my hotel, waiting. I glance at my watch for a third time, 6:29 a.m. Where is this guy? He did say 6:30 a.m. I just need to be patient. As I nervously glance around, I finally see headlights approaching, and once again I look down at my watch, 6:30 a.m., right on time. The black town car pulls up to my hotel door, and the driver emerges. He walks around the back of the car and meets me at the hotel door. The driver is calm and composed; he looks at me and asks, "Mr. Mitchem?" "Yes," I reply. He stretches out his hand and shakes mine. As if on cue, we both start to walk to the parked car. The driver opens the back passenger-side door for me, and I drop a thick presentation folder on the seat and close the door. The driver wishes me a good day, gets in the car, and drives off. As the town car exits the hotel parking lot and turns the corner, I could feel a rush of calm wash over me. I had just taken a huge risk, the next big step, and all I had to do was wait and hear what the results were. If it works, it will be a powerful turning point in my already very exciting career. If not, I hope I get another chance.

Later that evening, after a day full of meetings and conversations, I sat down with the CEO of the company I was working for to discuss the merits of my proposal. The very same proposal I had dropped in the backseat of the town car that morning. The basis for my action was to change and expand my role in the company. Unbeknownst to the CEO, I had spent weeks preparing the proposal. I had it edited several times, added images, graphs, and all my past achievements at the company to show him that I was capable of handling this new and much larger role. I had even reached out to clients from Nestle, Marriott, and Microsoft for recommendations that I added to the proposal. I saw myself excelling in this new role, and I was ready for it to start, now. How could he say *no* to me? I am ready! But, after the nearly two-hour conversation, he did say no. My heart sank for a nanosecond, but it felt like a lifetime.

Quickly I pulled myself together, and my inner voice forcefully said, "It's now or never, Todd." So, in the most confident voice I had ever used, I said to the CEO, "At this company we talk about corporate change all the time—it's what we sell to our clients. So my question to you, sir, is: do you believe people can change and grow?" That was it. That one statement sent a shockwave of reality into his heart and moved the needle in my favor. The CEO pondered my statement for a few seconds, looked at me, and said the one word I was hoping to hear for over two weeks: "Yes." After a moment of careful consideration, the CEO looked at me and said, "Okay, here's your chance, so don't mess it up." With that, the whole conversation was over and we moved on to chat about the conference and other business matters. In that moment, I realized my car accident, my recovery, and all I had gone through was worth it, because it created a drive within me. That car accident caused me to reset my mind, regroup my future, and refocus in ways I could never have conceived. Everything had led me to this moment, the point in my life when I was moving up in the company and was going to get a chance to be mentored by the CEO himself!

I wonder sometimes what would have become of me had I simply done nothing that day, or had I accepted his first answer. What if I had never worked on that proposal and pushed for the new step in my career? Or what if I had simply quit because of my car accident? However, I am thankful that, instead of backing down, I seized the moment because I felt the instinct to go after this new position, planned for it, and had the attitude to take the risk. The timing felt right, and that feeling and curiosity about future possibilities was much more powerful than my fear.

WHEN IS NOW!

You will get sick of me repeating this phrase over and over. But it's the formula for getting your life to the place where you want it to be. In the work of disrupting everything for the better, this is critical: you can't move to the next phase of your life of enrichment if you stick to where you are now, because you feel that "someday" you will take the chance and brave the unknown. That "someday" is now. The time for planning is now. The time for an attitude adjustment is now. The time for tapping into your instinct is now. To jump in and start or go in the direction you wanted is now. In the next chapter, I will lay out a strategy to seize these moments. However, be aware, you are not ready for a new path or new beginnings until you are prepared to sincerely let go of the "someday" thinking. As long as fear and negativity dominate your mind, you are not ready to engage a new initiative in your life.

I have told this story about the CEO and my proposal to many people. They often ask me an interesting question, which actually tells me where their minds are. "But, Todd, didn't that proposal take a ton of time?" Well, yes. But, really? That's your biggest takeaway from the story? I just told you a story of how I called a limo company a week earlier and asked them to meet me all the way on the other end of town in Seattle PRIOR to picking up the CEO. I tell you how I arranged to pay for that detour and then how I placed a proposal into the car that was going to pick up the CEO from his hotel and take him to his meeting that morning. I talked about the great chance I had that morning, because, as he got in the car to head over to his meetings, he was going to find the proposal. The proposal I had spent weeks writing and perfecting. I then continue to talk about how I researched the role I wanted to have and outlined how I would succeed in it, if I was just given a chance. How I contacted my past clients to write referrals for me so I could put them in the proposal. And finally, I go on to explain how excited I was during the discussion with the CEO about my future and the moment where I pushed back on the *no* response with the CEO's own words, "Do you think people can change?" in order to close the deal. After all of that, if all you can wrap your minds around is the time it took me to prepare the proposal, and then say to me, "If it had been me, I probably wouldn't have put so much work into it, just in case the CEO said *no*." If that's where your thoughts are after hearing the story, it shows me that you are not ready to see the big picture of your future and work hard for it, because you are still hung up on the details, elbow grease, and time that this project was going to take. It shows me you aren't ready to leave the comfort of your current safety zone and take a risk to go for what you want the most. Well, the CEO did say *no*, and then I pushed back anyway. I actually poured my entire self into the preparation and the discussion of the new prospect for my career, and, in the end, everything I did, and the time I spent, and the courage I had to find to do it was worth it.

It's not mind reading when I say I know where people's thoughts are when they ask the question about how long it took me to prepare the proposal. It's simple: the people who can only focus on how long it took me to prepare that proposal are NOT ready or willing to change their lives now. If they can't fathom spending a couple of weeks of unsolicited work on a project to give them a chance to radically change their lives for the better, then they have no business thinking that they are ready to improve their lives. It takes work, people. It doesn't happen overnight; it doesn't always come easy; and you have to spend time and effort if you want it. But, if you want it and are willing to do the work, you CAN do it and you CAN have whatever you are striving for.

In order to truly take on the parameters of this learning, you need to realize that your useless complaining, anger, and countless excuses are destroying your ability to find motivation to move forward in your life—to thrive and to become a better you. Your politics are useless, unless you are a politician. Your divisive nature on social media is pointless, unless you are truly, positively, and physically making a change in whatever area you are complaining about and not just posting your opinion. Your never-ending arguments at work are simply a time drain and a stressor. There are better ways to improve or change what you don't like. Complaining is just another way of procrastinating. You are not doing anything beneficial; you are not fixing the problem; and you are definitely not changing the outcome you are upset about. What you are doing is burning the time in your already limited life while getting more and more depressed and falling further and further into a victim role. Success, happiness, and joy take work. They take work, because removing the habitual ways of interacting with the world is work. It is work on yourself, work on controlling your emotions, and work in figuring out what it is that will truly make you feel that you are thriving and not just existing. It's as if right now your life is tied in a huge knot and you need to take time unraveling it and figuring it out before you pull hard on the strings sticking out.

ON THE RUN

When I entered the cannabis industry, one thing became clear immediately: the entire industry was moving fast, faster than anything I had ever experienced. But the question I kept asking myself was: Why? Why is this industry moving at a breakneck speed? And why are its founders so risk-centric? Why is it like an addiction to come to work every day and work with more passion than I had ever felt in my career? To say the least, my head was swirling with these questions until one day, after fourteen hours of amazing and purpose-driven work, it hit me. The reason we were all working so fast, and on purpose, with a phenomenal drive for success, was because we all felt something I had never felt at any other job or even when I was disrupting as much as I had in the corporate world. It was because we were purpose driven, fearlessly accountable to every moment of the day, and building an industry for people who needed it the most: patients, veterans, and consumers who used cannabis to improve their lives, abandoning the alternative of chemo drugs, antidepressants, antianxiety medications, sleep aids, and many more pharmaceuticals that took away from their daily joy. The marijuana industry, at that time, was still mostly illegal, and we were forging our way to a new era. Imagine today if your bank account was suddenly closed. What would you do when you went to the ATM to withdraw cash, but you couldn't? How would you pay for gas when you pull in at the gas station with a completely empty tank? When I entered the marijuana industry, it was still not very mainstream and having my bank accounts being suddenly closed was a common occurrence. There were moments when many of the marijuana industry leaders and I felt like we were being treated as criminals. We had to pay employees in cash after seven of our business bank accounts were suddenly closed. Imagine paying over 150 people in cash; would you feel safe counting out hundreds of thousands of dollars in your office? This led to personal challenges as well. One day, I was driving to the gym and stopped to get gas. As I went to pay for my gas, my card was declined. I attempted to use it a second time, and again the card was declined. So I did what anyone would do, I called the bank to see what the problem was. To my surprise, all of my accounts were closed. I had no access to any of my money, all because I was depositing my paychecks in cash, which caused a warning to go off regarding my accounts. Those cash deposits were my salary! However, the bank saw the large cash amounts as potential drug money or cash laundering. This was and still is a regular occurrence for people in the marijuana industry. The industry was still growing and becoming more mainstream, but all of us who worked in this industry felt as if we were very much on the edge of acceptance. It's a funny thing to suddenly be thrust into a world so drastically different from the one you have been used to, doing something no longer routine to you. Imagine if today all of your friends, your neighbors, the parents at your kid's school, and your bank saw you as a bit of an outlaw. You would feel very isolated, very fast. But at the same time, you would be engulfed by this new energy of helping to make a change in the world. A feeling that you are pressed for time because you have no idea how fast anything will change or what problems you will face, so the only choice left is to succeed in every present moment.

On January 1, 2014, when Colorado became the first state to allow recreational adult use of cannabis, my colleagues and I were, in fact, blazing the trail. The laws and regulations at that time were literally being created around our efforts, even though cannabis remained and still remains, at the time of writing, a federally illegal substance. This industry wasn't built on decades of rules and business models. It was brand-new, with no rules, no standards, and an everyone-for-himself environment. While most industries may have a gray area that they run into once in a while, the cannabis industry WAS the gray area. It felt as if we were the pioneers of the industry—renegades and outlaws by the standards of other industries—because we were on the raw and ragged edge of a new industry filled with taboo, and we had to figure everything out on our own. The cannabis industry often gets compared to the alcohol industry, but this is a poor comparison. Yes, both alcohol and cannabis had to go through prohibition and, at one point in time, both substances were illegal everywhere in the United States. Other than those few similarities, the industries branch off into different directions. We all knew right away that this plant was unlike anything we had ever witnessed before, because it was amazingly diverse. Can you name another substance that is enjoyed recreationally, while it is also reported, as in the case of Dr. Sanjay Gupta's many CNN specials on the matter, as having life-changing medicinal benefits like preventing seizures and many other ailments?[1] It's difficult to come up with something else that has so many uses and so many divided opinions. So, suggesting that cannabis could use the same model as the alcohol industry is completely out of the question. Alcohol is used only as a beverage and, while it can offer some health benefits, if used in moderation, for many people, it has one purpose—inebriation. Meanwhile, cannabis consumers all over states like Colorado tell me personally when I visit dispensaries or speak at events that this plant helps them relieve many ailments, and they are adamant that cannabis is the reason their physical well-being is back on track. So, you see, we had to forge new territory within a federal system that did not support us; thus, we felt like renegades and outlaws. That outlaw mentality was a huge reason the cannabis industry even existed when it was mostly illegal. If people long before me had not taken even bigger risks, built businesses, and dared to grow cannabis in the face of federal prosecution, the current $5.5+ billion industry would not exist. This industry was created by bending the rules, and now it was actually helping regulators create and regulate itself, just as responsible business owners do. What I realized was, because the bulk of business leaders in this industry treated their world as if they were outlaws on the run, the passion to succeed was always engaged. As powerful Disruptors, they had to burn bridges between themselves and "normal" society at the time. Even I—when I entered the industry—became isolated from all the people I once knew and worked with. That day, when the CNN story with Miguel Marquez called "Colorado Pot Big Businesses" broke with me in the forefront as the new spokesperson for cannabis, my life changed.[2] I became an outlaw in the eyes of the corporate world; but at the same time, I started feeling the exhilaration of working fast to create incredible results, or, as I call it, "living on the run." On the run to create an industry at a breakneck speed that will one day become just another industry without its current stigma.

The feeling of being on the run is a profound one. As you think about your "When" for doing something, consider what it means to feel like an outlaw. When outlaws are on the run, they are living today as if their lives depend on it, because there may not be time tomorrow to do what should have been done today. As an outlaw, you always feel as if you could have it all taken away, yet you go forward because there is no turning back. Think about any movie you have watched in which you are pulling for the outlaw to succeed. Why do they ultimately win in the end? Because they are on the run toward the future, and they never turn to look back. They literally have nothing to lose. Knowing that to go backward would mean the loss of all their hard work, they push in the only direction they can: forward. And they do it when? NOW!

Am I saying you should set out to break laws, break rules, and fight the system at every turn to win at all costs? Absolutely not! I am stating, however, that the fire in your belly you seek is based on the mental state of outlaws. You will need to attach your Intentional Why to your goal and ride like a stallion into the sunset. Of course, the biggest thing to be very afraid of, which will come to get you in the end is death. We are all on that same run. But you are also on the run from a life of mediocrity, from a life of simply existing, and toward a life of truly living.

NOW THAT'S THE HIGH LIFE

Before I left my corporate career, there was a string of events that turned me in the direction of the cannabis industry. As I mentioned before, after my car accident, my mother—the survivor, the powerhouse, the cancer-beating, positive influence who helped me recover—called to tell me that her doctor diagnosed her with a second cancer, and this time it was terminal. In fact, the prognosis was that she had a maximum of six months to live. I traveled to see her in the hospital, met her doctor, and started to plan for the end of her life. This second cancer diagnosis brought back all the gut-wrenching memories from when she had her first cancer; but this time, she wasn't going to make it. It was the most painful experience in my life. I remember the doctor telling us privately that there was no way she would make it, that this cancer most likely was caused by the radiation treatment from her previous cancer, and this time it was a "definite fatal event." He was a kind man, and he did his best to comfort all of us, but the fact that my mother had six months to live could not be comforted away by anyone.

A massive chemo treatment was going to be useless in this fight, so my mother opted for a holistic center that could help prepare her body and mind for the agony she was about to face before her imminent death. A nurse at that facility told my mother to get her hands on some "good weed," because it would help her with pain relief as she slowly deteriorated. But my mother had no access to legal cannabis, nor had she ever consumed it. In fact, if I had been caught smoking weed as a teen, I would have been certainly, swiftly, and severely punished. So, my mother, being the Disruptor that she was, found a way to obtain marijuana, which she used to make muffins— from my great grandmother's recipe, no doubt—and ate one of her infused edibles each night. All at once, I was witnessing the impact of cannabis on a cancer patient's pain firsthand, and my mother was engaging in real outlaw behavior.

Exactly to the day, six months after my mother was diagnosed with terminal cancer, I received a call that would serve to catapult my life to a whole new level. When I answered the phone, the voice on the other end was crying; it was my mother. She told me that the doctor who diagnosed her with terminal cancer had been in a terrible car accident; his car was pinned against a guardrail by a semi-truck, and it had exploded. He and his young daughter were both tragically killed. My mother broke from her crying to tell me one statement I keep with me today: "No one gets to tell me when I die or when I am done!" She was alive, and someone who had medically served her the death sentence was no longer with us.

That was nearly seven years ago as I write this, and I am elated to tell you that my mother is STILL ALIVE. That's right, those cannabis muffins not only helped her to defeat the deteriorating body pain caused by the cancer but also helped her to go into full remission. Once again, I was motivated by her story; and I saw cannabis working in action, on my mother. I was interested in pursuing involvement with the cannabis industry, after having witnessed the life-changing effect cannabis had on my mother. At the time, however, I had no idea how to start or how to transition into the cannabis industry to make the most use of my specialized skills and experience. I started constantly researching the industry and learning about it. I knew that the right opportunity would present itself, but how, when, and where were mysteries. I just wanted to be ready. I was always clear about my goals once I got an opportunity to enter the cannabis arena: I wanted to improve the industry by teaching the companies how to build better, smarter, stronger, healthier organizations focusing on consumer health and safety, standards, and quality. On behalf of people like my mother, I was going to dedicate the next phase of my career to an industry ready to be legitimized. I just had to get into the cannabis industry and leave my corporate career behind.

It was not until 2013 that I ran into someone who suggested I call a colleague of his who desperately needed my unique style of business coaching, leadership, and business building skills. The person who needed my help was one of the leaders in the cannabis industry. This was just the opportunity I had been waiting for, over the three years prior, so I jumped on it. Keep in mind, I did not sit idle for this entire three years. In fact, I researched the plant, studied the medical marijuana framework at the time, and even reached out to several people I knew who grew their own marijuana at home. I was working to create a chance for me to work in the marijuana industry, and it took me the entire time to finally align with the right opportunity. When the moment came, I was ready to take the shot at this new industry, and my fuel was my mother's remission from cancer. Talk about an Intentional Why! I was leveraging my mother's cancer-fighting victory utilizing marijuana to catapult and pivot myself to a new world where all of my disruption skills would be tested in ways even I couldn't even believe. This is why I stated earlier that your Intentional Why MUST be stronger than the Habitual Why. If you don't engage a reason for doing new, often scary, things, you run the risk of falling back into your habitual ways of thinking that will stop you in your tracks. If you don't have a powerful Intentional Why, then you will never leave the security of your current career, which is not fulfilling you, or change other things in your life that are holding you back from your fullest potential. The power of your Intentional Why is critical and must connect to you emotionally.

When I entered the cannabis industry, I was challenged immediately. At each new demanding moment, I was inspired by my mother's story again and again. I talked about my mother's recovery every chance I got. I did this very intentionally at first to convince the public that my intentions were pure. Later, the story would serve to keep me focused in the face of adversity within an industry filled with risk and reward.

AFTER THIS, CLOSE THE BOOK OR TAKE THE JOURNEY

I don't want you to think that this will all be easy or simple. Your often-destructive behaviors, even if based on Habitual Whys, are still destructive. I know it may not seem that way, but every day, every moment, every second you waste on your damaging actions, no matter how small, those are wasted moments. It feels easier to stay where you are, even if you are stuck, because then you don't need to challenge yourself in meaningful ways and do all the hard work to change your habits. So what I am about to introduce to you is risky. When others tell the truth about someone else's destructive behavior, most people get mad. In today's world, it's difficult to find people who can take criticism and use it as a blueprint to improve themselves. Some people believe that they are fine the way they are, and nothing about themselves needs changing or improvement. However, there is another group which I am hoping you fall into. That's the group of people who see the world we live in, their own lives, and a never-ending sea of challenges, and say, "I am making a change in me, now." It seems that you are reading this book because you want to find that blueprint, to build on your experiences and polish yourself. If that describes you, then the next section will be about tough love and fuel for you to find your motivation to begin to do what I am suggesting and actually take real action.

Frankly, if you haven't been doing any of the exercises in the previous chapters and applying the lessons to new challenges, then there's no point continuing. If, after reading this chapter, you did not feel a stirring inside yourself to get up and start doing something now that will start you on a path of success immediately, then you need an intervention. When I give an audience a presentation with this key lesson, I stop here and say, "Okay. I need to know right now if you're willing to work hard to get to the next level. If you are sitting there thinking that this is a hypothetical question, if you just sit silently in your chair and cannot or will not take action, then you are holding yourself and everyone else back. Whatever reason is holding you anchored to the person you are now, you need to let go, because time is running shorter with every passing day." When I am on the stage asking thousands of people if they are ready to start taking action to improve their lives, I give them a choice, which is completely up to them: go home or take action. To make sure the message sinks in, I give everyone a few minutes of personal time to think about their options and perhaps a silent escape method. After most of the audience members return their focus to me, I tell them, "We are going to take a break and, when we come back in this room, you will engage with the next phase of learning to take your work, life, and focus to a new level. If you are not ready, then, for your sake and that of the rest of us, please don't come back. Go home, fall back into your mundane routine, and wake up tomorrow like this never happened. But if you are ready, take a break and come back, ready to transform." The funny thing is, everyone comes back. The question is: will you? Will you read on and apply the lessons from this book to launch yourself to a new level of living?

TOUGH LOVE

I have met a lot of people who are depressed, tired, and just drained from the same routine, a job they hate, family that is falling apart, and so on. Those people have hit rock bottom, but they keep on doing the same things because they're afraid their lives will get worse. Until they are dead, how can their lives get worse? They are at rock bottom; they cannot get lower than that. They are at their all-time worst, because they are the walking dead in their own lives and within their own choices. If they don't find whatever inner strength they have and start to change things, then their lives will always be the same and life will become mental hell. I bet staying in the same place and never getting out of debt or never getting that promotion is causing you pain and anger. In the next chapter, we will use these feelings as a motivator to inspire you to write down what you truly want in your life, and then create a plan on how to get it. *You, Disrupted* is all about you taking charge of the new ways of thinking I am outlining and stepping into a new world. You will, in the next section, begin to ask, "What steps do I need to take to get that promotion? What steps do I need to take to get out of debt? What steps do I need to take to finally go on the vacation of my dreams?"

Here's another hard fact: it's difficult to change. Why is it hard to alter our behavior when the changes we are about to achieve could be so positive? What I have learned is that we stall because those changes can also trigger anger and denial that lead to deflection of the true facts of our behavior. We become frustrated in those moments, out of fear of facing the reality of our Habitual Why origins. So we tell ourselves we are fine just the way we are. But those days are over for you. The exercises coming up will squash those Habitual Whys and replace them with purpose-driven Intentional Whys powered by the fuel of realizing you have nothing to lose. If you are experiencing this and you are here, reading this book, it's because you want to make your life better—because you are trying to find a way to live the life you have always imagined.

I know very well what it's like to have things keep piling on top of you. I get it. You're sitting right there with the feeling of the world crushing down on you, your bills are mounting, someone's dying, someone's sick, your kids are struggling, you're getting let go from your job, you're getting this and losing that, you are frustrated with society—or, worse than all of that, you are simply and totally bored. I have been there and I understand that you have a lot of things happening in your life. But here is the important question: So, what? Do you think you are the only person struggling? What are you doing to get yourself out of this situation? Are you using every excuse in the world for why things aren't working? Here's a hard fact: no one cares about your story, unless you are using it to build something better for yourself. Unless you're going to do something with your story and inspire others, don't share it just to be a victim. My story is only valuable if you learn something from it; your story is only valuable if you learn something from it and do something with it. If not, it's just a story, just another story you add to your life portfolio about how you were victimized by sad and unfortunate circumstances.

If you can feel my energy as you are reading this, then you are finally understanding that I am writing this section only to yell this phrase out to you: WAKE UP! (Okay, you can read the rest in a normal tone.) We have become drones, shells of who we used to be, and now all we are capable of is just surviving life. If your mentality is "I just want to survive life," then you are dead already. All you are going to achieve is survival. Period. If your whole thinking is "I hope I make it to work, I hope I get to work on time, I hope my boss doesn't yell at me . . . ," then that's all you will get, because you are not taking action to improve your life. It's just complaining and wishful thinking. If you don't start taking action to get yourself to a better life, then, frankly, you don't deserve one.

You have gotten a glimpse of what I have been through in my life and some of the things I've done. Do you think all of those things happened through a series of accidents? Do you think everything was just given to me? Well, I worked hard and never gave up, and that's how I got to where I am today. I never stopped working toward something I wanted until I got it. I was fearlessly accountable to my own future, and I have never let society dictate the rules. I live a life on purpose, loving others, uplifting the people around me, taking risks, and finding new adventures because I live life like I am on the run from the end of it. I have harnessed my renegade spirit—which you will do next—and take life on, headfirst.

So many people today are waiting for that hero or heroine or magic unicorn to come and save them, to give them the promotion, to take them to the next level in their life, to force them to stop being habitual. Well, that person (or unicorn) isn't coming, because the only person who can do all of that is already inside each of us. Your personal beliefs can compromise your success, but all that can change if you start believing in YOU.

The urgency of this critical chapter MUST not be lost on you. If you didn't read the story from the beginning of this chapter and think to yourself, "Holy shit, this is unbelievable. I forgot how precious my life and EVERY interaction is." If that wasn't enough, how about the story of my mother reminding me when I was falling apart after my accident, that she wasn't going to let a doctor tell her when she is going to die? If that doesn't motivate you, then all I have left for you is a forced call for action: Either turn the page and let's go to the next level, or slam this book shut and give it to someone who is ready! If you're not ready to take responsibility for your life, if you're not ready to wake up with a sense of urgency, if you are not ready to apply the exercises from this book to your life, then put the book down. I only want to deal with people who are ready to grab their life; realize it's special, rare, and short; and actually *do* something with it. No one has time for continuing to live a life they don't want, and the person who has the least amount of time to do this is YOU.

UP NEXT. THE REBOOT!

I will end this chapter with the same ending as my presentations. Word for word, here it goes. I hope to see you in the next chapter, but if not, I wish you well.

> The problem is that your system needs to be restarted, and we can't restart your system if you don't recognize and realize it's time to go to that next level. It means, once you pass through that door toward a better life, you cannot go back to the way you were; it's impossible. So you are either going to take a break and stay in your comfort zone of despair, excuses, fear, sadness, and the BS you keep telling yourself, OR walk through the door of opportunity, close it behind you, lock it, and never go back to that old self. Because there is no going back. Does that mean you will never feel like you are wavering or that you're afraid? Of course not, you are a human being. What it means is that you never go back through that door of change, even though something is trying to pull you back. You make a stand for yourself to never go back to whatever you left behind, because you realize that life is short.
>
> Now, if I did my job today, that should empower you to realize that you can't mess it up and you can't finish it; you are always working on yourself, and you're always in the process of working on something. There is no finish line, all you can do is to make everything as amazing as possible and do all the great stuff inside of you. Since none of us knows what will happen to us when we die, imagine that you die and the first person you have to answer to is yourself. And, let me tell you, that self is pissed off at you because you never lived up to your highest potential. And that pissed-off self is going to haunt you for eternity.
>
> Inside of me is that self who had desire, potential, excitement, and energy. Who wanted to do great things. Who talked to me repeatedly in that little inside voice, saying, "You really should write a book. You should go speak to share the message. You should go and join the can-

nabis industry to make it great. You should take a big risk!" My answer to my inner voice is, "HELL YES!" And your answer now MUST be the same. We don't get to do it over or go back and change things.

So, before I let you go on this break and make the critical decision whether to continue or leave, let's take a moment of complete silence for you to ask yourself, "Am I ready?" Think about it for at least ten seconds. The next step is up to you. Keep in mind, both steps will take you in wildly different directions. It's your choice! What do YOU want to DO?

Let's take a break, and I hope to see you all, here, on the other side of your everyday normal.

HOW TO APPLY IT

If you are still reading, I can guess you desire to continue on the journey to becoming a different, better, version of yourself. But in order to truly move down this new path, you need to now take a hard look at your life, the people in it, and the things you spend your time on. Think about how much time you waste on a daily basis, and list these out on a separate piece of paper or a document on your computer. Are you on social media for hours on end? Do you spend a great deal of time complaining? Do you waste the day away texting, sending e-mails, or focusing on countless distractions that steal your life? Whatever these are, list them. Next to each one, list the many ways you could seize your new disruptive self instead. For example, if you spend over an hour a day on social media, write:

Activity	Time Spent	Alternative Activity Toward Disruption
Browsing Social Media	2 Hours a Day	Spend Two Hours Researching My New Idea

Keep going through your day, listing all of the activities that are time drainers, and come up with a better and more intentional way to spend that time to improve your life. I know this seems like a simple activity, but it changes the way you use your time. If you have a long list of time-draining activities, you will start to find new ways to replace them with something more in line with your new goals and vision. If you don't have the time to do this important, "Now"-driven exercise, when will you have time to turn the page to the next chapter? You won't. So if you are ready to do the work on yourself, turn the page; if not, close the book and keep browsing social media. After all, I bet there is a new cat video that needs one more "like."

CHAPTER 5

THE REBOOT

reboot: to restart; to produce a distinctly new version

What do you do when your computer locks up? You reboot. *Reboot* is just another name for an entire system reset. On my Mac computer, rebooting is a simple process that requires pushing and holding down the power button. In that instant, as my finger is on the power button, I have started to completely reset the system. Why does a computer lock up and need this important reset in the first place? A client of mine at Microsoft explained to me, in simple terms, the reasoning behind the computer reboot.

Picture your computer as a rubber band that you are holding with your hands on opposite sides. If you pull your hands apart from one another very gently, the rubber band doesn't exert too much resistance and thus doesn't stretch to its maximum elasticity. However, if you begin to pull and stretch the rubber band with considerable force in every direction and, as your hands move farther and farther apart, the rubber band gets more and more stretched. This, in turn, makes it very rigid and not as flexible as it is when the rubber band is relaxed. The analogy he was trying to explain with the rubber band example is that the more programs you operate on your computer, the more stretched the "rubber band" will get. When you have too many programs opened on your computer, the processor and the available memory can't function efficiently, slowing everything down and sometimes even freezing up. Going back to the rubber band analogy, eventually, after the rubber band has reached its elasticity limit and can't take any more stretching—SNAP!—the band breaks and you must get a new one. It's a good thing that a computer can reboot instead of snapping like a rubber band and requiring a replacement.

Your life is a great deal like that computer and rubber band analogy. You keep adding more and more items to your life: work, kids, relationships, activities, and on and on. This adds stress to your life—even though many of the items might be positive. However, all of the added parts keep on functioning in tandem with one another. You need to make sure that you have enough time and money and energy to do everything on your list, which in itself can be stressful. You may be familiar with the constant buzz of many reminders about things that need to be done. For example, if one of your tasks is to do the laundry, then logically after the laundry has been done, this task should remove itself from your brain and be marked as a task that has been completed. Unfortunately, these repetitive tasks don't shut themselves off when they are "done," because you'll just have to repeat the same process of washing your clothes in a couple of days; instead of being eliminated, this task has been filed at the back of your brain, still running in the background just like a computer program. This happens in many areas of your life, so without any clear direction on how to shut down parts of the stressors and problems in your life, you end up with many moving parts constantly bombarding your brain. Eventually your personal rubber band— your mental stability—snaps. You get overwhelmed and just think to yourself, "Forget all of this, I will never have a better life." or "Why am I even trying? I'll never get to where I want to be." This is the time in your day-to-day life when the problems and stress get the best of you and could break your will to keep on pushing and striving to do better. At these moments, without you even knowing it—even though it's tough to think, because at this point you may feel brain-dead—you are ready for a reboot.

When you read the end of the last chapter (welcome back, by the way) and were finally ready to move forward with this chapter, my goal was for you to understand this very important concept: *it's time for you to reboot*. It's time to take action, today, so you can begin to reboot your personal system. While I was tough on you in that last chapter, it was necessary for me to show you the essential nature of rebooting your life. A computer can simply be restarted and function well after a few quick minutes of powering down. But when a person's life crashes, in any area, it can be painful, devastating, and often very difficult to recover. However, your life is not over; it's just waiting for a new beginning. Remember, you are in control of your stressors, and your ability to manage them is to disrupt them. This is also true for you as a worker or a leader in your current profession. If your team is off track, it is up to you to reboot the initiative, or the entire team. If you don't, Habitual Whys will dominate your team.

You may or may not know this: when you reboot your computer, there is a pre-programmed process the system follows to test and restart each program and, overall, get itself running again. A very similar protocol is also used for people when they are in the reboot process. This chapter is literally a step-by-step process for rebooting yourself. I have personally followed this technique again and again to reset all or parts of my life. Many times, the intensity of rebooting depends on where you are in life. If you are happy, and the only area in which you are struggling right now is your health, then you need to reboot only your "health program." It's almost like a New Year's resolution to start eating healthy and working out, but instead of waiting for the first day of January to start your plan, you start it right now (and you don't give up by February). For your continuous success in the rebooting process, I have laid out the steps in a specific order. I have found this process to be the best formula for resetting a person and directing him or her toward the life, circumstances, and desires he or she seeks. For you to be more disrupted in all aspects of life, I suggest following the steps in this chapter to the letter. Just because you read the following steps doesn't mean you will change and have a better life instantly. That's because the most important and last piece of this formula for success and a brighter tomorrow is *action*. Taking action is the most important step in any area where you want to see progress. Let's not kid ourselves; change is difficult. If you are here and still reading, then I believe you want to change and, most importantly, you finally believe you can change. Get ready for a reboot. Step one: attitude.

ATTITUDE

> *What attitude is not:* Attitude is not as simple as positive vibes or faking happiness until you become happy down the road.
> *What attitude is:* Attitude is your emotional and behavioral state, which you can personally control.

A few years ago, I was coaching a leader whose challenge was that he would suddenly become very frustrated with his co-workers, friends, and literally everyone around him. Throughout the day, many little annoyances would build up and, while he could control his frustrations in front of his team, bosses, and select family members, the negativity inside him was consuming him more with each passing day. For the sake of his privacy, let's call him David. David knew he had a problem that would prevent him from living a less stressful life, and the best part of this story is that he wanted to change his behavior and figure out why he was annoyed with everything. He also knew that for him to change his behavior, he actually had to take action. Unfortunately, David could not act—because he had no idea how he was going to elicit and execute the change. Or where to start. Or, worst of all, where to look for the triggers that would set him off. This is where I come into the story. While coaching leaders, I always utilize the same foolproof process but change it to fit an individual person's need for improvement and which challenges he or she needs to overcome. The first step is to listen to the person's goals, watch her behaviors, listen to what she says, and observe her body language in meetings with her team and with her bosses. Then, after the initial observation, I implement a series of steps to help this specific leader elicit her needed change. This is a straightforward process, where I observe and figure out what the leader's Habitual Why is and then help her turn it into an Intentional Why. I would work on this change by implementing daily coaching adjustments to rewire her thinking and help her achieve better results. Throughout my years of coaching top-notch leaders, I have had much success with this program, but this particular leader, David, was different and I was doubtful that the same program would work for him. David was so darn good at hiding how he felt when he was in public that even I could not differentiate between when he was deeply frustrated and when he was deeply content. The dysfunction and Habitual Why in his life were hiding his emotions until he had an opportunity to unleash his anger. To say the least, he was a mystery—until one day, it hit me. I needed to shadow him for an entire day in both environments—when he interacted with colleagues and when he worked alone behind closed doors.

While observing him working on a spreadsheet at his computer, the desktop system suddenly locked up. I didn't notice at first, because I was writing down some notes, but I certainly heard it. Now, I don't mean I heard the computer lock up; I heard David lose his mind. The first sound was a loud smack on the side of the computer. *WHACK!* The second sound was a loud, "Oh, f—you! You stupid computer!" Next came a series of, "This always happens to me!" and "This computer hates me!" I watched as David spun in his chair and, after a 360-degree rotation, returned to face his computer. That's when he flipped both of his middle fingers at the computer and said, "YOU WIN! AHHHHHHH!" It was 8:35 a.m., and our day had just begun.

After David screamed and flipped off his computer, there was a knock on his door. I was guessing that the person on the other side of the door was going to get a rude awakening to David's mood—I prayed that the poor soul would leave the office in one piece. I braced myself as David walked over and opened his office door to see one of his colleagues. Instead of keeping the momentum of his anger and rage going, he completely changed and acted as if the insane burst of anger and frustration, the completely negative tantrum, had never happened. David smiled at his co-worker, talked for five minutes about a work issue, and closed the door. I was confused, and I can't say that I had seen this fast of a mood switch before, so I stayed quiet and kept observing him further, trying to figure out what had just happened. As the day progressed, we moved from one meeting to another meeting with short breaks of going back to David's office. Every time we would move back to his office, I started to layer small conversational elements that would help me to get to the bottom of his angst. I would ask, "So, David, what's next on today's agenda?" and each time he would say something like, "Well, I need to go meet and deal with a real mess of a situation. I swear that person [a colleague of his] hates me, and I am so mad about it." David never answered my questions with anything positive or constructive; his responses were always negative and indicated that he felt bogged down by the situation and that he was surrounded by idiots at work who could not get work done the right way. While the specifics of his agenda would change every day, the tone and attitude were always the same: total shit.

ME MAD! ME MAD! ME MAD!

The only thing we can completely control is ourselves. We can't control any other person or an outside circumstance the slightest bit, but we can control our personal feelings and the attitude we have about life. There is a common illusion that we don't have this control and that we are the victims of other people's actions and outside circumstances. The phrases, "You made me mad," "You are causing me to be upset," and so on, are all phrases that give away our power to others. We live in a world of instant reactions, lack of impulse control, and blaming others when we don't see life unfolding as perfectly as we had planned. This is what was happening with David. To help him, I asked David to perform the Me Mad! exercise and, after practicing it, he literally changed his life. If you will practice this exercise, your life will change for the better, and you will regain power over your personal emotions. It's a simple attitude-adjustment exercise, and it will transform the way you own your attitude. You may feel a bit silly while doing this exercise the first few times, but you must let go of certain beliefs in order to make room for new ones.

"YOU ARE MAKING ME MAD!"

If we view one of the most common statements of negative attitude, we can see just how ineffective our thinking is and how out of control our attitudes are. As we look at the above statement, "You are making me mad," I want you to ask yourself which words stand out to you? *Mad*? *Me*? *You*? *Making*? If you said *You*, then you are on the right track. The first word I want to examine is *You*. When you utter the phrase "You are making me mad," you have made the statement that someone else is in control of you. Instead of being accountable to the feelings, actions, and attitude inside your own mind, you have granted another person ultimate control over your emotions. We all complain about privacy being taken from us, or bemoan that the government controls our lives, yet we quickly give up control of ourselves to others. We do this even faster when faced with a difficult person or situation.

Let's look at the statement again, "You are MAKING me mad," and notice that I have brought the next problem to your attention. To make someone do something with the power of your mind is a trick stolen from the Jedi in *Star Wars* movies. If you have ever uttered the words "You are MAKING me mad," then you must have been the victim of some Jedi mind trick. How else can you explain someone gaining access to your mind and *making* you do something? Frankly, you can't, because the ONLY way for someone to have this power over you is for you to allow it. The truth is NO ONE can "make" you mentally do anything without your permission. What you do when you use the above statement is take the easy way out of attitude adjustment. You give up and blame the other person or circumstance. "You are MAKING me mad." "This car is MAKING me mad." "THE TRAFFIC IS MAKING ME MAD!!!" These statements, and those like it, are simply your attempt to deflect your negativity and lack of ability to change your attitude onto something else.

What is the truth of the statement "You are making me mad!"? Think about it. If you said, "Me mad!" then you are on your way to your positive attitude adjustment. The truth of the statement and your attitude is YOU are MAD, and you alone control this feeling. To become a true Disruptor of your own life, you need to—and I mean today—take control of your feelings, including being mad. Have you ever been mad at someone who does not care in the slightest about your anger? Sure you have. Every day you most likely are mad at the guy in traffic, the politician of the day, the latest news story, and the closest people in your life whom you allow to drive you to madness. Most people have the attitude in which they feel as if all these outside circumstances victimize them, because it's harder to admit the simple truth of "ME MAD!" So take action: immediately take ownership over your personal feelings, because you, and you alone, can control them.

MAKE THE SHIFT, YOU CRYING BABY!

Now, for the exercise. The next time you are faced with a negative attitude, which will happen at some point in your day, I want you to start rebooting yourself with an attitude shift. When you say or think, "You are making me mad!" or "He/She is making me mad," scream out loud (perhaps in the privacy of your home), "ME MAD! ME MAD! ME MAD!" Stomp your feet like a crying two-year-old, because you are mad, indeed. By *mad*, I mean lost-your-mind, feel-out-of-control, breaking-things mad. If, at first, you are not ready to take the leap to screaming "ME MAD!" out loud, then, at the very least, do it internally. You will find it hard to have a negative attitude when you are stomping and yelling "ME MAD!" By doing this, you are putting ownership of your emotions on the one person responsible for them: you. Great news! You have now started down the path of taking control of your emotional state.

It's just that simple.

After I teach this exercise to my audiences, some people say to me, "Well, Todd, life is not simple. I am not mad all the time." I understand that you are not mad all the time, but the real reason for this exercise is to make a point: you give control of your positive attitude to others, to outside circumstances, and to things over which you have zero control. Here are some more examples of how you give others power over you and your positive attitude. When you say:

- "The kids are driving me crazy." You allow your kids to control your sanity.
- "This traffic is causing me to be late." You allow traffic and the driving actions of others to cause you to be angry that you are late. It's your responsibility to leave home to get to the office on time.
- "My work is stressing me out." No. You are stressing yourself out, and the work is your excuse.

- "I can't become a leader in my company, because no one is helping me." No one is supposed to just come and help you. You need to find someone who can work with you to reach your goals. Stop putting so much effort into complaining about others not doing things for you and start putting more effort into yourself to get to where you want to go.

Every negative word you speak is a virus eating at your disruptive spirit like a cancer. It's time to shift, stop complaining and bitching, and move toward a life in which you take ownership over your actions.

VISIONING

What visioning is not: Visioning is not just having hopes, wishes, or dreams based on a lack of something. For example, "I wish I wasn't broke and could afford a vacation." That is not a vision.

What visioning is: Visioning is having a specific, positive outcome for your many situations in life based on the belief that you can and will achieve it. "I will take the vacation of my dreams, to the island of my choice, in less than a year, which I will pay for easily and effortlessly." A vision requires perseverance and strength to get to your goal.

Every day, when you wake up, what are the three things you think about first? Do you wake up and say, "Great! Another day at the grind!" or "I need coffee?" Do you think about the mounting bills or the stress at work you must face? If you start your day with your first thoughts being negative, how do you expect to have a great day, change your attitude, and fulfill your dreams? We tend to think in connected patterns, so one negative thought usually brings another negative thought trailing behind it. So, if one of the first thoughts you have as you get out of bed is about your medical bills, the next thought is usually about the actual bills or how much further away you are from having enough money for your dream vacation. Then you just fall down the tunnel of unhappiness and despair because you can't afford the things you want. It all started with one negative thought about one bill. This expanded exponentially in your mind, and your thoughts are only focused on your debt, more debt, credit cards, and on and on. Jumping on the train of negative thoughts before you have the first cup of coffee puts you on the track toward making your day awful and negative. The agitation you are feeling from these thoughts will determine how your day will go and how you will respond in certain situations.

People who have adopted this visioning, learning from my presentations and coaching, wake up with a bigger goal. They wake up saying, "Today will be an amazing day!" and "I see my vision for each of the areas of my life, and I will see progress in those areas today." They want their day to begin with a positive attitude and want to see their vision coming to life. The reason they do this is because they take the time to craft a detailed vision for their life and go far beyond the daily grind of simply surviving. Achieving the life of You, Disrupted is all about the vision. This is not to say that you will only be happy once your vision is achieved; it is to say that you become excited by the vision itself and will be happy as you progress down the path toward it.

MACRO VISIONING—SEEING THE BIG PICTURE

When I wake up each day, the first three things I say to myself are:

- "Today will be a powerful and positive day."
- "I am thankful for being alive and healthy."

- "Today I will live toward all the positive things I see for my life."

Fourth is ALWAYS, "Coffee time," but that's not important right now.

If you notice, those three statements are about Macro Visioning for the entire day and life. I call them "macro" because they lack detail and specificity for each moment of my life. We will discuss Micro Visioning shortly. When you are starting each day with a vision of your life in a positive context, you are poised to be the Disruptor who seizes each moment of the day. It has been stated many ways and by many different people, but the truth is, what you focus on is what you get. One of my mentors often talked about the need to focus on the final outcome of projects so our planning would be more targeted to achieve the desired vision. Your life, and the direction you want it to start moving in is the same: "What you focus on is what you get." From a macro perspective, you MUST focus on the most positive aspects of each day. This is the case no matter what mental state you are currently in, because I am not expecting a depressed person to ignore being depressed and fake being happy. However, a depressed person can wake up tomorrow and, from a Macro Visioning perspective, say, "Today I will work to feel better" or "Today I will find at least one thing to appreciate." All of these statements depend on the person and what that person needs to do to get to a better mental state. Statements are simple ways to declare a change you want to occur. Regardless of where you are in life, you can find at least three positive Macro Visions for the day.

But Macro Visioning doesn't stop there. As you begin to apply the learning from this chapter, you will need to have visioning time. You will need to make time every day to sit down and map out all the positive things, people, and circumstances you want to see coming into your life. My fiancée, Diana, and I do this individually and together as we set a vision for our family, our relationship, and all the experiences we want to share together. The process is very straight-forward, but it requires us to act. You start by sitting wherever you are most comfortable and will not be disturbed. Then you start to think about what you want in your life and what you would like to change in certain areas of your life. As you are figuring these things out, write them down or type them up. To get you started, use these seven categories:

- Health and Fitness
- Family
- Spouse/Partner Relationship
- Financial
- Material Possessions
- Career/Work
- Self-Knowledge

These are the key areas of your life, so take them seriously and take time to explore all of them and what you want to change and maintain in each one. It's important to note, as you map a vision for yourself in all of the areas of your life, that you need to then look at each one and list your reason—your Intentional Why—for that vision. By finding your Intentional Why, you will find your motivation for reaching that goal. How will it feel when you reach your goal? This will also cause you to ask yourself if the why is strong enough to overcome obstacles, challenges, and struggles around the vision. If you don't ask these questions of yourself, it will be difficult to keep moving toward your goal when things become challenging. It's not enough to envision what you want, you must also know *why* you want it.

Remember, you are not to map this out from a negative perspec-tive. Hence the reason this chapter started with changing your attitude. Here is an example of my personal vision for my career when I was ready for a change:

Macro Career Vision 1/1/2013

> I see my career changing for the better, where I feel excited and fulfilled each day, work on projects impacting millions of people, and achieve even more financial success. I see this to be something truly groundbreaking. It will feel powerful and exciting to watch this unfold. I want to have an opportunity to change my career, because what I am doing now is not fulfilling.

After the vision is written out, in a Macro Vision way, think about it each day and look for opportunities for it to reveal itself. Personally, I would say the following every day until I reached my goal: "Today I will get one step closer to my career vision and will meet the right people to bring it to life." Taking a Macro Vision and simplifying it down to one statement, which can be spoken each day, retrains your mind to focus on the new thing or changing situation you want. As 2013 progressed, I would say this statement as part of my daily waking routine. No matter how frustrated I would get by things not moving fast enough or how much extra work I had to put into being successful, I would stay focused on the positive (the part of HOW my life will change when I reach the intended goal). I was lucky, because I was open to two options: either my current career becoming more fulfilling and exciting, or starting a new career in the cannabis industry, where I would be learning new things and helping advance the cannabis frontier. By the end of that year, I was out of my then current career, because it didn't become more ful-filling; I had become a leader in the emerging cannabis industry; and I was being interviewed about my work on major news outlets around the world. My vision for a fulfilling and exciting career had come true, and a new career path was underway. That is the power of the Macro Visioning process. You must know what you want, and then use these tools to figure out a way to get it.

A Macro Vision does not necessarily need to be earth-shattering or intensely life-changing. You can always start slowly with something small. If you simply want to speak up more at work and share your ideas, your Macro Vision may be, "I see myself as being a more outspoken contributor who freely shares ideas and positive input and seeks to learn more ways to add value to the company each day." The point of this exercise is seeing in your mind with total clarity what you want in certain areas of your life, and it's how you begin to move toward your new life, self, and focus.

MICRO VISIONING—HOW'S THIS GOING TO GO?

There is another powerful technique I go through just prior to a meeting, presentation, or other experiences in my life in which I want a favorable outcome. I take a few minutes to Micro Vision how I see the experience going. For example: "I see this meeting being very useful, and the outcome will be acquiring this client as a long-term customer." I have learned that I am not the only one who uses this exercise; in fact, there are millions of people already doing it. Unfortunately, they do this habitually and, 90 percent of the time, the Micro Visioning is negative. Think again about how you start your day. Do you head into a meeting while complaining to yourself about how badly it will go? Do you go to dinner with friends, knowing how annoying another person is surely going to be? Do you drive to work, already saying, "I bet traffic will suck today?" If so, congratulations, you are Micro Visioning—albeit in a negative manner. And, as I mentioned before, what you focus on is what you get!

What if the negative Micro Visioning happened in life more openly? Instead of people just thinking negative thoughts, they actually said them out loud like it wasn't a big deal. Imagine that you board a plane, and the pilot announces, "Good morning, everyone. We are flying to Denver today and I, for one, expect it will be a terrible flight. I know this airport very well, and the weather there is terrible; we will have delays and will sit on the tarmac for at least thirty minutes. Also, they usually make me circle the airport for an hour, because I am certain the air traffic control person hates me." If you heard that right before your flight, you would probably think to yourself, "Wow. I am on the wrong flight! I need to get off this plane before something horrible happens!" This is why it's important to be positive when you are Micro or Macro Visioning, especially when you are doing this silently in your head. The negative visioning you run through your head creates more and more negative situations, and they will be the only focus of your day. No wonder we are stuck in a victim story; we keep focusing on and living in the negative things happening in our lives.

Now imagine the same pilot with a positive and thoughtful Micro Vision. In this case, he would say, "Good morning, everyone. We are heading to Denver; what a beautiful day, the sky is clear with 75-degree weather. The airport is great, and the staff and I work hard to have the least amount of delays possible. We will have an amazing flight today, and we will be on time so you can all get to your destinations safely." Now that's the kind of flight I want to be on.

What about all the garbage inside your head? The negative self-talk, the negative beliefs, and the constant complaining are damaging you from the inside out. If your car looked beautiful on the outside, but you put the dirtiest oil and fuel into it, your car would not run well for long. Just because you are not speaking negative thoughts out loud does not mean they are less damaging to your new direction or vision. People may not be able to hear and see your negative garbage, but, make no mistake, it *is* damaging you. Imagine for a moment if every one of your negative thoughts flew out of your mouth as soon as you thought them. How would that impact your life, relationships, work, and the way you interact with society?

Below is an example of how I Micro Vision just before giving a presentation.

- "This will be the best and most impactful presentation I have ever given."
- "The audience will connect to the learning because I will be clear, on point, and logical in my teaching approach."
- "I see this presentation rolling off my tongue fluently, and I will be confident in my movements."

Each moment of each day, you should be Micro Visioning. In fact, you can start practicing this today by going into at least three situations at work or at home with a positive Micro Vision. You are going to be amazed at how positive Micro Visioning will change your experiences for the better.

PLANNING

What planning is not: Planning is not hoping or wishing. Planning is not saying, "*Someday* I will . . ."

What planning is: Planning is laying out steps, setting time lines, and finding resources needed to achieve your goals and visions. And WHEN do you do it? NOW!

When I entered the marijuana industry, I had assumptions about certain things that are not exactly as they sound. First, I thought a "grow," where the plants are cultivated, would be largely unsophisticated and look more like a basement with pots of marijuana plants in it. Well, if you illegally grow pot, this may be the situation. However, industrial grows are incredibly complex. The first grow I walked into was a sophisticated facility with security, protocols, and many procedures for each stage of the plants' development. There was a very carefully planned system, backed by intense research, to ensure that the plants would get everything needed to result in the desired end product.

This level of planning was incredibly detailed, because marijuana plants can't just be placed in soil and watered to get maximum results. At a cannabis grow facility, minimum results won't cut it. To get more yield at every harvest, the owners of indoor grows need to plan for proper lighting, ventilation, daily watering, purification of water, what nutrients are used, finding the right staff to cultivate the plants, finding the right team that will properly trim and cure the harvested plants, and a pipeline for how this product will be sold. Before a consumer purchases the final product, a very long list of protocols and instructions must be executed. If the owners didn't have a detailed plan for every stage of the marijuana plant's development, they would quickly be out of business because they would not get the results they wanted. All because they didn't plan the steps leading up to their goal.

When you see a successful person, chances are that you don't see the rigor, planning, and visioning that went into his success. What you see is only his success, and you say, "Wow, he got lucky." When, in fact, he worked tirelessly to plan, execute, and stay focused on his vision of the end result. This method applies to the marijuana business and any business focused on a set of goals. This same planning process also applies to your personal life and the goals you set. If you want to go to the next level, where certain areas of your life are more fulfilled, you will need to spend time creating, focusing on, and executing your plan.

FINALLY, WE SAID, HIGH THERE!

In the winter of 2015, the project called High There! was about to be born. I had signed on to be a cofounder and CEO of what I believed could be a game changer for the legal cannabis industry. I was working with people who wanted to create a social network to give cannabis-loving people all over the world an opportunity to connect with each other and talk about what they were going through regarding cancer and chronic pain, or (for veterans, specifically) to share their stories about PTSD. The app was also for connecting people who wanted to date and/or to build lasting friendships with other folks who also used marijuana in their day-to-day lives. I was excited about the project and felt that our team, my fellow cofounders, developers, and media liaison, were all ready to take our app to market. It's hard to explain just how much work and planning goes into building a company and an app from the ground up, as well as a simultaneous execution of a public-relations (PR) strategy. At any moment, one misstep could derail the entire plan. Despite the fear of something going wrong, I knew that all the delicate pieces of the rollout had to come together perfectly. Just as in my own life and my personal planning, I laid out the details of how our team would execute and launch the app in the middle of January 2015. Personally, I have never been one to adopt complicated execution strategies, so I kept it simple, to the point, and on target.

For High There! to be successful, we had to have a simple and clear plan, which we placed into two buckets:

- The App
- The Marketing Launch

By focusing on these two areas of the master plan, we stayed centered on the execution of each item so we would be more likely to hit our targets. Timing was critical to every step as we moved into the first two weeks of January; any mistakes could destroy our launch strategy while burning valuable resources. We had to be successful because—just like in your life—we all had a great deal on the line when launching High There! My business partners had put in a significant amount of funding. Our development team had put in countless hours of work. I personally was also sacrificing time and money, caused by decreased pay, massive hours spent on the project, and travel back and forth to our team in Florida as well as in New York. I did this just to engage with the High There! opportunity, and we were at a fragile stage of development. The stakes could not have been higher or the risk greater. If successful, we would launch a groundbreaking technology for the new movement of legal cannabis. High There! was, at its heart, being designed to remove stigmas associated with the marijuana consumer in ways we had never witnessed.

THE APP BUCKET

In the early stages, the app was clunky, to say the least. With little interaction other than connection and chatting, we were not getting the robust tech we needed to truly make High There! an app to remember. So I quickly set goals with the development team for the app to meet the following criteria:

- Be user-friendly, interesting, and fun
- Tell the app consumer's story in a way that creates engagement with others
- Stop the glitching and crashing

With those simple guidelines, the team went to work to get us ready for launch in both the Apple and Google formats. The app was developing quickly, but I was still not sure about the second goal of "Tell the app consumer's story in a way that creates engagement with others." We had not figured out how we should format the consumer's personal story on the app, or if it would even make a difference to anyone using the app. I had no idea what would be the best option, until I sat down and thought about the marijuana consumer. To solve this dilemma, I imagined a party where everyone in the room consumed cannabis. I further divided the party in my mind by having an area where people consumed for medical reasons, and another area for a group of people who consumed marijuana for fun. As I visualized this event in my head, I realized that all of those people had a story to tell about their lives, who they were, and why they consumed. There was and still is a heavy stigma about consuming marijuana. This, in turn, makes it hard for people who are cannabis consumers to meet people who will not judge them or look down on them because of what they choose to do in their free time. Weed consumers, just like any other people, have a story to tell about themselves, their preferences, their reasons for consuming, or why they love cannabis—and everyone likes to share their story with people they meet. Think about me, even I had a story to tell at this imaginary party. I shared my reason for being in the industry and how it helped my mother. With this mental exercise, I had finally figured it out: the story feature in the app would let the consumers share their personal story. This would let them feel free to be who they are without being judged; share stories and not feel like they did something wrong because it involved marijuana; and share experiences so that other medical consumers could find a strain that could alleviate their chronic pain. Something personal like this also added the human factor back into the app, which, up until then, was only based on the collected preference data from the users.

Because I had put each goal in a specific order in the app bucket, I was able to focus completely on solving just one goal at a time and ask the right questions to find a solution. To satisfy the second goal in the bucket, we created a new feature called "My Story." The app was on its way to adhering to our guidelines for improvement, and it was on schedule.

THE MARKETING LAUNCH BUCKET

Because our budget was low, and we were burning resources at a rapid pace (hell, my coffee habit alone was painful for the company), we needed to be very efficient when it came to the use of funds. At the same time, we had to leverage what we had and get the attention we needed so High There! would become a widely recognized product. For the marketing plan, we utilized both my past success with other brands in the media and a top PR specialist to help us leverage free publicity as a main strategy for building awareness. The precision and timing of our PR were critical. If we missed a window of opportunity or a news cycle, we risked missing our chance to have a successful launch. So the team prepared a plan that included a stint on CNBC's *Power Pitch*, which one of my reporter friends helped us land. In addition, we had a set of thoughtful and strategic articles that our PR strategist prepared in advance. Everything was ready to go, so when a great opportunity showed itself, we could hit the ground running. Because our plan was detailed and focused, the High There! launch was on target and on time. It was exciting to see the plan working and to feel the momentum of the pending launch. Everything was coming together!

How Do You Like Them Apples?

There is a strange excitement mixed with anticipation when you submit an app to an app store for approval. Whether it is for Google or Apple, developers take pride in sending the completed app for review and, hopefully, approval to be featured in an app store. Still, there is a process each reviewer must follow to ensure that the app works; they have to make sure that the app is not inappropriate and that the app developers have followed strict guidelines. For us, we had to adhere to two sets of guidelines, because when a company makes an app, it must make it for both platforms: Google and Apple. Those two platforms each have app stores for purchasing all apps for smartphones. The app store someone visits to download the app depends on the kind of phone that person has. Because the Google and Apple apps had to be developed differently, through a long and difficult process, it took over six months to build both of them. After they were completed, my team finally submitted our version of High There!, and we finally had a chance to breathe. We were excited and anxious as we waited for approval by both stores. Google approved the app quickly, which caused our hopes and excitement to rise to the roof while we waited for Apple to also approve the app.

A week after the Google Store approved the High There! app, I received an e-mail from our lead developer and, after reading the first few sentences, my heart sank. Our app had been denied by Apple and would not be featured in its app store. The reason? At the time of our submission, Apple was denying all cannabis-related apps. The bad news hit our small company like a brick through a window. For the first twenty-four hours, we talked about contingency plans: going forward without Apple by only deploying the app in the Google Play Store. We even temporarily entertained the bad idea of launching a PR campaign attempting to move Apple in our direction by calling out their policy around marijuana. Trust me when I say that emotions in the face of depleting resources, a giant roadblock in the way of progress, and a feeling of rejection can destroy hope. A roadblock so critical to the app launch felt like the end of High There! But, just as with anything in life, you need to be ready to make a pivot, pick up your pieces, and move toward a better position so that you don't lose everything you've worked for. After

I had time to rethink what we should do to save the company and still make High There! a huge success, I instructed the team to keep working on the app in both formats, so we could be ready to launch in the Google app store as well as in Apple's store, just in case Apple changed course and approved the app. I took ownership of the Apple situation and went to work to see if it could be made to work for the positive. Not one to take no for an answer, I proceeded to reach out to every contact I had at Apple from my past life as an executive consultant. Finally, after a few days of countless calls, conversations, and e-mails, I found the right contact and we started talking about what could be done to the app so that it would be compliant with Apple's rules.

FLEXIBILITY AND COLLABORATION IS THE KEY

Every great plan should always have an embedded backbone of flexibility and a mind-set of collaboration. I know that a multitude of outside circumstances and forces beyond anyone's control can disrupt plans and derail hope. A great example of this phenomenon is a plane that must divert around a terrible storm to get you to your destination safely. The pilot must be flexible, efficient, and knowledgeable of the fuel capacity and flight trajectory to overcome the obstacle. This flexibility also applies to your personal plan; you will need to be flexible to navigate around obstacles that you can't just ram through to get to your goal. In our High There! launch plan, I was working to make our development team be flexible around Apple's needs so that Apple would grant us access to its app store. Because I approached the conversation as a logical and business-focused collaborator, we were able to talk openly about the concerns Apple had about our app. As it turned out, the concerns were not as catastrophic as everyone thought initially. In fact, all that needed to be done was to implement a set of simple changes to the app to make it available only in the states where medical marijuana was currently legal. I also made the point to Apple that we were not selling anything weed-related nor directing people to a dispensary. We were simply a responsible social-networking tool for all marijuana enthusiasts, enabling them to enjoy and connect with one another.

Before resubmitting the app to Apple, I made sure that it complied with everything Apple was requesting; I had the app updated to meet the specific criteria; and I redesigned the launch strategy with my PR liaison. Only then did I resubmit High There! for review. In the office, we all carried on as if everything was going to work out. Each day, my attitude was positive, even when certain investors reminded me—countless times—about how bad it would be if we did not get into the Apple store. There were concerns that Apple would reject the app a second time, even though we had revised it to meet all the necessary criteria. It also didn't help that we were not the only cannabis-related app company to be turned down by Apple. I watched as other app companies in the industry tried to protest and went so far as to openly attack and bash Apple. Needless to say, the last two weeks of January 2015 were among the most stressful weeks ever. The entire success of our company hung in the balance. Then, at the end of January, I got a call from Apple that would send chills down my spine.

I had just landed in Denver from my New York City media trip, where I had recorded a segment for CNBC that was going to air at the same time as our High There! app launch, even if it meant we had to launch without getting into the Apple store. As I glanced at my phone, I saw a missed call from an unknown number, and a new voicemail message. I didn't pay too much attention to it since it was the end of a very long day, it was my birthday, and I was exhaustedly driving to pick up the kids so we could celebrate together. It should have been a very happy day, but, under my positive exterior, I was scared and feeling as if I would fail my team on this project. Our investors could leave, my cofounders could drop out, the app could fail, my ideas could be total failures, and on and on went the negative self-talk. I was naysaying myself so much that I forgot about the pending voicemail message. With all the energy I had, I finally snapped out of it. I was just leaving the airport, trying to find a way to get through this mentally tough situation, so I could reboot and explore other options that would take us to the same goal. I was telling myself, "Todd, you can manage this. You have been through far more stressful situations. There's always a way, you just have to look for it." Then I turned on some music and, for the better part of the drive, I tried to relax.

As one of the songs ended, I felt a little better and finally started to have a more positive outlook in general. I finally reached for my phone and listened to the voicemail. It said, "Todd, this is Apple. I wanted you to know we looked at your app again and feel, with the local function changes, and the fact we see your app as a social network, I am happy to tell you we have accepted you into the app store. Oh, and, Todd, Happy Birthday!"

WHAT?!?! I was overjoyed. I called the Apple rep back immediately. I just happened to catch him at the office before he left for the day, but he took his time and told me the good news all over again in more detail than he had in the voicemail. After thanking him and the team at Apple again and again, I hung up the phone, and, with excitement surging through my body, I looked to my left just in time to see the Denver skyline and the sun setting over the mountains. Everything was great, and I started celebrating the wonderful news by screaming and yelling "Whoooohooo!" at the top of my lungs. I actually got teary-eyed at the sheer excitement of the achievement. My emotions were over the top as I reminisced about the success of a plan built on flexibility and tenacity.

When High There! launched, it was the world's first cannabis app for social connections, dating, and interacting while being the only cannabis app in Apple and Google stores simultaneously. Even the other app I mentioned earlier, which had protested Apple, was not allowed in the Apple store for another two weeks. I was proud of the team, the execution strategy, and the plan, but, most of all, I proved to myself that a great plan, built with flexibility, only works if you are calm, patient, positive, and ready for anything.

REMEMBER MICRO AND MACRO VISIONING

So how do you plan to find a new job, business, or partner, or achieve the long list of accomplishments you want in your life? You take the same approach:

Match your plan with your macro and micro vision. If you don't know the destination, how can you possibly arrive there? If you want a new career, what kind of career do you want? How much money will you earn? What type of office will you have? What kind of team, boss, or environment do you want supporting you? If you want to be able to stand up in meetings at work and offer your opinions, what do you look like when you do that? How do you feel? If you want to find a great partner in your personal life, what is that person like? What qualities do you want him or her to have? For you to target your goal and successfully reach it, you must have a very detailed and specific outline of the goal that matches your vision. Once you have a clear goal, you can begin the process of attainment.

Put the plan in "buckets." Once you have your goal articulated, you must break the goal down into achievable and manageable priorities, or buckets, where each bucket has a deliverable. If you want a new career, but it is in a new field of work with which you are unfamiliar, or you want to start your own business, you will need to learn all about the world you want to enter. For example, before going into the cannabis industry, I met with the team members who wanted to hire me, I spent time in their grow operation, and then I spent days and weeks researching the plant, the industry, and the media around it. When I executed my plan to enter the industry, I organized my ideas into separate category buckets. It's almost like having a to-do list that's separated into different categories so you know what needs to be done and in what order each item needs to be completed. To make sure that I succeeded in this industry and executed the plans, I created a bucket called the "Learning Bucket." I also had buckets for "Salary," "Proposal," and "Defined Position Responsibilities," among others.

Manage your resources. This was a step I missed, because I did not plan properly for the huge depletion of my financial resources and it caught up to me, making navigating a new industry very difficult. For example, I was accustomed to earning a significant amount of money. I made the mistaken assumption that this same level of income would continue in the new industry. I was wrong, and the lesser income I initially had to accept took a toll on my available funds. This added stress to my life because I needed to be aggressive with my spending and networking without depleting all of my monthly income. I liken it to deciding to drive from Denver to Los Angeles with a full tank of gas but no wallet. Around 250 miles into the trip, you will need to get creative about how you will pay for the rest of the journey. When you deplete your resources fast, it may cause you to jump from "thrive" back to "survive" as you begin figuring out where your next meal will come from. While each situation has a varying degree of resources needed (finding a new life partner as opposed to starting a new business), each situation will deplete you of resources to a different degree and in a different way. Also, carefully define your resources: time, money, energy, possessions, and any other key resources fitting your scenario. Because I did not plan properly in this area (and have met many people who miss this also),

I can tell you that running out of money on the path to a new goal or vision can make life very difficult.

Focus on what is going right and change only the challenge. When we launched High There!, we had much going right and one very big thing going wrong: Apple denying our app the first time. Just as you should do in your life, I did not throw out all the good along with the challenge. I respected what was going right and built on it. When Apple denied our app, I went to work and figured out what we needed to do for Apple to say yes to the High There! app. This was just a challenge that needed further review and a different approach. When I focused on keeping the good things good and solving the challenge, I could stay on the path and ultimately drive the company to success.

Know when to quit, but never give up. These are two very different concepts: knowing when to move on from a project or an idea because it has become a useless drain, and knowing when you should keep on going with the project or the idea because it has so much potential. For example, when you want to move out of your current job or career into a new one, it is good to know the proper timing of when to quit your current job. Unless you have significant resources ready to go, quitting haphazardly in a flurry of passion may not be the best and smartest method for getting to your dream career. So, if you need to stay in your current job a little longer, do it. If you despise that job, never give up on your vision, goals, and planning. Although a plan may take longer to accomplish, that does not mean it is not worthy of working toward and achieving. While you continue working at your current job, you can be researching and preparing for a new career, and learning everything you can at your current one, so you have more experiences and skills when you are ready to make that switch.

INSTINCT

What instinct is not: Instinct is not reactivity caused by fear, nor is it panic caused by lack of planning.

What instinct is: When you dial into your gut feeling, you are dialing into instinct. It's that strange feeling you get when something feels right or doesn't feel right, and then acting based on those feelings. Instinct is the way your inner self (or subconscious) communicates with you, so you act with flexibility and stay true to your vision.

Many people before me have spoken of instinct in greater depth, so I won't attempt to outdo them. I will say this, however: it takes practice to listen to your instinct and hear what it's really saying. Once you do, you will reach outcomes you never imagined and feel more in charge of your life than you ever thought possible.

You may remember my story about the huge Pizza Hut leadership conference, where I disrupted the meeting with engaging entertainment, audience interaction, and energy, in a way no one was expecting to see in the corporate world. What you don't know is that I had to kick my instincts into gear leading up to the actual event. By using my intuition at that time, I learned the most valuable lesson about instinct: when you hear your instincts loud and clear, you MUST go with it. That may mean you have to go out and get the facts, not just other people's opinions.

A day prior to the big four-day conference with Pizza Hut, my team and I were delivering a pre-training lesson for the fifty or so managers from Pizza Hut. The managers attending this pre-training lesson would be responsible for supporting our leadership learning modules for the next four days. In my true style, I trained these managers for nearly six hours, interacting and lighting up the room with energy. I was over the top at times, because I had an instinct that this conference was going to need such a level of energy. I also knew a conference of this size was very expensive for the client, and I had to keep my focus on hitting the client's targets and ensuring overall success.

The stakes were high, so I turned up the volume and stepped on the gas pedal. It turned out that our client was observing the session that day. Nicole (not her real name) was a kind yet determined woman who knew exactly what she wanted as an outcome for this conference. As I watched her at the back of the room, I noticed she would laugh at times. At other times, she would reflect what I thought was a strange and disgusted look. Still, I went with my instinct to keep up a high level of energy and kept the training session going. Several hours into the training session, my leader, let's call her Cathy (to protect her privacy), came up to me in a huff. She was visibly upset and wanted to have a very important and serious chat with me immediately. The look of disapproval on her face told me she was coming to give me a directive, because something wasn't working. When we walked off to the side of the room to have a quiet conversation, she said, "Let's talk." Thinking I had made some horrible mistake of an unknown origin, I stood and listened as Cathy started in with her issue. "Todd, do you see Nicole's face back there? She looks absolutely disgusted by your behavior and energy. You need to tone it down now and get focused on a more business-centered presentation. Less energy and antics, and more business content!" For a moment, I stood there dumbfounded. Had my instinct betrayed me? Was I dead wrong? Should I have just followed the dry program outline without adding in the energy and interaction? Just then a question popped into my head, and it is one you need to remember when you are faced with people who want you to ignore your instinct. All I could say to Cathy was, "Are you sure?" Cathy paused and said, "YES!" I then responded with "Are you really sure? Have you asked Nicole if she is, in fact, upset about the energy level with which I am training this class?" Cathy didn't even have to think about it; she had an automatic answer: "No, but look at her face." To which I then responded, "So you assume she is upset and wants me to change my behavior?" Cathy nodded. To make sure I was doing everything in my power to make the client happy and produce the expected results, I asked Cathy, "Well, with your permission, I think we should go and ask her."

We walked over to Nicole, and I asked how everything was coming along for the four-day training—what she thought about today, and did the look on her face indicate we were perhaps needing to change something in the presentation? Nicole looked at both of us with a surprised grin on her face and said, "Gosh no! I was just watching you, your energy, and the way you are controlling the room, and I thought to myself, 'Man, our other speakers are not nearly this good.' Definitely keep it up, Todd!" My instinct was right.

I believe the little voice inside you telling you to go for it, take the risk, and make the plan now, is a voice you should not ignore. The way to tap into this instinct is to listen, write down what it tells you, and take the risk. My risk to listen to my instinct and elevate my energy would not have cost me my job, or money. It was a safe risk. But had I not listened to it at pre-conference training, I would have suffered a long and dry teaching plan, and we would have failed to produce the desired results for the client. Had I listened to the advice of my superior, Cathy, and toned it down without verifying her assumption, I would have failed. In the end, the only person who can tell you if your instinct is right for you, is you!

HOW TO APPLY IT

You have been at this book for a while now, and I bet your head is spinning. You are starting to understand the Disruptor inside you, the *You, Disrupted* person is getting more and more primed to take action. In fact, I want you to act right now. Either on your computer, on a piece of scrap paper, or on a flip chart, go back through this chapter and, no matter what, do not keep reading further until you improve your attitude, create a new vision for at least one thing in your life, build a plan to achieve it, and find one way to listen to your instinct today. Then and only then, do I encourage you to turn the page to learn more about integrating these lessons into your life. It's time for you to do the work outlined in this chapter, so you can begin applying it to your world. NOW! No one can do this for you. You are the only one who can change your attitude, figure out what you truly want, and create a plan to reach your goal. The consequences of doing nothing are dire—you will not engage in learning and, in turn, you will make no changes in your life. That is not why you picked up this book. The time for engaging is *now*, the lessons to get started are here, and you, ONLY you, can take the next step. Are you ready?

CHAPTER 6

YOU WILL FAIL, SOMETIMES

failure: taking a risk and not accomplishing a goal the way you had planned to

What failure is not: Failure is not being finished. Failure is not your end. Failure is not defeat.

What failure is: Failure is learning. Failure is fuel for the next chapter of your life.

In this book, I have often started a chapter by jumping into a story of one of the many experiences of my life. For this particular chapter, I am going to first introduce you to some concepts you will need to take time to understand. You need to understand the seriousness of the impact that the word *failure* has on your mind and, more importantly, your subconscious. Because you will be taking new risks in your life after reading this book, you will need to understand how to manage what you call failure, so those risks are not some terrifying monster you work to avoid. We have all attached a slightly different meaning to the word *failure*; overall, it means "defeat" to most. There were moments while I was writing this book when I felt that I shouldn't even use the word *failure*, because it carries such negativity. Being the kind of person who despises the status quo, I made the conscious decision to keep the word in my repertoire. The Disruptor in me would rather see the word redefined than avoided. Also, the frequency with which we all use that word means it is very difficult to ignore. After you have read this chapter and have consciously redefined what the word *failure* means to you, any time you hear the word—every time someone says it to you or about someone else—you will feel a different set of emotions. Therefore, for the duration of this entire chapter, I want you to focus on redefining the word. Make a new definition. For example, "Failure is fuel for the next chapter of my life." By the time you finish this chapter, I trust you will redefine failure as: opportunity, learning, or one of countless other positive words. The goal of redefining this word is to positively describe what happens during the so-called failure and utilize it to get to the next phase of life. If you do this, your failure will become a beautiful start toward your success.

One of the core reasons I am who I am today lies in the power of a simple phrase taught to me by my first teacher, my father. For as long as I can remember, every time I faced a situation in which I could fail, I would say something like, "I can't do it," or "I don't have enough skills to succeed," and my father, without hesitation, would say to me, "Son, there is NO such word as *can't* in this family." If you think about it for a moment, saying *can't* in the context of your risk taking can be a devastating situation, in that *can't* gives you an excuse to stop. Those simple words stuck with me and became bedrock for my Intentional Why, thereby helping me push through fear of failure in my life. When I wanted to learn how to ride a bike, I kept uttering the phrase "I can't," and again, my father would say, "There is no such word as *can't*." Think about how many times in a day or a week you say the word *can't*. By just uttering the word, you are mentally submitting to your defeat even before you make an attempt! Similarly, you can't always *try*, either, because you don't really "try" anything. You either do it or you don't. For example, you can say you "tried" to get in shape. Well, if you got in shape, then you "did" it; if you didn't get in shape, then you "did not." So *try* and *can't* are the ultimate defeats of success. You might as well just give up; with such minor determination as "I'll try," you won't accomplish what you really want. Say to yourself, as my father said to me and now I say to my own kids, "There is no such word as *can't.*" If you start to believe the word *can't* doesn't exist, then you will suddenly see all of your excuses vanish, and only two options will remain: do or don't. This is the epitome of what I mean about reversing your mentality around the meaning of *failure.* Taking the word *can't* out of your vocabulary does not mean that you will never miss the mark or feel defeated. Rather, it means that you will push forward with your best effort until you get what you have been working for. If you don't succeed, start again, but this time, take into consideration why it didn't work the first time. Remember, all you can do in the absence of knowing is to keep going! Therefore, in an unexpected way, a failure is teaching you a lesson to pay more attention or asking you one more time "are you sure this is what you want?" Most of the time, people give up after failing once or twice to achieve their "dream," but isn't a true dream worth never giving up on? In your life of fulfillment, "There is NO such word as CAN'T." To understand the power of this phrase, you need to understand my father from my perspective.

Dad grew up in the rural coal-mining town of Bluefield, West Virginia. To understand the background, I have to travel even farther back than my father's childhood. My grandfather married my grand-mother, who was eight years older, shortly after he returned from World War II. During the war, my grandfather was stationed and fighting in the Philippines for three years. Now, I do not mean that he was living in a barracks for three years and occasionally had to fight. I mean he literally lived in a foxhole (essentially a dirt hole dug for protection on the front lines of battle) for the entire three years. He fought, day in and day out, from that hole in the ground. After he returned to the United States, he met my grandmother. Even though she was older, already had four children she was raising on her own, and was tough as nails, he fell in love. After they got married, my grandfather took over the role of father to her children. They also had two children together. One of those new kids was my father. I should also mention that my grandfather built his family's home by himself, worked in the coal mines to provide a decent life, and led the family with strength.

It's no wonder my father grew up to be a man of strength, fire, and an unwavering sense of purpose. Dad joined the US Navy to serve his country during the Vietnam War; he was nearly killed at sea, and he too learned about resilience. The idea that there is no such word as *can't* was imbued in him at a young age by his own father. That is what carried forward into my dad's adult years and later become his lesson for me. When I faced anything difficult, I would hear that phrase blast into my mind: "There is no such word as *can't*." After my dad returned from Vietnam, he went into a career for the water company, where he was employed for nearly thirty-eight years. He started out as a meter reader and eventually worked his way up to a senior leadership role. With unwavering purpose, a tough managing style, and his talent for navigating a negotiation or difficult situation at work, Dad retired as one of the most respected leaders the company had ever experienced. Throughout my life and his career, my father taught me much about defying and redefining failure. He has always supported my decisions, worked to give me valuable knowledge, and supported me financially during various mishaps; he never once told me to quit, give up, or stop doing something I cared about. He was, and still is, my personal Disruptive Influencer. It was no wonder, when I hit a major failure in my life, that my father's and grandfather's advice rang in my ear, motivating me to the next levels of fulfilling my potential.

As you read on, know this: you will fail. What I mean is that you will miss the mark, not get what you want, or, frankly, choose a path that is frustrating and may not get you to where you want to go. You will make mistakes, fall down, and get hit hard by opinions. The question is, when you face the next idea you want to bring to life—from speaking up at work to starting your own business—will you let your negative definition of *failure* cause you to stop? Or will you see the opportunity as growth, recognizing that failure is a gift of learning and not the end?

You will always find a situation in which life hits you so hard it knocks the wind out of you. In that moment, you will say either "I can't get back up" or "There is no such word as *can't.*" It's a choice. What is about to follow are some circumstances I found painful to write but necessary to share. Admittedly, a moment came for me when I said, "This is a book meant to uplift, I CAN'T talk about my failures." Well, surely you can guess how that went, because here we are, talking about me not being perfect.

CRASH . . . LANDING

After a few days of traveling, the feeling of the plane landing at our home airport is usually a wonderful feeling. We are home. But on this this day, I was a mess. Distracted and "off." As I went about packing up my laptop and some of the other belongings I had pulled out of my bag for the flight, I could feel anxiety coming down on me like a ton of bricks. Even though I had slept through most of the three-hour flight, I was still mentally beaten as well as physically exhausted. As the people in front of me deplaned, I just sat in my seat, not sure what else today would bring. With my fiancée at my side, I was quiet—which is not normal for me. I was confused about why I was feeling this way, because, after all, in the few days we were gone, we had experienced an amazing trip from coast to coast. We had celebrated Diana's birthday, made presentations about the cannabis industry to top regulators of several states, and developed new business contacts. You would think I should have been on top of the world, but I was internally off.

My fiancée and business partner, Diana, was working to cheer me up. She asked me to talk through what was going on, so she could help me find the center of myself again. My attitude was at a low point and I knew, if I did not shift to a better mental state quickly, I was going to focus only on bad things and get sucked into the vortex of despair. What was I so upset about? The trip we had taken was powerful and positive. First, the panel in Rhode Island with the attorney general had been a huge success. I had been asked to speak on the panel to regulators, the media, and a huge group of law-enforcement professionals about the unintended consequences of marijuana systems that do not have thoughtful regulation criteria. I was, once again, representing an entire industry, and my comments would reverberate around the nation of regulators. That day would serve to further establish me as a voice of reason in what would become a legal national framework for the marijuana industry. As if being on the panel was not enough, we went to Los Angeles to meet the California attorney general for a fundraiser as well. For the first time, someone in the cannabis industry had an audience with this influential regulator and was having a conversation about marijuana policy. I was able to hear her concerns for the federal system, the unintended consequences, and the need for smart policies. There were moments at that event during which I felt humbled, honored, and as if all of my hard work was paying off. In fact, if you were watching my life as if it were a TV show, you would think I was at the peak of my business performance and at the top of my game. Well, all of that was on the outside looking in; personally, when looking from the inside out, I was falling apart and was a total mess.

While so much good was happening, there was simultaneously a mounting assault of negatives swirling around me. For three years in the industry, I had gone from that first day on camera representing and building one of the largest brands in the marijuana space, O.penVAPE, to consulting for other companies to elevate their brands, to co-founding and leading High There!—and at every turn I was finding success. To build on all those successes, I was about to launch a new venture introducing the cleanest e-cig/cannabis vaporizing hardware imaginable. With my experience in running companies, our team developing an amazing device, and the risk I took to launch it, you can imagine how devastated I was to find out that the FDA was about to release new guidelines for e-cig hardware, which would cost us millions to comply with and, even though our product was a clean alternative, we would not have the funding to comply. Diana and I had worked tirelessly to take a huge risk, research, plan, and work with a team to devise a safe product that would protect consumers from the dangers of most e-cig and vape hardware. Even with that positive design, this FDA standard was going to kill us before we could even get started properly. As the CEO of the new venture, I could see the writing on the wall. The business was crashing.

It felt as if doors were closing all around me, and, to add to my secret frustration, the constant roadblocks I was hitting with other companies in the marijuana industry were getting out of hand. Some of the brands I was advising decided to get into verbal and political fights with local government. Another company, led by someone I had trusted, invited me to discuss carrying our e-cig/vape hardware, only to eventually copy the hardware and sell its version at a cheaper price because it was made from less-safe parts.

At that point, I had hit a wall. I was frustrated and tired, not to mention wondering who I was even supposed to trust in this industry. So when those airplane wheels hit the runway, I was on the edge and it felt as if I had hit rock bottom. The last three years of my life, all the hard work I had done, and the many groundbreaking achievements I brought about into my life, seemed as if they had happened so long ago, especially in the face of such adversity, heartache, and struggle.

The funny thing about life is, like a computer about to crash, the whole system is in jeopardy, not just the negative things or the individual programs that need to be restarted. When a computer crashes, it locks up *in toto*, and that's what happened to me; my full system lockdown was upon me. I was terrified and afraid of what my life had become. I was a shadow and a shell of a guy who had been on top of the world. It felt as if I finally got to the top of the success mountain, and, after a very hard and stressful time working to get there, I just fell straight off the cliff. I was afraid something else was going to go wrong, and I didn't know how I was going to deal with one more thing that wasn't working. I did not want even one message on the phone or via e-mail, or even news media, because it might signal that another area of my life was about to shatter into pieces. All of the failures happening around me surrounded me in a suffocating cloud of despair.

LETTING GO OF THE FAILURE

Not all risks are completely successful, even ones you calculate as much as possible, but that is OK if you have the right perspective. You need to begin to look at risk as a natural part of a dynamic life. For example, if you work outside the home, you cannot get from your house to your current place of work unless you are willing to take the risk of walking out the door. Unless you understand that you take risks each day and the ones you will take as a result of reading this book will simply be part of your life, it will be difficult for you to move forward successfully. Part of applying the learning in this book to your life is realizing that moving past a feeling of failure or fear often takes awareness and strength. We often force ourselves to do things in the name of tenacity, when, in reality, we should stop doing them altogether. While I agree with the necessity of tenacity for success, sometimes you need to realize when to stop working on something—because it just won't work no matter how many resources and how much time you keep putting into it. Instead, you need to apply all of that energy to starting on a new path, finding new opportunities, and gaining a new perspective.

Other times, a change or failure is forced on you by losing your job, getting into an accident, or experiencing a breakup. However the change occurs, and no matter how painful the change that is forced on you, you can use that opportunity to build a new vision and plan something new in your life. For example, I am sure Steve Jobs was not happy when he was fired from his own company, Apple. But later he stated that, during those ten years between being forced to leave and coming back to the company, he had some of the most creative and inspiring moments of his life. You have to look at what you see as "failure" to be a *growth opportunity* now, and a new and maybe even better path to future success.

I will often reflect back on my perceived failures to view them as learning opportunities, which helps me gain a new perspective when I need it most. Sometimes I didn't even realize how much I needed an opportunity to change until I was forced to find a new way and gain a fresh perspective on life. To do this, I analyze one of my past "failures" and ask myself if I would change anything if I had a chance to do it over. If I say, "Yes, I would change something," then I will play out the many different directions my life could have gone and the many different experiences I would have missed, had I not "failed." The truth is, you can't be happy where you are now but regret how you got there—even if you made a mistake, picked the wrong people to be around, or faced some terrible life-altering situation. Every mistake, misstep, or misfortune has taught you a lesson and put you where you are today. If you like one thing, even just *one* thing, about where you are, about yourself, or about a skill you gained, then you can never complain about how you got there. By complaining, you are putting yourself in a complete victim mentality that becomes an obstacle on a road to success. Instead, view failure as a positive. Even if you learn a sometimes-difficult lesson, that brings you wisdom, understanding, and knowledge of missteps, and helps you discover new directions you didn't know were out there until you failed. In sum, failure becomes only what you perceive it to be; and that is all about attitude.

When I came back from my trip in the story above, I was dealing simultaneously with fear as well as failure. It took all of my energy to try to figure out what was happening and where all of this internal negativity had come from. On our way to the baggage claim, Diana and I worked hard to try to make sense of all the closing doors, while working to stay focused on what doors were being opened. It felt as if this giant fear was an evil force working to kill me and take my power to move forward. During our walk, my conversation was random and certainly not confident. I was in the dumps, and it was very difficult to change my attitude, because I was completely frozen by the fear of feeling that my many projects were failing. I worked on positive thoughts to attempt to redirect my attitude with a recap of the trip we had just taken. After all, this week was big. I was the only one in the industry who was granted the honor to speak to the attorney general and all of Rhode Island about marijuana policy. And I was the only one in the industry who met with other important officials who were talking about a national framework for a legal marijuana business environment focused on consumer safety. The relationships I had forged at that time with key people were very strong.

New doors were opening, but I couldn't see them through the fog of fear. I had so many things running through my mind at the same time, lots of competing priorities, and a flurry of habitual self-talk of "What are you doing in this industry when it's so hard?" and "You are stupid for trusting the bad players in this industry." My negative talk was running wild, and as we walked through the airport toward baggage claim I had hit a wall. My personal operating system and computer of my life had locked up. I could not take another step. I put my phone in my pocket, let out a deep breath, and mentally went blank. I was overwhelmed with a feeling that I had allowed my career to fail. I feared that I was putting my family at risk financially and not being able to provide everyone with what he or she needed. I wanted to quit and run away to a deserted island—just forget everything about my career and start completely over.

I want you to know that life will sometimes hit you from all sides. The feeling that you are drowning in a sea of fear can set in very quickly, hit you mercilessly, and then beat you down. In these moments, remember that you need a reset. Actually, you need a total system reboot. You need something to get your mind and your attitude back on track. In these moments, you must remember to make the fear of not moving forward to a better vision stronger than the fear of being stuck in the same place or being afraid that you might fail. When you reset and refocus, only then can you start working on a new plan. The most important lesson is: You should NEVER build a new plan that comes from a place of fear. You must reset first and get out of the horrible place of despair.

LOCKDOWN CREATED LOOK UP

Isn't it interesting how life, the universe, or whatever you call it, throws people and circumstances in your way just when you need to encounter them? Sometimes knowing you need an attitude shift is all it takes to set in motion the countless small, seemingly meaningless actions needed to land you right where you need to be at the exact moment you need to be there. Maybe some things aren't meant to happen except to put you on the right path and steer you toward something better. So, as Diana and I approached the baggage claim,

I put my phone in my pocket, put my arm around her, and waited for the carousel to bring up our luggage. By not obsessing with my phone or my challenges for a moment, I was more focused on the surroundings. As I tried my best to breathe and concentrate on things other than the failing venture and what to do next, I caught a glimpse of someone who looked familiar. Standing in front of the same luggage carousel was a former client of mine—a client whom I had when I was still working in the corporate coaching world. She was at the airport with her daughter, and they were coming back from a trip and just happened to have their luggage routed to the same carousel as ours. In an instant, I remembered the amazing and powerful work we had accomplished together. We were friends and colleagues for four years, before I suddenly left the corporate coaching industry to embark on my cannabis-industry adventure. You see, I was so excited to dive into the cannabis industry that I exited the corporate world in a rush, with very short notice to my clients that I was leaving. I did not provide the best closure of my contracts that I could have and should have. After my departure, the friendship ended. In fact, you'll recall, at the beginning of this book, when I was getting ready to be interviewed on CNN, I was receiving text messages from former clients stating they would never work with me again—one of those texts was from her. I do not believe in coincidences; this was a sign, a sign of a possible direction. Admittedly, I regretted the way I had abruptly exited our business relationship, and I had felt badly every time I thought about it. Even though I had been excited about the path I went on, I could have treated her better on the way to my new career. When I was thrust into the marijuana spotlight three years earlier, I left clients behind much the same way many had since left me behind. Clearly, I wasn't sure what she was going to say when I approached her after several years with no communication after my very jarring departure.

When Diana and I approached her, she was surprisingly kind

to me. I introduced her to Diana, and we proceeded to discuss the usual catch-up dialogue most people share after a long time of no interaction. Unbeknownst to her, our chance meeting was a wake-up call for me and sparked an amazing conversation between Diana and me on the drive home; both my attitude and direction changed once again. We often ignore the signs that are put in front of us. If you had been in my shoes, would you have talked to her? Would you have run the other direction and hid behind a stack of luggage until she left? Oftentimes we miss the opportunity to grow because we are fearful about dealing with a past mistake. I am here to tell you that because I made a decision to stand and talk, everything changed for me again. The Disruptor is not afraid of any interaction, even one in which his or her mistakes must be faced. I could feel that disruptive power rushing in me again.

SYSTEM REBOOT—USING THE LEARNING TO PUSH PAST FEAR

On the ride home, it was Diana who uttered the most powerful statement I needed to hear: "What would you coach me to do if I were in your situation right now?" I wasn't expecting this question, so I looked at Diana and said "What?" She looked at me from the passenger seat and said, "Well, you are obviously not happy, and we are not getting where we want to be. So, just for a minute, pretend I am you, and you are my coach; what would you tell me I should do?" That simple question was just the spark I was looking for to start my engine and finally drive away from the fear that was holding me back. All the events that had led to this point, coupled with seeing and talking with my former client, slowly began to pivot me in a new direction. My feeling of needing a new plan grew stronger. This is how my reset began. It didn't take just one day or one week; it took a while, because I had to go through all of the steps of the reboot. After all, I had taught others the reboot learning and had taken risks for a long time as a corporate speaker, so reapplying it to my situation took more effort than I anticipated, mostly because this reset was unexpected. Suddenly the realization that I MUST keep going forward overpowered my fear of failure, judgment, and negative thoughts. Here is a play-by-play of how I reset myself using the learning I had stored away for a brief time, and then went on a new path toward the next phase of a fearless future.

ATTITUDE

When I got into the car at the airport initially, I felt doomed and as if I had hit rock bottom. To say the least, I was expecting the rest of the week to be awful and depressing while I found new opportunities to pursue. All of that changed on the drive home, when I realized that there were other opportunities right in front of me. I didn't comprehend that they were there the entire time, just waiting for me to take them. It was time to go in a new direction. If I were to shift my attitude, I would need to remember the warrior inside me who had driven me to accomplish very disruptive things in my life. That warrior, I believe, sits in all of us and emerges at times when we need him or her the most. In order to be focused on the new path and keep my attitude where it needed to be, I had to split from all the negative people in my life as well as from those who were hanging on only so they could use me. As one example, those people who were only hanging on to me because of my success, and not to enrich my life, needed to be cut loose. In other words, I needed to intentionally burn some bridges to protect my future. And as for the people I had wronged in any way on my way out of the corporate world, I needed to apologize to them and repair our friendships.

Looking back, I see that changing my attitude was actually the easiest part once I remembered who I was and told myself that the attitude shift MUST occur. I literally coached myself, as Diana directed questions concerning the new direction and what I wanted as an outcome. While she sat beside me in the car and took notes about my answers to each question, I launched into a positive-attitude-change rant exploring new directions and outcomes. The most powerful part of this process was finally reminding myself who I was and what I was here to do. I started the rant by acknowledging all of the good things happening in our lives and deciding to focus on those. I focused on the positive feelings I had about speaking, coaching, and working with good companies in the marijuana space. At one point, I reminisced about what I had accomplished in many successes throughout my career to find powerful positive emotions that I then leveraged to turn my attitude around. Essentially, I remembered my power. It's interesting to me how people will often have no problem tapping into negative emotions and bad memories when it suits their victim story and unconscious desire to demonstrate a bad attitude, but how difficult it is for people to tap into positive memories and emotions when they need to reset their attitude. Look at your own life. When you need an attitude adjustment, do you find it difficult because all you can concentrate on are negative memories? In other words, if you smack your foot on the bed in the morning, do you immediately remember a positive thought to feel better? Like how great it felt to have a foot massage? Or do you talk about the foot pain all the way to the coffeemaker? The point is that it takes the same amount of effort to be positive as it does to be negative—why not go positive?

VISION

To go to the next phase of my career and life, I reset my vision. This is what you will need to do after you reboot. With my attitude in a good place again, I started to bounce ideas off of my Disruptive Influencer, Diana. On the drive home, we were starting to get excited that things would start to look up again. While we were talking, I realized that I needed a break from the marijuana business until I found positive companies that truly wanted to go to a new mainstream level, far away from the negative players. Based on the government-affairs work I was doing, there was no doubt in my mind that the industry was about to get a wake-up call in such a way that only the good companies would survive. So, I decided to cut ties with the old contacts who weren't moving forward or setting higher standards for the industry, and to wait for the best business operators to emerge.

Sometimes, when you are resetting your vision, you need to free yourself of the old world you are trying to move away from (burn a bridge) and stop focusing on old things that are not working. Still working through the reboot/reset on the drive home, Diana and I decided that our new company venture had to be shut down. This was the most difficult decision of my recent career. A total failure. However, realizing and acknowledging that something isn't working and cutting it loose is better done sooner rather than later, so you can begin on something new. Ending the company was the only way we could remove the massive distraction of it not working and the stress it was bringing to our lives.

Because I started to reboot myself, I had a new, clean mental framework with which I could build a new vision. I organized my new vision in the following way, by having Diana write these words in her notebook as I continued to drive:

I will immediately focus on key areas of the next phase of my career. I will move to rebuild a speaking career with which I can share all of my experiences from the marijuana industry, government affairs, and business in order to help other people and their businesses. I will work to build our company division around government affairs for all industries and for all sizes of companies. I will build a successful coaching business for both cannabis and mainstream companies.

I want you to know that when you go through this process, new ideas will start to flow. Past goals, unfulfilled dreams, and other possibilities that you weren't even aware of will come to mind so that you can start to thrive again. One of my goals in life was to finish a book I had started about a year earlier. So I had Diana write down an additional goal: "I will focus on finishing the book I started and launching a new phase of my career, life, and focus."

By the time we arrived home, a new vision was emerging. I was ready to put together a plan. Keep in mind that, as a Disruptor, I may have many ideas and goals in my mind, but I also listen to my positive Disruptive Influencers like Diana. I was excited, full of energy, and ready to start; but I knew I had to think about my vision and all the aspects of what needed to be done and how. I had learned from my earlier mistake of jumping ship too fast when I left the corporate world to join the cannabis industry. I now knew that I needed an exit strategy from the projects that weren't working, and the strategy needed to be thoughtful and careful. Just because I had a new plan didn't mean I could just quit everything; we still had bills and employees, and the new plan hadn't started to unfold. The reason I want you to understand about how careful we needed to be as we transitioned was so you understand that being a Disruptor does not mean you put at risk your well-being or the well-being of those closest to you. You can disrupt your career, for example, by rebooting AND including how and when you will exit something. I recently gave the Reboot Your Life presentation, and one of the key questions from a member of the audience was about this very topic: "How do I start a new business but still keep my job until I am financially stable in the new business?" The answer is the reboot, but you add in the plan for the transition. Many people forget this simple yet important step.

If you reread the section above, you can pick out the critical Disruptive Influencers in my life who helped get me to a new place mentally. Sometimes the smallest events or interactions can be very large Disruptive Influences, so start watching for opportunities in all forms. For me, it was the client I had not seen in some time; she was more of a Disruptive Influencer than she knew, because her presence reminded me of things about myself that needed to reemerge. The most powerful Disruptive Influencer of all was Diana. Her positive attitude, unwavering faith, and a fighting spirit that can face any challenge in life were like a flame igniting my soul. As I mentioned earlier in the book (see chapter 2), this type of person is critical in your life, especially if you want to make big changes. Doing everything alone is not practical, but more importantly, by finding a positive Disruptive Influencer, you are allowing new ideas, accountability, and positivity to flow into your life.

PLAN

The next morning, I started to focus on my new vision and kicked off the day with a walk outside to keep my attitude focused. After a morning meditation, Diana and I started designing the new plan based on the new vision, both macro and micro, that we created in the car. I need you to understand that this is the work. You can't simply change your attitude and vision in your head and then go back to the same old routine as the day before. You need a reboot, and that means you need to take action. You must do the work of devising and writing out the plan in detail. We broke our plan for our company's new directions into segments and areas of the vision needing attention. Before I walk you through the process, you need to understand that this plan did not start to look complete for nearly three weeks. You see, the vision process we outlined earlier, both macro and micro, is the easy part from a physical work standpoint, in that you determine the vision and then move forward to the plan. But the planning is the core of the process, because it outlines the steps it will take to actually achieve the new result.

As we were developing the plan to match my vision, we would keep adding details—unexpected turns and twists and ideas—into the appropriate categories. This flexibility and constant modification of the plan created a way for me to seek out more refined and focused opportunities that would not have arisen if we had established a very rigid plan allowing for absolutely no changes. As long as you keep to the original vision of what you want, there is more than one path or plan to get there; you just have to pick the one that fits in with your needs at the time. While we were working on and tweaking the plan for a new path, I was still working on current projects so that we could make ends meet. This is an important point when creating a new plan for your life, situation, work, or family: you do not need to make it all happen in a day, or a week, a month, or even a year. Taking your time to be specific in the plan is critical to your future success in any area, large or small. If you want to be a better employee and speak up more, you need a very well thought-out plan to mitigate the fear of feeling stupid when you speak up. If you want to change careers, you need to take time to plan the next career move, timing, financial security, what new skills you need to acquire, and so on. You will need a plan, which may include where to live, how to support yourself, and what changes you need to make inside yourself in order to be the kind of person you want to be. The point is, planning takes time upfront if you truly want to be successful in the long term. If you want the change to stick, you must take time to plan.

For the next three weeks, Diana and I planned each phase of the new change. All throughout that month, I executed small changes that seemed minuscule at the time but made a huge difference in the long run. I changed my cell number and e-mail address, and I completely redesigned my website. Because I wanted to take total control over my situation, I did those tasks on my own. The initial feeling of control added more momentum to execution of the plan. Each week, I made a new strategic change in both my current career as well my newly developing one, based on our emerging plan. It took us a while to design new content for presentations while revamping my coaching content. The next week was all about the structure of the plan, which was simply:

- Write a proposal for a book Diana and I had talked about, utilizing my previous attempts at writing it.
- Begin speaking to corporations full-time again based on my old relationships and contacts.
- Engage new coaching clients, pulling from current marijuana-company clients, new ones, and past corporate clients.
- Articulate a new speaking message about what I have learned as a leader and founder in the marijuana industry and in the start-up world.
- Leverage my skills and relationships working alongside government officials to build out a government-affairs part of the business.
- Disengage from all people and activities that are not working toward the new focus.

I did not complete every single task in one day. Some tasks overflowed into the second and third week of the plan because they had so many moving parts that they had to be managed separately.

To be sure, this new plan would require taking many new risks, but the plan itself creates a critical direction, which pushes me away from the fear of the risk. It is through your plan that the risk *you* will need to take goes from risky to calculated and careful.

VIEW FAILURE AS POWER

As the flip charts that we used for our planning started to accumulate around the office and the plan unfolded, I realized an important lesson: my failures drove me to reboot myself. Think about failures throughout your life. Did you look at them as a time of deep regret and anguish? Do the memories of those moments still cause you to shudder and fall into despair? Is there still guilt that you are holding onto? This is your moment to look more positively at these failures and use them as fuel to power you forward. The fear I felt around rebooting my life was not nearly as scary as the fear I felt about continuing on a path that was not serving me or our company. In fact, once we had the outline for the basic plan, it was time to fill it in completely, which we did over the following four weeks. In four weeks, with Diana as my Disruptive Influencer and partner, we had redesigned the company direction and our own lives, and we had started to head in a new direction. And that was just the planning phase; it may take much longer than four weeks to revamp your entire business career or major parts of your personal life. If you want it badly enough, and it's a big change, it will take time. I utilized failure as a lesson and fear as my fuel. I discovered how to convert the angst and fear into energy to move forward. Even if you love most situations in your life and only want to change small things, fear and doubt can still arise. That is when you need to look deeper and ask yourself, "What can I learn from this fear or this failure?" That simple statement can get you closer to your fulfillment, as it has for me.

THIS BOOK IS BORN

One example that changed everything was this very book you are reading. Because our most valuable asset is time, Diana and I did not want to waste it on attempting to self-publish. We knew that in order for this very book to come to fruition, the skills of a book agent would be needed to secure us a publishing deal. But how would I find this person and get him or her to represent me? After all, I had never completely written a book like this—or completed any book for that matter—let alone researched what it would take to find a literary agent. So Diana and I went to work investigating how to secure a literary agent. While searching for the right agent online and in catalogues, we simultaneously started to build a book proposal that we could send to the literary agent (after we found her or him), based on a sample Diana had found in her research. We spent countless hours writing, crafting, and preparing this proposal, all while raising three kids, taking them to school, and managing our other business needs. Let's just say we were really busy; it was not easy, but we stayed with it. To make sure that the book was as good as it could be, we harnessed the power of the best editor I know: my stepmom. She is a brilliant editor and wields the English language like a pro. She has always been one of my Disruptive Influencers, and as I mention throughout the chapters, you need positive people who will be your Disruptive Influencers in order to succeed. The process went like this: I would write parts of the proposal, Diana would help me refine them, and my stepmom would then make it as perfect as possible. It was a true team effort and, in the end, produced the book proposal I sent to the agents who I found through our online research.

With every opportunity comes fear. I found a new fear right out of the gate, before we even finished the proposal for the book. Fear of rejection. What if the book was not liked? What if someone told me it sucked? What if we never got a deal and I wasted all that time?

These were all self-sabotaging statements emerging like a river of poison and sucking me into the muck. Still, I was operating on a new set of rules in which I measured the fear of staying where I was, deeply dissatisfied, against the fear of failure. I then harnessed the force of being more fearful of staying where I was and leveraged it to find success. After all, failure is learning, right? So what if I failed at writing the book—at least I was working toward my vision and goal. After a long week of work, I sent the completed proposal to forty agents all over the United States and then waited for an answer. A week after I sent out the proposal, I tallied up: ten nos, twenty-eight "not at this time" responses, and two yesses! After chatting with the two agents who saw potential in our book proposal, I went with the one my gut instinct told me was the right match for me, my style, and my desire to bring my history, lessons, career, and all the positive things I had accomplished to life. The day we signed the agreement with the agent was only the start. While this may seem like it happened fast, make no mistake, it took a great deal of time to draft the right proposal that an agent would appreciate and feel confident marketing. The tedious upfront planning and execution made all the difference, while removing the fear from my heart, and that opened the door even wider to seize this opportunity. I had to do the one thing I am calling for you to do. I had to believe this book would find an agent and a publisher. I knew someone was going to champion my book. By remaining focused on the outcome and executing the plan, I was able to steer away from fear, because I had unwavering faith that I would get an agent, eventually. And I did. Well, I and my Disruptive Influencers did.

Because we had put so much time and effort into the proposal, when the agent submitted it to a select number of publishers, we had two publishers come back with offers to publish the book. In the end, we picked the best one, which was aligned with our values of taking risks, doing a project the right way, and working collaboratively. We also found the one who believed in our vision. You have this book in your hand because of a collection of positive attitudes, Macro and Micro Visioning, and a detailed plan. I, the Disruptor, and my Disruptive Influencers, made this work. If you need proof that everything we are discussing about disruption actually works in the real world, well, you are holding that proof in your hands right now.

A JOURNEY OF MISSES, OR WERE THEY?

The following stories have no specific sequence. They are independent of one another, and are proof that failures are really learning possibilities for the willing and teachable Disruptor. I write them as independent stories so that you can relate, regardless of where you are in life. Each is a free-standing piece of learning to make the point that beautiful lessons are everywhere. Enjoy!

I have "failed" more times than I have succeeded, but I had never viewed my misses as failures; rather, I saw them as expensive lessons. I always see them as learning engines to rev up the next phase of my life. I have learned so much in all of my experiences that in order to help you, the reader, I MUST be authentic and truthful about my journey. I must share not only how I have won at life but also how badly I lost when I took a chance and missed the mark, but learned lessons in the effort. Had I not risked myself in these ways, I would not be benefiting from the knowledge I gained. I want you to understand that your life, too, can be filled with learning failures and STILL be amazing. Here we go on a short journey of a few more misfortunes, complete with what I learned from them.

1997–Chuck

In 1997, I was on top of the world. My career as an entertainer was flying high in Chicago, I was attending Second City Training School (for comedy and improvisation classes), and I was loving my life. But, somewhere in my heart, I felt that I deserved more. The feeling was almost one of entitlement. For a young entertainer making more money than I had ever had, it was easy to get caught in the trap of "give me more … now." I guess it was fitting that I ran into a con artist named Chuck (this is not his real name). Chuck was a slick Italian man who drove around in limos, flashed large wads of cash, and, coincidently, wanted to take my entertainment skills on the road to Florida to open a new entertainment venue. How could this possibly go wrong? To top it all off, he offered me even more money, slapped a stack of hundred-dollar bills in my hand, and said, "Come to the airport, we are going to take a cruise with you and my team to discuss the future." This felt too good to be true, but I wanted the adventure. I ran home, packed a bag, and could not get to the airport fast enough! I thought the universe had rained down good stuff upon me and it was my time to shine.

The cruise was amazing. All expenses paid, and then a stop in Florida to set up our deal. Next came setting up the office, shopping for property and a location for the club, and driving expensive cars. It just kept getting better and better. Chuck's story about becoming a well-heeled businessman was based on reinvesting the money of a very wealthy benefactor who wanted to own nightclubs and who trusted Chuck with his money. I was in love with the lifestyle Chuck and his team kept piling on. His slick and obviously expensive suits, fast-talking style, and unwavering confidence was intoxicating to a young performer. I wanted him to be my mentor and friend, and to lead me to success. I was hooked by Chuck. It's funny how we can get caught up in something we think—or even know—we deserve. We become blind very quickly when cruises, stacks of money, fast cars, and all the fun we can handle are just given to us. But even after a phone call with my father during which he said, "Todd, it just sounds too good to be true," I was undeterred from continuing on this path. After all, this guy had money, was successful, and had credibility. What could go wrong?

In my first week of working with Chuck, he blew my mind with his level of conviction to get what he wanted. As a team of five people, we walked into a bank in Florida. Chuck sat with the manager of the bank and said these words, which I will never forget: "I am working to reinvest $18 million into this community by the person I represent. That money will be wired here in the next week; well, hopefully to this bank. It really depends on the relationship we have with you in this moment." The bank manager's jaw hit the floor, and he started to treat us like royalty. You would have thought I had walked into the room accompanied by the wealthiest man in the world. Chuck's mastery of persuasion sticks with me to this day; from him I learned the power of unwavering confidence. After Chuck and the banker closed the deal in which Chuck would transfer $18 million into this bank, they signed the paperwork and exchanged business cards. As Chuck stood up to leave, he looked at the banker and said, "There is one more thing you can help me with; we need eight thousand dollars in cash to set up our office and such. Could you give us that amount in advance of the $18 million transfer?" The bank manager said, "No problem, sir," and within a matter of moments, he handed Chuck the cash, merely on the promise of the big wire transfer.

We were only two months into our journey, and I had a new car, job, and house, and I was putting my skills to use preparing our plan, touring properties, and generally feeling excited. Then a telephone call came that changed everything. "Todd, this is the dealership. Chuck's payment on the three cars did not come through. I want those cars back NOW!" You see, Chuck had paid $20,000 in cash upfront for three brand-new Corvettes. Chuck, another guy I will call Jason, and I drove off with them solely on Chuck's promise to the dealership that a bank transfer would come through. Well, the money never came, and the dealership wanted its cars back. I was shocked. Literally an hour later, I got a call from my bank telling me that my paycheck had bounced. What!? What was happening? The entire world around me started to spin out of control.

My calls to Chuck went unanswered. I drove to his house, but it was empty. So I called back the car dealership, told the staff where the car was, and left the keys in it. Then I rushed home and tried to find out more about Chuck on the computer. Back then, the Internet was in its infancy; however, with persistent research and some of Chuck's personal information (I had his full name), I found him. Chuck was actually a wanted felon who had conned many people in huge check fraud and investment scams. He had actually served time in prison for the felonies and had recently gotten out. He had used his charm, wit, passion, confidence, and skills to swindle not only me but also other investors, as well as the bank manager and the car dealer, to acquire loads of money and a brand-new car. By the time I realized what was happening, Chuck was gone and I was stuck in a new state without a way to make money and with many bills piling up. Going for the quick money, I had found a so-called failure; searching for the fast success, I had found fear of being completely lost—but I learned some amazing lessons in reading people better, keeping myself safe, and being smarter about business partners.

So why do I not call this a failure? Because I actually learned a great deal from this experience. I learned to verify who I was dealing with, and I gained an understanding of how to use confidence in conversations and negotiations. Chuck was a gifted negotiator and could get anyone to do anything.

When I found out what had happened and that I had been used—sure, bitching, complaining, and whining were all options, but to what end? Instead, I picked myself up, borrowed money from my family to cover the bills I couldn't pay due to the bounced paycheck, and kept moving. Again, my fear of standing still was greater than my fear of additional failure, so the only way I could go was forward.

I moved from the coast of Florida to Orlando. I eventually found a new career at Universal Studios as a lead manager and entertainer for some of the largest audiences I had ever encountered. How was I able to secure this new work, you ask? Well, with my newly acquired, savvy expertise in negotiation, persuasion, and confidence, all combined with how to dress to impress. Getting swindled by Chuck was one huge failure that actually gave me even bigger benefits. Now pause and look at your life. What is in your life right now that is teaching you something valuable? What lessons are right in front of your face? Perhaps you can't see these lessons because you are blinded by negativity. You have choices, and one of those choices should be to find the positives of every perceived failure. Many people have said this many ways, but just remember, you can't be happy with where you are and still curse how you got there.

A Night on the Town

A night out with Diana's friends, that's what motivated me for a week. Diana and I work hard and long hours because we are driven to get to the next stages of success. On top of that, we are also parenting three amazing kids. You can imagine how much extra time we wish we had to just go out and be together, unencumbered by responsibilities. So, when we were invited, a week in advance, to go to an event with some of Diana's friends, I decided that we needed to make the time to go. These were friends Diana had had for a few years, so, in my heart, it was important to make the night special for her. For a week straight, my reminders to her about the event came like clockwork. "Aren't you excited to hang out with your friends next week?" "Are you excited for a night out?" "I bet we will have so much fun at this event, I can't wait!" In my mind, this was supporting her need to spend time out on the town with her dearest friends so she could catch up and be a part of their lives. This was also my chance to demonstrate my love for Diana, by going somewhere important to her. I wanted nothing to ruin this occasion, so fear rose inside me. Why? Well, frankly speaking, I wasn't really excited to go. We were already having a long week with the kids and countless hours of work; the last thing I wanted to do was head out for an entire night on the town. Every time that thought would enter my mind, I would say to myself, "Todd, stop! If you screw up this night for her, she will be really sad. Man up and make it happen . . . for love!" Far too afraid of screwing it up, I remained outwardly steadfast around pumping enthusiasm into the anticipation of the pending evening.

On the day of the event, we started getting ready, and every few minutes I would think to myself, "I really don't want to go out." Then I noticed that Diana was definitely distracted by selecting her outfit. It seemed that she was frustrated about what to wear and seemed really upset by her choices, which is not like her. I suddenly realized that maybe my silent negative attitude was impacting her, so I poured on some more excitement and said, "You look amazing. We will have so much fun, and I love you!" After she found an exquisite outfit and was ready to go, we were finally on our way downtown, with the music playing loudly in the car and enjoying the wonderful drive. Still, Diana seemed really distracted and not thrilled with something. Leaning over and turning down the music, I said, "What's on your mind?" The next words out of her mouth were priceless. "Well, I really don't want to go out tonight. I never wanted to go, because we have been working so hard and nonstop; on top of that, the week has been so long and exhausting. I want to see my friends, catch up, and have a great time, but tonight I would just rather have a second to breathe and relax with you at home. You were so excited the entire week that I am trying to suck it up and go out so you can have a great time. I was so afraid to tell you, because I didn't want to ruin your night." After I burst out laughing, my next comment changed the entire night, "Me either. I only wanted to go out so you could have a great night. And I was so afraid of telling you I didn't want to go, because I didn't want to ruin *your* night. I would rather go home, drink wine, and just hang out." By this time, we were laughing hysterically in a car headed to a destination neither one of us wanted to reach. So we turned the car around and laughed all the way home.

The point is, when you allow your fear to take over, it's almost like allowing a crazy person to rule your decisions. The decisions you make when you are in control are drastically different from the ones you make from a place of fear. When you consider that your assumptions are driving your fear, you realize all of the nonsense and fear-based actions you take are draining time, energy, and resources from your life. It may be time for you to squash your fear by removing your assumptions. You do this by verifying the assumption to be true or not true, and then you make decisions based on that answer. Had I verified my assumption that Diana really wanted to go out for that special evening—and found out that my assumption was, in fact, not true—neither one of us would have wasted a week pretending we were excited about doing something neither one of us really wanted to do.

Batman

It was 1991—before it all really began. . . . OK. Audition time. I had to leave early from my job as a manager at Kohl's to audition for the role of a lifetime. I drove for an hour, got out of the car, practiced my lines, and walked into the audition space. The fateful word, "Next," rang out. Here I go to my new acting future. At the time, I was living in Ohio, not really the acting mecca for a twenty-year-old guy with hopes of having a robust career in the arts. Nonetheless, I went for it. I said the lines like a pro and, right away, the director said every actor's dream phrase, "We love it, you have the part. You will be our Batman!"

Now, this was not some role in a movie or new TV show, but I didn't care. I was going to be the Batman! A guy who traveled the country dressed as the caped crusader, pulling up to movie theaters in an actual Batmobile from the newly released movie. More important than all of that, I had learned how to act the part, audition, and show up without letting fear drive me out the door. To top it off, my skills had worked. I did everything right to land the part. This fun, marketing acting role would not be winning me an Oscar, but surely it was to be a powerful experience for a new career path. The following day, I came in for the costume fitting. Just putting on the cowl, the chest plate, and the cape made me feel like a superhero; well, until I had to put on the pants and the arms. You see, Michael Keaton, the actor who played Batman, was only 5 feet 10 inches tall, and I was 6 feet 5 inches. Basically, the suit was far too small for me. In a flash, my Batman hopes died in the dressing room. What was to be the single most fun and exciting experience of my young career was crushed in that moment.

The point here is you can do it all right, you can prepare, plan, and have a great attitude, and still fail. In your life, you can get the part you have been dreaming about, and then lose it even faster. It was sad, and, of course, I was down in the dumps. I mean, who wouldn't want to drive the new Batmobile? I have always believed that sometimes things don't work out for a reason. In this example, I learned preparedness was key to success and focusing on the end result matters. I learned to overcome rejection, even when I did everything right. Your life is the same way; even if you do everything the right way, you can still fail because of things that are out of your control. Remember, it's not personal. It's learning.

HOW TO APPLY THIS CHAPTER

Failure. The best way to overcome the failure mentality is to go back and look at a failure in your life and then map out all the things that the particular failure taught you. You may structure it like this:

> I failed at _____.
> But I learned _____.

List the skills you learned, opportunities you created, ideas you generated, or people you met during your path to that specific failure who are still positively impacting you. Then, each time you experience a failure, simply take a moment to think about what you are learning, write it down, and keep it where you can see it each day. Soon, you will get to a place where there are only opportunities that come as lessons instead of failures.

Another thing you will take away from this exercise is that every perceived failure is actually filled with a new way of looking at the problem. No matter how seemingly trivial the misstep or how epic the miss, in the end you gain more experience in how to deal with things that don't go your way and how to create better solutions to future problems. The key to applying a new mind-set around failure is to adopt the acceptance that each time you fail, you will learn something new. Then you simply apply that lesson the next time you embark on a new adventure.

We live in a society that constantly reminds us of our failures. We are told to check our credit score so we can see our failures in finance. We post our entire lives on Facebook and other social media outlets, and if we just happen to share a mistake with the world, then we are reminded of it forever. When we fail at a job, we are not able to put it as a reference on our resume, so we are forced to remember it in our minds as a miss, a failure. When we make mistakes at work, someone will certainly remind us sarcastically of our "track record" in the future when we want to make another attempt. We become fearful of taking risks, because of the judgment by others of our choices. Society is always reminding us of these mistakes, but it is up to us to remind ourselves of the lessons we have learned. If you look at your life and the work you just accomplished in the "Apply It" section of this chapter, you will see clearly the learning you have achieved from your mistakes. My advice: keep staying focused on lessons learned and the good things achieved from those lessons, and never curse how you got there.

CHAPTER 7

A LITTLE CHAPTER ABOUT FEAR

Oh, Fear, you worthless mental state, tying people in knots and causing them to make terrible life choices. Fear, you hungry demon feeding on the negative internal dialogue I have created for a lifetime. Fear, you mental support for the complaining victim to hide behind while continuing to live small. How do you rule our lives? If failure is to be redefined, as we talked about in the last chapter, fear gets its own small chapter, but only big enough to make the point: it cannot control you—the Disruptor—unless you allow it. What is fear, really?

> *What fear is:* Fear is based on assumptions, negative self-talk, and constructs that tell you a negative story. Fear is a myth your mind creates to justify why you will always flounder in an ocean of dread, anxiety, and panic, and you will never succeed in anything you do. Fear is a lie, a lie you have created in your own head. Fear is a construct. It is an emotion that we choose to feel in a situation of danger, either perceived or real.
>
> *What fear is not:* Fear is not in control.

When faced with something unknown, we immediately allow fear to take us over, but make no mistake, the only power that fear wields is the power that you give it. If you want to become a Disruptor and live a thriving life to its fullest, you MUST recognize that you are in control of your fear. To me, fear is not real, it's just an emotion and it's something that I can control.

When I am faced with any perceived threat, danger, or anxiety-inducing situation, I make a choice to work toward not allowing the fear to take me over. I look at this choice as either a decision to be scared or a decision to move forward. It's hard to start to control fear, because society has engrained it into our minds that we are supposed to be afraid. Instead, I think the smarter action is to manage the future risk, which starts with discovery, use of caution moving forward, and remaining calm.

Fear may feel necessary, at times, for physical survival, but to a person who wants to make a difference at work, at home, or toward their own fulfillment, fear is a dangerous lie that will not truly serve you. At least not if you want to thrive in the game of life. We are born with an involuntary reaction in our bodies as an evolutionary response to keep us safe. It is not until later in childhood that prolonged fears or being taught to fear begins to build foundational pain, which then affects our decisions for the rest of our very limited time on this planet. As we age, it becomes more and more difficult to cast off the fear; we start to use it like a blanket to protect ourselves. Afraid, we—as adults—seek ways to feel safe. We choose friends, jobs, coffee, alcohol, TV, and countless other coping tools to feel safe, loved, and less afraid of everything. This manifests in different ways for each of us, but without a conscious understanding of what fear is and how to stop it, we meander headfirst on a collision course with mediocrity. We give fear more credit than it deserves.

DIANA

Like you, I have faced fear many times; these experiences have taught me how to overcome it and not give it power in my mind. For this chapter, I was prepared to tell you all about my personal fears at each stage of life, as well as how I overcame them; but then I paused. I paused because it hit me: I am not the right person to talk about fear. Why? Because someone near and dear to me has overcome far more fear than I have. She has faced fears that would knock most people to their knees, begging for a savior. And then, when facing her biggest fears, she attacked life in a way that truly defined her as a powerful Disruptor. Surely that is why she is so amazing at being a Disruptive Influence in my life. Her name is Diana, but to me, she is so much more.

Diana is my better half and partner in all things life and work. Since the very first day we met, she has inspired greatness in me unlike any I have experienced in even the best situations in my life. It is her passion and love that pulled me out of some very dark mental places. More important, it is her own personal journey past defeat and fear that inspires me to parent, love, and live even more fiercely than before, without any excuses. She demonstrates a fearless way to live life and experiences self-forgiveness for her mistakes that is unparalleled.

Emigrating from Lithuania at the age of twelve, Diana spent the first part of her childhood in difficult and trying situations. After the Soviet Union fell and life was hard in the Baltic states, her mother came to America to seek a better life for herself as well as for her daughter. Diana was just five years old when she had to say good-bye to her mother. She was a child who couldn't understand quite yet that sometimes life asks people to sacrifice the most important things in their lives in order to have a better tomorrow. In this case, it wasn't as fast of a trip to a better tomorrow as everyone had hoped. Due to massive amounts of Lithuanians fleeing to different countries because of the country's economic instability, Diana did not gain permission to leave the country alongside her mother. Diana's mother had a grim choice: stay and live in poverty for the rest of their lives with little hope of survival, or leave her daughter behind to be raised by her grandmother until they could be reunited in America. Making the single most difficult decision of her life at that

201

time, Diana's mother said good-bye to all she knew, and headed to America, overcoming pain and fear to build a future for her daughter. Diana's seventy-year-old grandmother became a full-time caregiver, raising a child of five all alone, thousands of miles away.

It would be nearly seven years before Diana would be reunited with her mother. In the meantime, the only contact they had was through letters, pictures, and phone calls that kept the bond alive. In America, we simply do not understand the perils people in many foreign countries face. For example, when Diana's mother left the country, she couldn't return to Lithuania because she would not be able to leave again. She had her green card and needed to have American citizenship in order to start the paperwork process required to get Diana to the United States. It took countless denials, constant pleadings by her grandmother and mother to the Lithuanian embassy, almost all the money her mother earned working in the United States, two lawyers, and seven long years for Diana to be reunited with her mother. These are challenges most of us will never face; however, these are the same challenges that can shape a person in so many different ways. We have all met people with far less challenging starts in life who complain about how hard they had it and use their past as fuel for fear to tell their victim story of why they will never succeed. Can you imagine the fear Diana, her grandmother, and her mother must have felt during those seven years?

When Diana and her grandmother finally arrived in America, Diana was twelve. She had waited seven years to be reunited with a mother who now was someone she barely knew. After three weeks of adjusting, Diana found herself in an American middle school with no friends, learning a language she did not understand. Again, for many kids who might find themselves in this circumstance, defeat would be imminent. Diana has told me about the fear she felt on every level: the fear of seeing a mother she really did not know and had to learn about, the fear of a new school, the fear of a new country, the fear of having to leave all of her personal possessions behind, and the fear of not understanding English, let alone being able to speak it. Because Lithuania is a small country and has its own language, there was not another Lithuanian to help her with school or to help her learn English. A translator was also not available. What happened next should be a lesson to all of us about taking action to overcome fear. Using her instincts and a giant dictionary she carried everywhere, she learned basic English in her first semester of middle school! After that, she mastered English in two years, to the point of being fluent. She even worked to remove her accent to fit in. It would be an amazing world if most kids were taught the courage, passion, and determination Diana exhibited in those early days and that she still conveys today. At twelve, in that all-American middle school, immigrant Diana taught herself English—spending countless hours into late nights studying and memorizing words, doing homework she didn't understand, and hoping that maybe she got it right, and making friends who had some compassion for this foreign kid. By the time she was in high school, Diana was more than fluent in the language and the culture. If you had met her then, you would think she was born and raised in America. She became so skilled at turning her fear into determination that she graduated from high school as a junior—a full year early! She was the first student in her school to convince the principal to let her graduate as a junior, as long as she took senior-level classes that were required to graduate at a nearby college: Diana was a Disruptor of epic proportions.

Pause for a moment and think about yourself and any fears that you may be feeling in life right now. What are those fears? Do you think that you will accomplish what you set out to do, or will you let the dread and anxiety of failure stop you? Sometimes all we need to pull ourselves out of the construct, or what I call the lie, of fear, and into a more thoughtful direction is to hear another person's struggle. Not because they may have a worse story than yours or to make you feel bad about complaining, but to start thinking in terms of what's possible. Without a positive outlook for your goals, you will develop your feelings of uncertainty into true negative reactions, actions, and misguided interactions. If you were in Diana's shoes when she was a child, would you have chosen the path of achievement like she did, or would you have chosen to tell a victim story to feed your fear-based life? Again, in the world of a person who begins to take calculated risks that spill over into all aspects of life, you MUST see fear as not real, but as a perceived thing that you either move past or allow to control you. Luckily for Diana, she had the attitude of "I can overcome this" and then set out to reach a goal. When times would get hard, her story of "I can" would change to "I must," because, to her, there was no other option than to break through whatever obstacle was in her way to reach the goal.

She did not stop there. Setting out to complete college in a big way, Diana got her loans, obtained two jobs, then proceeded to put herself through college and graduated with not one, but two degrees—one in molecular, cellular, and developmental biology, and another in integrated physiology. This woman has a great deal to teach us about overcoming fear, but, more important, she did so with her heart of gold intact. I have never met a kinder or more compassionate woman who loves the people and world around her. As we work together to raise three kids, I see how powerfully she impacts their lives each day with her love as well as with her disdain for excuses. She inspires me each and every day. It is no surprise that, in this new phase of our careers, she has been the most valuable business partner imaginable.

Diana's story has a great deal to teach us about fear. Many people in her circumstances would have collapsed from fear and used it as a crutch to limp along in life. Many kids today fall into despair simply because they have lost their phones. They are blind to the challenges of others. Growing into adults, these same kids lack the skills needed to become Disruptors like Diana. This collective illness of fear has created a society filled with complainers, people wanting to be rescued, and kids obsessed with mindless games and activities. If you reread Diana's journey again, you will see one fundamental difference you can utilize right now to stomp fear to the ground. Your will. It was Diana's will that moved her past fear each time she faced it. It was the greater fear of staying lost in the new world of America that she leveraged to overcome her fear of the unknown. To her, staying where she was and not moving forward was never an option. Your will can be the same if you energize it with your vision and a plan. You can't control when fear will appear in your mind, but you damn sure can control how you use your willpower to push past it with action.

So what's your excuse for letting fear take you over? What will you find to complain about when it comes to your failures? It will be difficult, I assure you, to make those excuses now that you have seen that nothing is impossible—it just takes persistence. If you speak up at work and don't get it right, so what? Did you die from the experience? NO! You learned and grew. But what if you felt empowered? It is only when you believe that failure means something devastating that you succumb to a life of habitual thinking. So lose the fear of being wrong, being rejected, and feeling stupid, and, most importantly, lose the fear of failure.

REMEMBER—ACTION MATTERS

Perhaps if you start to understand what fear is actually doing to your life, and what it could do in the future, that thought may be enough to stop you from seriously wasting any more of your life on feeling afraid. I promise you this: a fear of failure without a corresponding action toward a vision can become the reality of only surviving life, not thriving. Something I say when Diana and I are sharing her story on stage at a conference is this: imagine if she had let her fear of failure dominate her decisions instead of taking action toward learning English, graduating early from high school, and excelling in college. Do you think she would still have the same life? If you ask her, she would tell you that had she chosen to be scared of everything new and personally unexplored, she would most likely still speak only limited English, live in an all-Lithuanian community here in America, and would have never gone after the many amazing achievements in her life thus far. It would have been very easy for her, after the first perceived failure to learn English, to say to herself, "I can't do this. I am stupid and English is hard. I will just be around people I know and survive this life." We all have aspirations for greatness, but in the face of perceived failure, difficult times, pressures of life, and the overwhelming society of people telling us that life is hard, we fall into a survival mind-set. However, by doing as Diana did—building a micro and macro vision, taking actions toward a new future, constantly rebooting the situation, and never stopping her progress toward her newly disrupted life—you will discover a different and more confident way of living.

Many people in this world, instead of working to succeed at a passion, will simply survive in fear of not being able to pay the bills and provide for family, or of looking stupid if not succeeding. Many people in our society are chained to their executive position, their cubicles, their factory lines, and their corner offices because they don't have an awareness that fear can be destroyed with action. That scary risk becomes the risk a person MUST take. Think about all of the things you fear. Are you afraid of failure or of looking stupid? Where did that fear come from? Who put that fear there? Diana was afraid of looking stupid when she came to America, but she did something about it. She took action. She mastered a new language, because she was tired of all the mean kids making fun of her English and her accent, and because she stood out. She beat the fear because she wanted more out of life. When you are faced with challenges or the desire to take a risk, it will be the inaction or lack of seeing yourself in charge that takes a small, perceived fear and makes it huge.

BREAKING DOWN AND CHANGING FEAR

OK, so now you see what fear really is: a construct. It's in your head, and you alone create it and feed it. And, just as Diana showed us, that fear can be overcome through focused action. I know what you are thinking—"Todd, that all sounds great, but how do I actually see fear for what it is in my own life and overcome it?" I'm glad you asked. Below are steps to overcome fear as you embark on your mission to achieve a vision and become your best Disruptor self.

Overcome the Cause. Fear starts as a construct to protect you. You fear failure, because the actual fear of failure protects you from actively going down a path where your mind will need to process the failure and turn it into learning. It is easier for your mind to stay static and for you to stay where you are, than it is to learn, so it throws fear at you to protect itself. To overcome this first stage of fear is to ask: "What is my fear?" For example, Diana had a terrible, recurring fear that if she spoke up at a work meeting or blurted out an idea, she or it would be shut down by other people. She was afraid of looking stupid and being labeled by other people as "the person without any good input."

After you identify the fear, you need to ask yourself, "What past experiences are causing this fear?" For Diana, it was early in her life in America and other kids making fun of her when she would mispronounce words or didn't understand what people were saying. Sometimes people would get irritated because they had to use simpler words to explain what they wanted to communicate to Diana, and sometimes they would just get mad, giving her the impression that she was too stupid to understand a simple idea. Even though all of this had happened while she was in the seventh and eighth grades, that irrational fear stuck with her for a very long time. So, for her, speaking up at meetings was difficult because she didn't want to be made fun of and, worst of all, to have people think that she was stupid and thus label her as the "dumb" employee of the year.

Now, start fixing your fear. Tell a different story. The only way you can stop being afraid of something is to change your story. Instead of thinking that she would look stupid, Diana told herself a new story: "I will speak up when I have a good idea, and, if it's not what everyone is looking for, at least I contributed and encouraged other people to share their ideas so we can all solve the problem at hand. After all, I taught myself English, I might as well use it." This was her story, and, after a while of telling this to herself, she finally believed it and kicked to the curb her fear of looking stupid at meetings.

Overcome the Excuses. As you implement the first step to stop, or at least dampen, your fear, you will feel the pull of excuses. Your subconscious mind has become brilliant at making up excuses to validate your fears, just so you don't start heading toward something unknown. To your brain, the unknown is translated as danger: a situation you haven't experienced or are not used to experiencing. Excuses take the shape of statements like, "I can't do that, I am too young/too old," "I won't be able to achieve that level of success, because I am not smart enough," and "I do not have enough money to start that business." The next step toward stopping fear is to just stop making excuses, or to turn the excuses around. I encourage you to come up with as many excuses as you can on your own to explain why you "can't" realize your goal or vision. You should write down on one side of a sheet of blank paper all of the excuses you can come up with about why you can't do something; then, on the other side, turn them into actions. So, when you find yourself saying something like, "I won't be able to achieve that level of success because I am not smart enough," replace it with something like, "I may not have the knowledge now, but I can at least begin to research what I need to learn in order to achieve that level of success and how others have done it." Then you can list the steps of how to achieve that level of knowledge so that you can go out and do what you previously thought was impossible. Demolish the excuses by turning them into action steps toward your vision. This is where your planning from earlier chapters is critical. Your plan toward your disruptive vision is also your excuse killer.

Overcome the Reactivity. The biggest amplifier of fear is reactivity. Reactivity shows in that moment when you trip and start to fall down a flight of stairs, and then attempt to stop your fall by quickly reaching out to grab something. When you are fearful about doing something new or branching out, you become reactive and attempt to reach for anything to make the fear stop. What I mean is, when you are afraid of looking stupid for speaking up, for example, then any time an opportunity to speak up at work presents itself, your mind will go into a litany of excuses about why you shouldn't open your mouth. You are reacting to a chance of failure. I have watched people in the work environment come up with all sorts of excuses to stay at their desks and protect themselves rather than attend a meeting in which they would need to speak up or contribute to a plan. To overcome reactivity, you pay attention to the stairs and take one step at a time so that you don't fall. You carefully plan actions to help you overcome the fear that can cause you to falter. Simply go back to your plan and determine actions that will force you to break out of the comfort zone you have created that was brought on by fear of something. This will lead you to take new actions. When I first spoke to a large group of government officials, I was afraid, but then I remembered how I spent hours planning my speech, constructing my PowerPoint presentation, and researching my notes. My fear was unfounded; it was a story I had created in my head. I was ready to take action and I stopped reacting to my fear.

JANUARY 30, 1971 - ?

That, above, is my feeble little timeline. I was born in 1971, and, on the other end of the dash will be the time in space that I will end. All my actions to overcome fear and achieve the life I want occur in the dash between those two dates. When you look at your life this way, you begin to see how small that dash really is. You have so little time to do amazing things. By taking actions toward your vision through planning, you become a Disruptor in your own life. When you overcome fear using the above technique, you start to ask bigger questions like, "Why not be the best leader in my company NOW?" "Why not be the best parent NOW?" "Why not be the best partner NOW?" When you overcome the fearful thinking, you will no longer be terrified to stand up, step up, and speak up.

That is all you get, Fear—a tiny chapter, because you don't deserve more. I put only Diana's story in this chapter because it is such a powerful demonstration of what is possible for anyone who can destroy fear with action. Diana had no advantages, no special privileges at the age of twelve when she came to America. The government does not give you a pass to an education in this country just because you are new. So Diana had to develop fear-eradicating skills. She learned to have a vision, build a plan, eradicate fear with action, and work hard each day because she knew that she, and she alone, was responsible for her life. The same goes for you. No one owes you a life without fear, and no one can give it to you. Fear may rise up at some strange time when your subconscious mind feels threatened or your ego believes it will lose, but fear after that point is a choice. What you do to move past it is also a choice.

Finally, take a moment after reading this chapter to look at the new plan you are making. You already know the fears that come to you frequently. Write those down and build action steps into your plan to move past the excuses that will pull you back down toward fear.

Humans have evolved from the days of being chased by dangerous animals and having to learn how to create fire and survive the harsh world. Still, many of our fellow humans, perhaps even you, think that we are still being chased by something. It is this nonsense thinking that causes humans to lie to themselves, as well as to others, about what fear truly is. We all need to stop the madness of negativity that allows fear of progress to take over our minds. We need to stop using fear as a crutch for failure, because it will never get us to our destination. As far as I can remember, I have never worked with a group, a leader, or a company that said, "We get the best ideas from the scared people."

CHAPTER 8

USE IT!

I hope you remember the story from chapter 1 where, in 1992, as a fledgling Disruptor, I took what felt like the biggest risk of my young life and headed to Chicago with a vision of creating an interactive comedy show. That show would eventually entertain audiences for over twenty years. You may remember my story about the way I overcame my deep fear of taking this huge risk. Looking back, when I sat in my car on the side of the road, contemplating my future and everything that could go wrong, I see that I almost allowed the fear of change to take me back to the comfort zone of my hometown. I could have turned around and gone home, gotten a regular job, and become someone else. But I had a positive attitude and excitement; I had built a plan supporting my vision; and I had my instinct, so I kept the car moving. And with every mile closer to Chicago, I was also getting closer to moving my life toward many failures and much success. If I had known back then about all the crazy turns my life was about to take, I wouldn't have changed my plans to go to Chicago; I still would have driven forward. So, while I told you all about the amazing achievements during my time in Chicago, I have a different type of story for this chapter. Why? Mostly because I want you to understand that just because you are stepping into a new life as a Disruptor—just because you have the right attitude, vision, and plan; are tapped into your instinct; have changed your definition of failure; and have taken action to overcome fear—you are still not yet equipped to manage the day-to-day challenges that will seek to ruin your progress toward your goal.

Are you surprised? Does that mean you will fail before you have even started? Or are you wondering, "Why should I do any of this if I'm still not ready, even when I have practiced and applied all of the steps in this book?" No. What I mean is that you are simply not ready until you read this chapter and apply USE IT! to your new adventure. As we have all experienced, obstacles will arise on your path to success, and those obstacles don't care about the fact that life is short and we have goals to reach. The many daily stressors, negative situations, and life circumstances do not care if you have an Intentional Why. The only person who cares about how the surroundings affect you is, well, *you*. It is therefore my responsibility to give you a simple, thoughtful tool to overcome any obstacle seeking to wipe out your progress and excitement for whatever you are disrupting. For this lesson, let's go back to 1993, Chicago, two months after I first arrived in the Windy City, back to the Excalibur Club's show called *Comedy You Can Dance To*.

JANUARY 29, 1993

Lights up. Music up. Microphone on. Audience ready. Go.

With the microphone in my hand at the largest entertainment venue in Chicago, I blazed a trail on stage and yelled out to the audience, "Everyone, put your hands up!" The crowd screamed and whistled with excitement, and, for a few moments, I owned the room. For this story to make the most sense, here is a description of the framework of what the new audience-interaction comedy show *Comedy You Can Dance To* was. Essentially, I would take the stage every quarter hour to interact with the audience members who, up until that point, were simply drinking and dancing. When I would get on stage, the audience would watch me, listen to my direction, and mimic my moves to the music. The musical part of our show was created so I could go on stage and interact with the audience in a way that led them on a dance journey during whatever song was picked for that day. So, for that portion of the show, everyone had to follow my dance moves and verbal instructions. In other segments, I would take the stage and run a contest that was also a game show, or some type of comedy sketch. So, there I stood, ready for one of my first shows. As I got up on the stage, I looked over the crowd and thought to myself, "Look how far I have come in such a short time." It was only a few months ago that I left my small town and drove to Chicago, and now my vision was actually my reality. I was doing it! Sure, it was not the Academy Awards or some new start-up company that would earn me a billion dollars, but it was my moment—a meal of life I cooked myself, and I was ready to eat it for dinner.

With the lights flashing and my first song blaring, I opened my mouth and … nothing. I was speaking into the microphone, but no sound was coming from the speakers. My microphone was dead. Staring around the stage with the lights up, I felt like a lost soul. I was disoriented, afraid I would be booed off the stage and probably fired. The protocol for dealing with a microphone not working was to run back to the sound booth and figure it out or find a new way, on the spot, to get the audience to pay attention and not even notice something was going wrong. I took a risk, chose to keep going and figure something out before the audience even had a clue that the microphone had gone out, but how? I realized I was in a serious crisis, my most desperate moment, and right then I had a memory pop into my head; I remembered that, about four years earlier, I had learned to whistle. I mean a loud-ass whistle that would deafen a dog. I know this sounds silly, but in that moment of crisis, I had to do something. I could not accept the idea of standing there in failure. I was going to take the audience back under my control and move the focus where I wanted it. The whistle was all I had in that moment, so the risk became the opportunity to shine. Under pressure, I could only think of that one thing to do to make some noise. I instantly put the microphone in my pocket and lit the room up with my whistle. Immediately, the entire audience looked in my direction. I had them. So then, as the song played, I moved around that stage with my dance routine, the song, and, of course, the whistle. Every time I wanted the audience to change directions during the song and dance another way, I would whistle. When I wanted the audience to stop and clap with me, I would whistle. Not only was it working—but it was even more fun than just yelling out directions over the microphone. After the song ended, and while the DJ played a set of dance music as a short intermission for the show, I ran back to the sound booth to find out what happened with my microphone. I had just completed the musical interactive portion, and up next was a comedy sketch. As I handed the microphone to the sound technician, I said, "Hey, the microphone is not working." He turned to me and with a snarl said, "I know, I turned it off, because I think your show is stupid." All I could do was just stare at him and try to figure out how I was going to perform for the rest of the night without a microphone. An obstacle was born.

As it turned out, the original team of performers at the club did not like me very much. Well, actually, they hated me. Really, though, who could blame them? I was a cocky, young entertainer with high aspirations, and I was now their new boss. In chapter 1, I told the story of how this entire Chicago entertainment adventure began and you may remember the Disruptive Influencer who allowed me to take the risk of going ahead with my idea. Well, after talking to Tim, the entertainment director, and having my trial for two weeks at another one of the clubs owned by the same company, he was so impressed with my performance and my idea that he made me the leader of all of the performers at the club. Tim loved my concepts; unfortunately, the existing team did not. To make matters worse, I was considered pushy, as I would stop at nothing to achieve my vision. Admittedly,

I was unrefined in my approach, and these guys wanted to get me fired. For the next few months of shows, they would engage in all sorts of shenanigans to ruin my act, and their antics would always be a surprise. I knew that on any night I was working, at any moment of the show, the lights could be turned off, the music stopped, or the microphone shut off; and sometimes a few objects would fly in my direction, courtesy of my teammates. All of these "distractions" and "pranks" were designed to make me quit, but I always pressed on. I took a risk to stay and learn from the chaos and crisis that had become my new job. It was one of the loneliest experiences of my life, but, at the same time, it was one of the most fulfilling challenges to overcome. I admit that the situation is funny now when I look back on it; but if you think about it, life is never done giving us reasons to give up. We can always get overwhelmed and feel like going forward is far too difficult, but when you want something disruptive in your life, you MUST take the risk, and find a way to push through. No one else will do it for you.

The crew was tireless with their challenges, but I treated their obstacles like a personal dare to get creative. After each show, I would go home and try to think of what they would do next and what I could do to overcome it. For example, if they shut off my microphone, I had my whistle. If they stopped the music, I would say to the audience, "I stopped the music for a reason." Then I would take them in a new direction, such as launching into an audience-interactive comedy improv sketch and, other times, bringing volunteers up on stage for an interactive contest. My reactions to whatever equipment failure was planned for that night became faster and faster. If the lights went out, I would grab a portable spot flashlight I had hidden on stage prior to the show. Soon, no matter what obstacle the crew threw at me, I had a way to use it to make something amazing happen. I didn't realize it at the time, but all of the attempted sabotage by my team had held me in a constant crisis mode, which pushed me to become better, to come up with great new ideas to overcome the obstacles, and to learn how to be a true performer. I took a risk that was nerve-wracking every time I walked into the club, but at that point, I had come too far and sacrificed too much to just quit. I was persistent and positive every time the show was on, because I was not about to let negative people derail my vision. I also believed that if the team would just work with me, the show would be even more amazing. So I pushed forward, night after night, defeating every obstacle. When the team was finally tired of failing to disrupt the show, they stopped. But during those few months of their mockery, my confidence on stage grew exponentially and, with that, so did my abilities.

This is a story where risk-taking and managing everyday crisis situations has a wonderful ending. After a year, the team finally got bored of the stage torture and my undying motivation to keep on going, and we all became friends. The team at Excalibur—the team that initially tried to get me fired—and I finally built something truly remarkable on that stage. Throughout the time I worked there, I never stopped focusing on my vision, and I continued to use all of the obstacles put in my path as building blocks for a strong foundation I could build on with time. Sometimes you have to be tested and pushed hard in life before you can truly learn the lessons you were supposed to learn. Out of this experience, I learned techniques to motivate any audience, regardless of size, and to engage in a memorable and fun experience. This foundation has actually carried me farther than just the show—I gained skills to deliver inspiring keynote presentations, leadership sessions, and many speaking engagements. It has fast-tracked me forward by decades into a speaking and coaching career. What I learned was applicable not just to the business world but to all areas of my life. When I have a personal plan based on a vision, I use the same set of tools I used in Chicago to overcome obstacles and use the parameters of that challenge to build something better.

This level of acceptance in all things pushes me to think creatively, innovatively, and as a Disruptor, instead of wallowing in "what if . . ." or "why me?" scenarios.

Years after I left Chicago, I was asked at a conference how I was able to be so nimble on stage, and to adapt fluidly in business, and to flourish in the face of obstacles. My response went on to become an important part of my future successes. I simply said, "I USE IT!"

This entire book, up to this point, has been a series of stories in which I took serious risks, accompanied by an outline of the steps of how I overcame them and lessons from my life, all of which will prepare you to bring on breakthrough results for any new vision you can dream up. But now you will need to master one final foundational tool to be equipped to live in a crazy world of obstacles. The tool is called "USE IT!" No matter how great your vision, plan, and attitude are, obstacles can still ignite fear and doubt. Through the practice of a USE IT! mentality, you will be prepared to overcome those obstacles, large or small.

As you embark on your journey to change even the smallest parts of your life, you too will hit roadblocks. Of course, people may not blatantly attempt to mess with your vision on purpose, but, nonetheless, you will hit obstacles that can slow you down and are completely out of your control.

IT'S TIME TO USE IT!

USE IT! is a simple, life-tested mind-set of five building blocks that works in the office, at home, on the road—and everywhere in between. Not only will it help you as you take the journey into disrupting your own life, but it will also help you redirect your road-raging, passive-aggressive, always-assuming ego by simply changing your perception of stressful moments. Because you are not in control of other people or outside circumstances, you will have this method for putting the world around you in perspective. Why are our brains always misfiring and taking us off course on the way to our vision? Well, because we're all a teensy-weensy bit too preoccupied, fighting stress, and trying to solve other people's problems. Have you ever lost it and barked at a co-worker? Assumed someone was out to "get you"? Fought just to prove you were right about something . . . something that ended up being trivial? Gotten mad because a stranger cut you off in traffic? USE IT!'s mental building blocks will help you laugh a lot more and lose it a lot less.

The sheer pace of our lives today makes for alarming levels of stress and crisis, which distracts us from applying the lessons in this book. There's always something to do, somewhere to go, some frustration around the corner; with the USE IT! mentality, you stop trying to fight these situations and negative stimuli and instead find ways to adapt and integrate the positive aspects of everything into your new way of living in this world.

YOUR LIFE, ONLY BETTER

Could you stick to a diet that only addressed what you ate and not why you ate it? I recently went on a bit of a health reboot. I realized I was snacking constantly, which was causing me to gain unnecessary weight. So I started my diet and detox plan by eliminating certain foods from my diet. Everything was outlined in the plan I used, called "The Fat Flush Plan." I thought this diet was great for me because it made me stop eating foods that are bad for me and replace them with balanced, healthy foods. So why are we talking about my dieting? Well, one of the mental changes the plan asks you to make is relevant to our discussion about USE IT! When you change your diet and remove certain foods that have become your comfort foods, it takes only about two weeks before your cravings start to diminish or are completely gone, and then you realize you have been eating non-nutritious food out of habit. Your life and your ability to change yourself are like a diet: it's hard at first and we all struggle and have withdrawals, but after a while, it becomes second nature. This is the same process to pursue if you want to make real change in your life. Like addiction to junk food, distractions are only mind games. One thing is certain for people who like to disrupt the world around them: life will relentlessly drop distraction after distraction in front of you before you are even close to achieving your vision. From simple traffic situations that create frustration, or the countless aggravations at the airport, distractions are everywhere and we cannot control them; we have to learn to deal with them. You may not like what's happening, but at least you can deal with whatever situation is at hand and have total control of your feelings with the USE IT! mind-set. In the real world, you will need fortitude—a strong nothing-sticks-to-me way of thinking—to help you create new visions and achieve new goals, and give you foundational support as you begin to disrupt the world in your own personal way. USE IT! is designed to rewire your brain to think differently. It will help you to pause during a stressful situation and recall five factors that lead to positive actions.

The theory behind USE IT! is to embrace everything. I am not saying that you should act as if nothing stressful is happening in your life, but rather that you should change the way you feel about these things. When you are at work and the boss does not let you speak up in a meeting, you USE IT! to write your thoughts down and send an e-mail with ideas. When you spend countless hours preparing a new plan for your career change and you encounter a naysayer who tells you five ways you will fail, you USE IT! You apply the mentality to every difficult situation so that you stay on target and eliminate the pain and suffering we tend to create for ourselves, which distracts us from success. This technique alone will change your life in huge ways—and all you are actually engaging in is a new way of interacting with the world. Even if you forget the rest of this book, which you won't, this life-tested, five-point mentality will put you back on track every time.

USE IT!

The five building blocks of USE IT! are:

U: Understand the big picture
S: Say, "My attitude dictates my experience"
E: Evict your ego

I: I make no assumptions
T: Take nothing personally

Seems simple, right? The problem is, while we all know these things from a conceptual standpoint, there is often a HUGE gap between what we know and what we actually do each day when faced with challenges. USE IT!, once you understand and adopt each component, is a base, a foundation of building blocks upon which you can start reframing your new disruptive self. Let's take some time and understand each component.

First, you need to keep in front of you what USE IT! stands for as you read this section. It's a proven process to bring the entire book to life, but you need to keep repeating it in your head to remind you of the focus required to overcome anything.

U – Understand the Big Picture
S – Say, "My attitude dictates my experience."
E – Evict your ego

I – I assume nothing

T – This is not personal

If you have written these steps down to keep them close, you are ready to move to the next stage of understanding each one in detail.

U: UNDERSTAND THE BIG PICTURE

What is most important when you are traveling to your vacation or business meeting? Is it the airport? Is it the security line? Is it getting the right seat? Is it getting your carry-on (that is slightly too big) in the overhead? Is it the taxi that took thirty minutes to show up? Is it the fact that your hotel room is not yet ready for you to check in upon your arrival? What is the most important part of your journey that you should be focused on at all times? If you answered "To get to my destination," you are correct. Nothing else matters. The rude ticket agent, the bad seat, the no-upgrade status, the upset security agent, the crying baby on the plane, the delay at the hotel—none of those things matter. Then why do we get so bent out of shape and distracted from getting to our destination safely and on time by these reoccurring situations? Mostly it is because we allow these distractions to invade our brains and take up precious space, all because we have lost sight of the big picture.

When you think about all of the work you have accomplished while reading this book and all of the new ways of thinking you are adopting, wouldn't it be a shame if, along the way, you allowed the simple distractions of life to throw you off course as you head down the path toward your new disrupted self? I, too, find myself in situations requiring me to constantly refocus my mind on what is most important; and, believe me, I deal with the exact same distractions and stressful situations as you do—from rude people working at restaurants to the countless ways I could become enraged in traffic by rude drivers. However, to make sure I stay focused, I always use the first element of USE IT! to remind me of what matters most on a moment-to-moment and day-to-day basis: Understand the big picture.

In 2003, I was working as a consultant, and I was leaving for a trip to Canada to meet my future client. With two of my colleagues alongside me, we all carpooled to the airport for an early flight in order to make an afternoon meeting. Unfortunately, I was in such a rush that morning that I had forgotten my passport at home. The worst part is that I did not realize this until we were quite a distance from my house. The only way I could get to Canada was to have that passport, so we had to turn around and go get it. We were too far from the airport for me to drop off my colleagues, and, if I did drop them off, I would never make it home in time to grab my passport and return to the airport. After I got my passport and we finally arrived at the airport and made it to the check-in counter, we discovered we had missed the forty-five minute check-in window literally by less than five minutes. I could have gotten enraged at the unfairness of it all; instead, I focused on the end result—the big picture—which was getting to Canada and the meeting with my client. Instead of starting to yell at everyone and demand that I be put on the plane, I stayed calm and demonstrated a humble level of remorse to the ticket agent, apologized, and, I'll admit it, begged to be allowed to get on the flight. When she said *no* for the fourth time, I kindly and calmly said, "We are so sorry again and it was, as I said, my fault. What do you suggest we do?" Without hesitation, and in the sternest voice I still to this day have ever heard from a ticket agent, she said, "I would not be late next time." Now, think to yourself for a moment. Would you be able to remain calm, or would you simply lose your temper and react? By staying focused (understanding the big picture), I held my temper back—even though it was hard—and requested that we be put on the standby list for the next available flight. The ticket agent accommodated that request.

Still dealing with the craziness of our morning, my colleagues and I pressed on, but security was a nightmare. Now we were going to be late for the second and final flight to Canada that day! But despite the circumstances, the only thing on my mind was making the last possible flight, because to miss it meant we would lose the opportunity with the new client. Once we finally made it to the gate agent, I was determined to get on that final plane, because my focus remained on the big picture: being on time for the meeting, which meant getting to Canada. With the standby tickets in hand, however, I was admittedly fearful that we would miss the flight. When we arrived at the gate, I looked at the older gate agent and said, "Hi, my name is Todd, and we have a huge meeting in Canada. I am hoping you can help us get on this flight. But before we talk more, I could really use a hug." I am not joking. That is precisely what I said. She looked up, laughed, and said, "Yes. I need one too!" After we hugged, the ticket agent moved back behind her desk, moved the paperwork she had on her terminal, looked up at me, and said, "Let's get you all to Canada." By the time she was done, we were booked on the flight and she gave us first-class seats.

While I do not encourage you to go around hugging people (although wouldn't it be a much nicer world if we did?) or expect all the doors of life to open if you just focus on the big picture, I do want you to fully embrace the idea that understanding the big picture is the first block of the USE IT! mentality. That's because if you focus on the big picture constantly, it will help you to stay focused on what matters most in any situation. If you are stuck in terrible traffic, do your best to understand the big picture—safely getting to where you are going. If you are planning a new business and the first client you seek tells you no, stay focused on that understanding of the big picture, because you will find great clients eventually. The key is to always stay focused on what needs to be accomplished and what is most important, no matter how hard it gets. Don't turn every small setback into an unfixable catastrophe, because that will only spin you out of control. When you take calculated risks after reading this book, you will need to keep yourself focused on understanding the big picture so you can keep your ship, metaphorically speaking, heading in the right direction during any real or perceived storm.

S: SAY, "MY ATTITUDE DICTATES MY EXPERIENCE"

We discussed attitude in an earlier chapter, so I don't need to go over it in as much detail now. I will, however, point out that in that earlier chapter I discussed attitude in the context of changing yours when creating a new vision or taking your life in some new direction. But in the context of USE IT!, attitude is a foundational element that will serve to keep you in check in the many micro situations of life. A negative attitude in the simplest of situations can completely take your life in the wrong direction, and fast.

Watching the world around me while I ride this amazing life journey is, in essence, like watching my favorite reality show in real time. The difference is that we get to interact with and impact the world around us the way we want to. One of my favorite places to observe people and their behaviors is at an airport. At an airport, you can observe a large conglomeration of people who don't know each other, have a wide variety of backgrounds, have different reasons for traveling, and are all on the road to achieving the common goal of getting wherever it is they're wanting to go—literally and figuratively. When you mix a lot of people who harbor fear, anger, personal importance, lack of vision, misguided priorities, selfish behavior, and years of egotistical storytelling, sprinkled with some happiness, great attitude, and excitement, it produces a scene that is unfailingly interesting to watch. Some people become completely distracted due to their lack of attitude control and a lost understanding of their big picture. So, as a bystander noticing someone who is yelling at the ticketing agent or being rude to TSA security, or even throwing a tantrum at the airport gift shop because the shop doesn't carry his favorite brand of chocolate—you can see that those people seem to lose their minds, albeit briefly. In that snippet of time, they are not applying USE IT!

One time, while traveling to speak at an annual marijuana-industry conference, I was passing through airport security. While waiting for my turn to place my items in bins and send them through the scanner, I observed a gentlemen arguing with a TSA agent about the procedural process. Essentially, this man was not thrilled with the rule about taking the computer out of his case and placing it into an empty bin by itself. He wanted to just pass his entire bag through the x-ray scanner. I had no clue as to what was agitating him, but I could definitely smell the aroma of some type of alcohol wafting off of him. The TSA agent, following normal procedures, informed the man that he was going to have to take his computer out of its case and send it through the x-ray machine separately. While TSA "service" can be hit-or-miss, this particular agent was both patient and kind. Still, the man became more and more enraged over time. After several minutes of what can be best described as huffing and puffing, he took the case with the computer still inside of it and threw it at the TSA officer while yelling, "Get it out yourself!" In an instant, airport security and more TSA agents walked up to defuse the situation. To any bystander, it was very clear that this angry man was about to have an even worse day than he had been having five minutes earlier. His attitude definitely dictated his experience; he forgot all about the big picture, and his mental blocks were keeping him from a more fulfilling life experience, not to mention a peaceful travel experience. Look, we all have bad days or bad situations that can turn our temperament sour, but only if we *allow* it to happen. A quick way to stop this is to admit that you are upset and find a way to react to the situation in a better and calmer fashion. The simple shortcut of saying to yourself, in times when your attitude is off track, "I admit I am upset and my attitude is off; now how can I make this situation more positive?" helps you put yourself back on the right track—where you are in control of your emotions.

Remember, we can't always control a situation, but we can control the way we FEEL while we are experiencing tough times. Our feelings in moments of perceived stress make all the difference in the world to our overall life experience. When the only thing you can control is your own attitude, by all means, assert that control. Say it aloud: My attitude dictates my experience. Say it as many times as you need to. First *understand the big picture*, then *say, "my attitude dictates my experience."*

E: EVICT YOUR EGO

I think the most damaging problem in modern society is the ego. I define the ego as the need to win or to make sure that others know they are wrong. Have you ever been in a relationship, arguing about some pointless topic when you suddenly realize your need to win and being right has far surpassed the positive attitude and the actual big picture of living in a happy relationship? We all have. Your ego is that need to win, regardless of what it is you think you are winning. So here is a great example of a stupid argument my fiancé and I have had a few times. The good news is, we have stopped arguing about stupid things like this because we have realized that it's a waste of time and energy. Here's a version of the stupid argument:

Her: "You never listen."
Him: "Yes, I do."
Her: "No, YOU don't."

Him: "I am listening right NOW."
Her: "I am telling you something important."
Him: "Yes, got it."
Her: "I don't think you do."
Him: "Well, you don't listen to me either."

Keeping the ego at bay is hard work, but I work every day to keep it out of my mind. Of course, this has not been easy or consistent; it's always a journey in which you keep learning what works and what doesn't. Often we are pulled into conflict and forget the simplest thing: winning is not the most important outcome. *Evicting your ego* is the next critical block in the USE IT! mentality, because when you remove the need to win and be right, you can correct your attitude at a rapid pace and stay focused on the big picture in the moment. I wish I could say that I have perfected this one, but even I falter with this important block.

For instance, Twitter is a great tool for communication of short facts and comments, and for sharing all sorts of stories about our business and especially ourselves. Admittedly, I am a fan of Twitter, and I use it daily for both entertainment as well as business-related functions. But like anything else, Twitter has its unintended consequences if used improperly. One of the best examples of my ego launching out of control happened one fateful day during the height of my new marijuana-industry experience. This one moment has been burned into my mind and serves as the reminder of the day I decided never to let my ego win again.

It's late May 2014. What a ride I was having. Marijuana had been legal in Colorado since January of that year; our company was now being called the "Google of Cannabis"; and we were the newly titled, "largest brand in weed." However, one day an activist started to protest our company on Twitter. The protest was based on a new drug-testing policy I had created to make the company safer. The details of the story around the drug policy are not nearly as important as my reaction to the Twitter posts. I hope my peril serves as a lesson to you as you encounter people or circumstances that can launch your self-centered ego into full overdrive.

Unlike the rational side of myself when using social media, my ego-centered self was overcome with anger. My attitude fell apart as I read the "#boycott" and other, more painful, words embedded in the tweets being directed at me and at our company by this activist. This was a multi-directional attack, and when it hit me I lost it. At the time, I didn't realize that I had a choice to put my ego away, adjust my attitude, and understand that the big picture was to make the company successful, which I could have done by simply asking the activist to meet one-on-one. A simple meeting could have given rise to a learning moment—to see if the person had input to make my policy better or to provide reasons why it should be scrapped. In fact, even one of my colleagues advised me to be cordial and see if the activist and I could find a solution to the issue. But I went the other way and ignored that sound advice. In fact, I more than ignored it—I started to tweet back. My tweet: "We are keeping people safe. So sorry you don't care about employee safety. Grown-ups need to behave differently."

That may not seem like a huge quote, but it was only the beginning. The back-and-forth of slams and hostility on Twitter, coupled with my out-of-control ego, the collective ego challenges with the founders of the company, and other factors led to a total meltdown of emotions. This was just another catalyst added to a mixture of behind-the-scenes events that eventually ended my time at the company. Besides the egos and attitudes to be dealt with, there was a lack of focus on what mattered most: building a great company. While I am thrilled to be where I am today, and more thrilled to have all the experiences I had after I left the company, I still wish I had put my ego in check that day. And I caution you here as well.

Your ego, that part of you that needs to win, can take over your decisions and will possibly damage your life or, at the very least, pull you off course. If you learn how to stop your ego, and can prevent yourself from writing a hateful tweet, Facebook post, text, or e-mail today because of my story, then it was all worth it. You're welcome. Look, I know that the ego is not some other person writing the story for you, but it is a real, unconscious part of you that can cause bizarre behaviors that will stir up a sea of regret if it pushes your ship off course.

We all make errors on behalf of that ego demon inside us. Believe me, it wants you to engage with hostility. That ego feeds on your anger and bad attitude as well as your total lack of focus. Replacing logic in those moments is a dire need to be right, to be vindicated, and to win. Just like me, however, you have a choice. You do not need to give in to it. And remember, once you give in, you tend to dig in. What I mean is that you dig in to a negative, forceful position in which even if you win . . . you lose—yourself.

So, we're nearly there with the USE IT! mentality: we understand the big picture; we say "my attitude dictates my experience;" and we evict the ego. What's next?

I: I MAKE NO ASSUMPTIONS

Have you ever made an assumption about another person or situation, only to find out later that your assumption was completely false? Worse, have you ever made an assumption, then taken action based on that false assumption, and made the situation worse? We all have. One of the key components to engaging this new foundational way of thinking is to eradicate from your mind the daily reactive snap judgments influencing your assumptions. When you submit a project or a plan to your boss for consideration, but your boss takes a week to get back to you, you make an assumption that your boss hated it. Then you may start thinking you are stupid for even believing that your plan was great in the first place. This also happens in your personal life: when you reach out to that new potential date you met last night at the singles' bar and she does not get back to you right away—well, you assume she doesn't want to talk to you, let alone see you again. And, of course, my favorite in the modern world is this: I send a text to someone, and when he doesn't respond immediately, I assume he is upset or doesn't care about the content of the message. All of these are just assumptions, unless they are later proven to be facts. Remember the *I* in USE IT!: *I make no assumptions.*

Recently, I called a government official I frequently meet with to discuss the cannabis industry. Instead of the person answering the call, I was sent a curt text message, "I'm in a meeting." Initially, I was a little taken aback; usually I get a full and detailed response. Suddenly, my mind was raging with assumptions. *What have I done to get such a short and not thoughtful response? Did my last negotiation with that person go in the wrong direction, without me realizing it?* I really thought about it for over thirty minutes. *What had I done? Did I say something wrong in our last meeting? Would this jeopardize our working collaboration?* I even took a moment to talk with my significant other, Diana, about it; she simply said, "I think you are overthinking it. That person is probably in a meeting; like the text message said, you will get a call when they have a free minute to chat." Of course, Diana was also just assuming that and trying to make me feel better, so off and on for much of the day I thought about this text and hoped I was wrong, but I had a bad feeling.

Later that afternoon, I met with a client. We were discussing his case, the situation he was having with the state, and how I could help him. At a critical part of the conversation, his phone rang and he grabbed it from his pocket, flipped his thumb on the screen and put the phone away. It wasn't the fact that he looked at the phone that caught my attention, but rather what he did with his thumb that changed my day and reminded me to do what I am about to instruct you to do when you face assumptions. When my client flipped his thumb on the screen, it was to instantly send the caller a quick pre-typed text. The text to his caller said, "I'm in a meeting." When I got back home that evening, I looked at my own phone and, sure enough, it, too, had the quick pre-filled text message "I'm in a meeting," so I could let people who call me get a quick response about my availability at that moment. You can imagine how silly I felt that I wasted so much energy on an assumption.

Since I still had a bad feeling about the curt text message and since I didn't receive a return call the same day, I wanted to prove to myself my negative assumption was false. So I texted my government colleague early the next morning and simply wrote, "Hey, I am hoping I've done nothing to upset you." Less than fifteen seconds after I hit the send button, the phone rang and the person on the other end was laughing and saying, "No, not at all! You have done nothing wrong in the slightest." My assumption of a negative situation was shattered and we had a great laugh about my ridiculous day of worrying. That is yet another situation in which I am reminded of my own learning. Assumptions MUST be verified or ignored, but they should never be acted upon without first getting a verification that the assumptions are really true. To say the least, this event taught me not just to stop assuming; it also taught me a little bit about the value of patience.

Not making assumptions is another building block that will help keep everyone sane while dealing with simple or even difficult situations. People will often ask me, "Todd, do you mean zero assumptions when you say, 'I make no assumptions'?" Yes. I mean zero assumptions. *I make no assumptions.* In theory, if you never made an assumption until you had all of your facts, your life would be less stressful; however, no one is perfect. We are evolutionarily programmed to make assumptions and evaluate people and situations to determine if we are in danger or if someone poses a risk to our safety.

Assumptions will be made unconsciously, or, as outlined above, made consciously—we're all human and we don't always follow even our own advice! But with the USE IT! mind-set, at least you can now realize what you're doing, then make sure that you clearly understand the reasons and get the real facts before you act.

Imagine a relationship or a marriage in which the two people never assume anything. Imagine the wife never assumes her husband will take out the trash. Imagine the husband never assumes his wife will always be ready for sex. I could go on with examples, but I think you get the point. These examples are here to signify the behavior these little daily assumptions build: dependence. We create our assumptions, almost like writing a script describing how the other person should respond to whatever we are dealing with. Then, when they don't, we blame them for not having the correct answer—the one that actually resides only inside our own minds.

Furthermore, sometimes we start to shift the blame of the real outcome, which is not what we expected or wanted, onto that other person by saying that the problem or circumstance was "caused" by them. In reality, we should blame ourselves for having made assumptions in the first place. For this building block to really sink in, we need to remember the "Me Mad! Me Mad! Me Mad!" exercise for attitude adjustment. If you find yourself upset in a situation in which you made an assumption, this tool also can be applied here, but by adding one important phrase: "Me mad!"

"You are making me mad."
"I am making me mad."
"I made an assumption that you did not get correct, and now I
     am mad."
"I am mad."
"Me mad! Me mad! Me mad!"

The bottom line is, if you are a person who makes assumptions on a regular basis and then gets mad at others for not doing what you have assumed they would do, you are getting really, and I mean really, good at being the victim. This, in turn, creates extra and unneeded stress in your life; stress you have created just for yourself, by yourself, by assuming what the outcome should be.

The Big Weed Assumption

While I was writing this book, my friend Mike came for a visit. Mike is literally my best friend; we have known each other since we were about nineteen years old. He and I have been through a ton of ups and downs in our lives. Even though he lives in a different state and we see each other only a few times a year, we chat at least once a month to keep each other in the loop about what is happening in our lives. To say the least, Mike saw me jump feet first into the marijuana space, so he was familiar with the industry. It turns out that he wasn't as in tune with everything as I thought he was, though. While Mike was here, he asked me if I could help him enter the marijuana industry. Mike, being a great sales leader and businessman, certainly has what it takes to be successful in the industry, so I set up a few meetings for him with some of the best players in the area. I knew he would do well, so we didn't really have a discussion about what to expect. His business acumen alone is superior to many of the business leaders who work in the industry; he is also attractive, personable, and kind. The reason Mike and I get along, and have for so many years, is because he is laid-back and easygoing. So, when we began talking about the meetings he just had with the industry leaders, I had to clear up some assumptions he was making about my life in weed. Mike was assuming that the industry was fast, fun, and easy. He had not witnessed my struggles and challenges, but he had felt the fun firsthand by spending time with me in the more entertaining aspects of the journey. His first assumption was that he would be able to keep his lifestyle the same as it was today, only with even more fun. So to clarify this gray area, I began to explain to Mike just what I meant about his first assumption.

When I entered the marijuana industry, I also made some wild assumptions that proved to be completely false. Unfortunately, my biggest assumption was about how easy it would be for me to make the transition from one industry to another, while continuing to work the same relaxed schedule. It finally hit me that I made an assumption just like Mike had, because I was looking from the outside in and the leaders at the time looked to be very successful and as if they were having a blast. Many of them were on TV, appeared to be making millions of dollars as if they had won the lottery, and went to wild and fun parties and vacations. But when I actually began working, I quickly realized that my life of working short hours from home and simply letting my already-honed skills do the hard work had come to a hasty halt. From the get-go, I was working twelve- to fifteen-hour days, traveling all over the United States, appearing in almost every major media outlet in the world, and feeling intense pressure from impulsive owners, investors, business partners, and old clients. That life of "chill" I had been living was abruptly over. So, when I shared my story with Mike, I could tell just by the look on his face that he needed to rethink this industry. You see, while I am a very outspoken Disruptive force, I keep many aspects of my struggles quiet and close to the vest. I like to share the big positives in my life rather than waste everyone's time with the negatives or the difficulties, so even my best friend was not aware of my struggles in the industry. Even though Mike and I are similar in many ways, we are different in very critical ones. One of them being that I am not a guy with hobbies. My hobby is my work. My goal with working is to change lives and disrupt everything I can to become better, faster, smarter, and wiser. Ever since I was a kid, I have been very bored with hobbies, except going to the movies, if you can even call that a hobby. What I love is being a great dad, going on dates with my amazing partner, and working my ass off. And here is Mike: he loves hobbies—one of his hobbies is having hobbies. He loves playing in a baseball league, hiking, exploring, hanging out, and working on old houses that he flips or rents out; and the list goes on. In between the hobbies and work, Mike also loves to be a great dad to his son, with whom he also has hobbies. So my reality check about the cannabis industry, and the amount of work it takes, caused him to pause and really consider the industry further before getting overly excited. I wish I had done the same. I would not have changed my decisions at all, because the marijuana industry was both one of the most challenging phases of my life as well as one of the most rewarding. However, had I truly understood the risks and qualified my assumptions a bit more before I entered the industry, I would have been even more prepared for the experience and would have been equipped to disrupt in even bigger ways.

Do I mean by this story that you should not get excited if things are fulfilling, yet you find out they will be more difficult than expected? NO! I am saying that you must get the information PRIOR to making a disruptive shift, so you are informed instead of just making wild assumptions about a new situation. I am hopeful that Mike will still join the industry in some capacity, but at least now he will be completely aware of what he is about to undertake. Remember, you need to ask the right questions, seek clear answers, and do a bit of discovery prior to making a jump to your new plan. As part of your new set of building blocks, you now have the "I make no assumptions" piece.

T: TAKE NOTHING PERSONALLY

One of the early career positions I held while working at a global training company was as a facilitator where I would deliver various corporate training sessions for large companies all over the world. This was one of the most rewarding career moves I could have made, because each week I would travel, meet amazing new people, and deliver sessions of experiential learning. Simply put, we would engage the audience in an activity designed to create mistakes in their behavior. Then, in a debrief, we would discuss "What happened, what does it mean to your life, and what are you going to do to fix this mistake?" These programs often contained a great deal of learning, while other times they were only for engagement and fun with an audience. Each session and each client was different, with different outcomes embedded in the presentation. Nothing in the workshops or presentations was an accident. Specific learning was created to engage and improve certain behaviors; however, if the facilitator failed, then the client could demand a refund. It was a high-stakes environment, to be sure, but it was extremely rewarding in return.

I was speaking in Dallas at a 350-person conference, delivering a highly interactive program. Basically, in this leadership program we trained people to be more thoughtful around planning by using a simulation in which they travel through a desert. It was similar to a huge, energized, interactive board game. During this particular session, a new salesperson, "Tom," was observing me. Tom's sole purpose was to observe the session for his own learning as a new team member, but he also had to give feedback to our team if necessary.

In addition to my logistics support, there were at least fifteen employees also supporting me in a fun, collaborative environment in which we had one mission: to guide and teach leaders what it means to have a maximized mind-set and how to plan more efficiently. The standards we were teaching them built a new framework for results focused on the emergence of better and more positive behaviors. The program itself was entertaining, but make no mistake, the learning was powerful. As the lead facilitator on the project, my job was to guide the program while delivering the lessons for all of the leaders of the company. In this case, the client wanted an even more fun atmosphere, and learning was not as critical. Following the client's specifications, we modified the session and debriefed the client about all of the changes. At 3 p.m., I started the presentation, and I thought the audience was enjoying the session and following along with the educational but fun activities that were bringing the four-day conference to a close. Since I was on stage and involved in the presentation, I wasn't aware that more than several participants got up and left before I was done with the presentation.

At the end of the session, I gathered my team and asked everyone, including Tom, for feedback. We all sat in a circle, and each person was given a chance to tell us what they liked about the session, and what we could do to improve. These feedback sessions were critical, since it was a great opportunity for our team to listen, capture each other's feedback, and then make necessary changes. Since the team was split up between so many different jobs (logistics, sound, lighting, material preparation, and so on), there were many perspectives that would benefit the later presentations as well as suggest how to improve them. When Tom's turn came, he simply said, "I would prefer to send you my feedback via e-mail." Before we continue with this story, I would like to clarify that, at this time in my career, I was speaking and doing workshops to large audiences at least two to three times a week, most of them in different cities. It was not uncommon for me to travel from coast to coast in the same week, so I thought Tom's feedback was not going to be very relevant when he got around to writing his e-mail, or at least not relevant for very long. I needed the feedback in real time, when it was highly relevant to the current situation and new plans and tweaks could be made to improve the next presentation, which was usually the next day. So, after several unsuccessful attempts at cajoling Tom to give his feedback at the group session, I let it go and moved on with the meeting.

Two weeks had passed by when I received Tom's feedback. Before receiving his e-mail, I had traveled from Denver to New York, then to the Netherlands, and then to India, and finally back home. Needless to say, I was exhausted. Tom's e-mail was short, but attached to it was a two-page, single-spaced Word document. As I read each heading and paragraph, I could feel myself unraveling and getting upset, but I also felt like I needed to apply the same principles I am asking you to apply: the foundational USE IT! mentality. Among Tom's statements in this very detailed e-mail were, "Todd has no skill as a facilitator." "Todd lacks the necessary business skill to have a thorough debrief." "Todd failed to use the debrief materials properly." "People were so dissatisfied with Todd that some left early." And the bad comments went on and on.

Admittedly, even though I was exhausted, I was very mad at Tom's comments and I forgot all about the "Me mad! Me mad! Me mad!" concept. I was fuming that Tom didn't share these comments just with me—adding insult to injury, on the same e-mail, he also copied the company's CEO, the global head of facilitations, the head of sales, the CFO, three random fellow facilitators, and three people I didn't even know. My anger was telling me to "reply all" and rip him apart. In fact, I almost felt the need to defend myself since Tom had discredited me to the top people of my company. It took everything I had for me to remain calm. I didn't know what to do or where to start. Did I need to defend myself? Did I need one of the team members from the presentation to be my witness and counteract Tom's statements? But the more I thought, the calmer I got. As I was finally more relaxed and had gathered myself, I remembered my own life's philosophy: USE IT! Understand the big picture; say, "my attitude dictates my experience"; evict your ego; I do not make assumptions; and take nothing personally. So in the end, I hit the "reply" button, rather than "reply all."

GETTING CONTROL OF THE ROADBLOCK

Just for a brief moment, think about yourself and put yourself in my position. Would you justifiably allow yourself to feel as though Tom's comments were personal in nature? Would you have hit the "reply all" button so you could justify yourself to everyone on the e-mail list, because of the personal nature of Tom's attack? Would you blast Tom in an e-mail to the CEO, trying to discredit him? It's easy for us to feel that we are being personally attacked by others. As in Tom's case, he felt he needed to blast me in public for reasons that were unknown to me. I could have certainly replied to everyone on his e-mail list and written a tirade of negativity, justification, and verbal slams about Tom. So I did what I am hoping you would do in this situation—I remembered that the big picture was to understand the client's needs and the attendees' and client's satisfaction about the presentation. It wasn't about Tom's satisfaction, even though we strive to be liked and please everyone in our lives. So, I did the only thing I could do: I checked my attitude. Then I put my ego in check and abandoned the need to win, thus, evicting my ego. The hard part was that I could have made wild assumptions, but I needed to understand why Tom was so upset and get the facts. The roadblock in my path to success and great presentations was Tom. Because I couldn't control Tom, I took control of the one person I could manage: myself. I wrote to Tom the following e-mail:

"Tom, thanks for your response. Let's set up a time to chat so I can address your concerns."

When I wrote Tom that e-mail, I had to abandon the thought

that this was personal. Even though I wanted to think Tom was an awful and vindictive person, I knew this wasn't personal. Tom and I had a phone call three days later. I was polite and civil with him, and, in order to get to what the real problem was, I asked Tom to take me through the document line by line so I could understand and shed some light on his concerns. As he explained his comments in the e-mail and where they stemmed from, I had to explain why I did what I did at the conference. First, I let him know that the company in question was not interested in the program for learning; they selected that particular program primarily for fun. Second, I told him about the client being very specific that I had to modify the program and no original client debrief materials were to be used in the presentation. The company wanted to make sure the participants would not feel as if they were supposed to learn something from the presentation but did not. Since I was explaining the behind-the-scenes facts of the presentation, I also told Tom the client wanted me to close out the four-day conference and make the audience feel like they didn't have to learn anything else. And, since this was the end of a very long and brain-straining four-day event, people had flights to catch and some had to leave early. Tom was silent. It took him a minute to process all of this information. After the initial shock wore off, he apologized. Tom's concern about my inability to facilitate a presentation turned into sheer horror about his assumptions about me. Worst of all, he had taken drastic actions to notify the CEO and other high-level people about my performance, based on his poor assumption of the event. It was clear to me that he had some explaining to do and apologies to send out to the recipients of his original e-mail. But the important piece of this new way of thinking is that you don't *need* someone like him to apologize. You become immune to offense because you do not take things personally.

As I hung up the phone, admittedly I felt relief. I felt relief not because Tom finally understood my context, but rather because I did not allow his reactive behavior to deter me in any way from a positive outcome. Yes, I was mad; but I also proved to myself once again that the USE IT! theory worked and I was the ONLY person in charge of how I felt or behaved. During the call with Tom, I decided not to mention to him that the same client had already called to book our company for the next year's event . . . and had requested that I be the facilitator. My decision to NOT add insult to injury for Tom is another layer of the overall mind-set of truly positive Disruptors like the one you want to become. We don't seek to punish people, even when we are correct in a situation. We refrain solely because it would mean our ego snuck back in and took over. Nothing is personal, and you don't need to win.

WHAT ABOUT YOUR BOSS?

When I tell that story to large conference audiences, people always want to know what happened with him and the CEO and the others copied on the e-mail. Were they upset? Did I have to write an explanation to all of those people about why Tom was wrong? What did I do about the fact that he sent the e-mail to all of those people? Simply put, I wrote to all of the people on the e-mail, saying that I would meet with Tom one-on-one and answer his questions about the conference. Since I was already booked by the same client for the next year's conference, it was obvious I did something right. No one ever questioned me on the matter; they each knew that if I was wrong, I would correct the mistake, and, if I wasn't wrong, I would explain to Tom what happened. By not REACTING and not taking this situation personally, I further strengthened the trust within the company and my team.

USE IT! NAVIGATES THE DISRUPTOR AROUND THE ROADBLOCKS IN LIFE

When we are driving from one destination to another and encounter a roadblock, we must take a detour; we do not reverse course or give up and go home. We find a way around the roadblock to get to our destination, and usually there is more than one way to do so. Life is filled—and will always be filled—with roadblocks. If, however, we learn to detour around them without letting them become stressful, we will find our way to the destination of our future disruptive self.

HOW TO APPLY THE USE IT! BUILDING BLOCKS

Apply: Understanding the Big Picture

But how do you refocus yourself on the big picture as you move through life on your way to new visions for yourself? The application is actually very simple and straightforward. When you are faced with some outside force, like a rude person whom you need to get past in order to achieve your vision, remind yourself of the most important element of this particular moment. For example, when writing this book I sometimes hit a wall where I just couldn't write any more. After spending so many hours on the focused activity of writing, it is easy to become distracted, which leads to frustration. I had a few choices: I could become frustrated because I am on a deadline to complete the book, and freak out about it by forcing myself to write when I am not ready mentally, OR I can calm down, relax, take a walk, and reset myself. Because I understand the big picture— completing this book, which is supposed to give you the tools to become a Disruptor—I need to make sure it has everything you need to succeed. That is my big picture; and by asking the question, "What is most important?" I keep myself focused.

Apply: Say, "My Attitude Dictates My Experience"

As we discussed in an earlier chapter, changing your attitude is often as simple as realizing that you have total control over your feelings and actions. You can control how you react to outside stressors in your life. I told you about the story of "Me mad!" in which you stop saying things like, "You are making me mad." When you say things like that, it demonstrates that you are completely giving up your control over your life to someone else, essentially so that others can control your life for you. And, as I have emphasized throughout this book, Disruptors DO NOT LET OTHERS CONTROL THEM. For the USE IT! mentality to work, you need to apply that same principle while simultaneously leveraging your attitude. In the case of the angry traveler at the airport, if he had only taken a moment to remember and fully understand that his big picture was to get to his destination, he would have had a very different experience. He would have been less likely to allow his attitude to respond with negativity and hostility toward the TSA agent's request. The right attitude is the most important element you can adopt to make your life and other challenges less stressful. So, for example, imagine that you are talking to your boss about an idea you have come up with to improve some part of your company—and I mean you are excited about this idea and you can't wait to tell your boss, in fact, you just want to start working on this idea now—but midway through the explanation to your boss, your conversation is interrupted by a co-worker. Naturally, this is absolutely upsetting. You may think that your co-worker is disrespectful or rude; and, worst of all, you may be hit with the feeling of fear, fear that the person will dominate your boss's attention and you and your idea will be disregarded. Now you could get flustered, start a barrage of passive-aggressive comments to make the co-worker go away, or exhibit some negative body language like crossing your arms and glaring at the person who stole your thunder. Or, even though you have been flooded by negative emotions, you can stay focused on getting your idea heard by the manager. When you turn your attitude to positively remembering to understand the big picture—which is getting your idea heard by the manager—you will be less likely to become agitated by the interruption, and then you can continue to relay your vision to your boss after the co-worker has left.

As you fully embrace them, you will start to feel each of the important building blocks in USE IT! stack on top of each other like a powerful foundation. So, next time, when you are faced with a difficult situation and you feel your attitude heading in the wrong direction, redirect it by asking, "What is my big picture?" This question will lead you to the conclusion that, for example, your big picture is not winning the argument about why people should not interrupt you at work, but actually accomplishing your original goal of communicating your new idea to your manager.

Apply: Evict Your Ego

I have studied my past for a long time in order to analyze why I have succeeded and why I have failed (or as I like to say—why I have had "learning opportunities"), to see where I could improve in the future. In the case of my need to win—in other words, my ego—I have found that I leverage the other blocks to guide me away from the "must win" mentality. If I am focused on understanding the big picture while putting my attitude in check, I will have a better chance to evict my ego. So, to evict your ego, you need to first build an awareness of when it takes you over and why. If you find yourself attempting to win in a situation or an argument, you need to stop immediately and refocus. In a relationship, it may look like this:

Her: "You never listen."
Him: "Yes, I do."

Her: "No, YOU don't."

Him: "I am listening right now" (he catches himself and thinks, "What is most important right now?" He answers his own thought with, "The big picture is most important: that I have a great relationship and actually try to listen to her.")

Her: "I am telling you something important."

Him: "I apologize. I thought I was listening; could you please repeat what you were saying? You have my full and complete attention."

Her: "Okay. Well, please focus on what I am saying."

Him: "Okay, I am all ears."

If you don't take responsibility for evicting your ego, who will? If you are in an argument, will you always wait for the other person to change his or her opinion or to come to a magical conclusion that you are right, or will you take control of your ego? If you remember the earlier foundational building blocks of USE IT! (understand the big picture and say, "my attitude dictates my experience"), you will be more equipped to keep your ego in check.

Apply: I Make No Assumptions

There is a simple method for removing assumptions from your mind. And even if you get off track, it will still serve to get you back on the path of making no more assumptions than you already have. That simple method is to ask yourself, "Do I know for certain my assumption is true?"

If the answer is no, and it most likely will be, then your assumption cannot be acted upon with certainty. That does not mean you shouldn't take a risk. In fact, if you look at the situation of Mike's assumptions about the weed industry, he could have done what I did: quit his job, jumped into the marijuana industry, and never looked back. He would do very well. But, with the information I gave him, he can now jump in more informed and better prepared for the difficult journey ahead. Imagine if you left your house this morning to drive from your town to a new city, but instead of getting directions, using your phone's mapping app, following your car's GPS, or asking anyone to tell you how to get there, you simply make the assumption that because the city is west, you should go west and, at some point, you will arrive at the city. That would not go well. Say you wanted to go to Los Angeles from Denver, but you ended up in San Francisco, over eight hours off course, all because you refused to get directions. I know some of the married couples out there know what I am talking about. You have that spouse, or you are that spouse, who gets lost and refuses to ask how to get somewhere due to not engaging the USE IT! mentality.

So, to engage the "I assume nothing" building block, you must gather information, ask the right questions, and qualify your assumptions. It will make the journey smoother and help you manage yourself in stressful situations.

Apply: This Is Not Personal

I created this building block of the USE IT! mentality last, for a reason. When you allow yourself to believe something is personal in any way, you allow yourself to become sucked into a vortex of reactive behavior in order to save your ego's need to win. The secret then in applying this block is in your ability to apply the others first. If you can refocus yourself on the things that matter most, understand the big picture; and if you then adjust your attitude by saying "my attitude dictates my experience," then you are set up to evict your ego. Once you get past these steps, you are then ready to qualify your assumptions about the situation (I make no assumptions). Believe me, over time, with a great deal of practice, the USE IT! mentality will help you to be successful. Once you have mastered these steps, you will be able to apply the final step easily, in this manner. As you review a stressful situation, a roadblock in your path, simply tell yourself, "This is not personal." Remember, when people lash out at you or attempt to stop you from acting on a disruptive dream, vision, or plan, they do so because of things inside of them that are not working; they do not do so because of you. They react in an attempt to destroy your situation only for a reason inside themselves about which you are unaware. This is one of the hardest steps for people to grasp at first, yet it is one of the easiest to implement once they do understand it. The truth is that NOTHING is personal, ever. You believing it to be personal is all that is causing a situation to be stressful.

THIS IS A LOT OF STUFF, TODD

Trust me, I know I have just thrown a lot of stuff (valuable stuff) your way. It's a lot to take in, especially added to all of the other information in this book. I've used this method daily for many years, and yet I've still given you examples of times when I didn't employ USE IT! as quickly or as completely as I should have. And what did it gain me? Nothing, except stress and frustration. So, take it a day at a time, a building block at a time if you must, and apply these steps. You, too, will get to the point where it gets easier and easier to USE IT! Remember, the purpose of these foundational building blocks is to help you over, around, and through the stressful life situations, the roadblocks, and the distractions that will inevitably get in your way as you forge your path toward your new vision. And what's more important than that?

CHAPTER 9

NOW WHAT?

As I look out at the audience, I can see that they are ready. I just took them on a journey of stories, anecdotes, and personal experiences, and bared my soul in a way designed to impact them forever. I worked the entire time to demonstrate that there was no need to be afraid of risk and, in fact, they should embrace it. *Disruptor.* This was a word they had heard in a passing conversation, saw it on a word-of-the-day calendar, or heard it used in some news sound bite to describe a tech start-up created by the latest twenty-something, or maybe it was a word they heard at work in some useless training class that never quite stuck. The word *Disruptor* was known, but the essence of the definition was never applied in their lives. Today, *Disruptor* took on a new meaning that is forever embedded in their minds. The goal was to empower, to uplift, and to help each participant understand how to unlock his or her inner fearless, powerful, forward-thinking, and risk-taking Disruptor.

From the stage, I notice a woman to my right wiping the tears from her eyes left over from the story of the man who carried his wife's remains home in a plastic Ziploc bag. To my left, a man is feverishly taking notes, and I can see his lips moving as he writes down the words, "USE IT!" The CEO of the company is sitting right in front of me and gives me a nod. After all, he had wanted me to teach his team that it was time to take their company to the next level, and he wanted them to understand that they all had a powerful part to play in that success. I see I have stirred different emotions in each one of the people in the audience, and now I need to make sure

I inspire them to want to change their lives, and their business for the better and have the courage to overcome obstacles in order to reach their goals. Especially when they leave the presentation.

I was about to close the talk, but a surprising thought enters my mind: "Did I give them all of the tools to reach their goals successfully?" I look down at my notes and recap the past several hours: we've been loud, excited, sad, and happy, and I have heard laughter, applause, and cheers fill the room. It's time . . . the close. Not a close for me, but a close for them. A final moment of answering the million-dollar question, "Now what?" Now, how do they go back to their current lives and situations and still have the strength and motivation to reach their visions? Now, how do they go back and look at those previously scary risks in a new way? While they sat in the audience, they completed a learning journey that had been hypothetical for them. They hadn't yet had the time to go out into the world and apply the exercises in order to change their lives. For the audience, the end of my presentation has marked the beginning of their application of the tools I've given them. Their disruptive journey was just beginning. I walk to the front of the stage, look straight ahead, and say, "Now what? . . . Now, you have a choice to make."

The end of a keynote speech, for me, is tough. It's tough because I put everything I have into it. I feel a huge sense of responsibility to give an audience all my heart, passion, and learning. I want to always exceed their expectations, because I know I do not get a second chance. Nearly every time I close out these discussions, no matter if there are two thousand people in the audience or twenty people, I am moved by emotions and thoughts about what else I can give them. How else can I inspire them to go to the next level? When I stand there on stage and hundreds or thousands of people are listening, taking notes, and are all ready to learn, I feel an overwhelming sense of responsibility, mainly because many speakers deliver talks and, to them, the event is just a transaction. They speak, the audience listens, the speaker collects payment, and everyone moves on with life. Not so for me. I make each delivery of supreme importance. Those people in the audience spent time to get to the conference, they took time from their busy schedules, they opened their minds to the new lessons, and they listened and participated for over ninety minutes. I asked them to take a risk the entire time to look inward at who they truly are, what drives their decisions, and how can they improve. I have disrupted them. Even with all of that preparation and passion to help and inspire others, I can only hope my words will help them change their lives for the better. I believe, if I connect to them, my lessons could potentially impact not just them personally, but every person they come into contact with for the rest of their lives. I want to build a sense of urgency within them, as I want to now build a sense of urgency in you.

DON'T BE THE FERRARI ON THE FREEWAY

My desire to be sharper and more effective with each audience, client, and person I come into contact with stems from me never wanting to simply be a Ferrari on the freeway. Confused? A Ferrari sounds really cool, right? In fact, if I gave most people a Ferrari to drive around their neighborhood, they would enjoy it and feel very excited to show it off. Some people purchase a car like a Ferrari as a symbol of "making it" in the world of business and finance, or simply to prove to others they have made it personally. So, then, why would I NOT want to be a Ferrari on the freeway, metaphorically speaking? Back in 2008, after my car accident and before I designed the strategy to convince the CEO of the company I worked for at the time to move me into a higher-level leadership role, he gave me a powerful lesson that still resonates with me today.

We were sitting in a small restaurant with few people around. I had asked to meet with him, my mentor, our CEO, to discuss how I could add more value to the company. In the midst of recovery from my accident, I was still regaining my confidence. I was speaking again, and my talent was shining through once more, but he was a figure I greatly respected. He and his abilities also intimidated me as a leader. Prior to building his own company, he had been a senior leader for a massive company with billion-dollar revenues, so asking my next question felt risky. When I asked the question, "How can I add more value?" the answer he gave me etched itself in my mind forever and made the risk of asking it well worth it. "Todd, you are like a Ferrari on the freeway." Right away, I was elated! "Boom!" I thought to myself, "I am a Ferrari and he sees it. Yes! I am a damn Ferrari on that freeway. I am sleek and fast. I like that!" But as he continued, it was apparent that I was missing the point.

"What I mean is, Todd, if you were a Ferrari, your talent as a speaker, personality, leader, etc., is sharp when compared to all of the other common cars on the freeway. On a busy roadway, the Ferrari stands out because it is surrounded by Toyotas, Chevrolets, and Hondas, but that is not what we need from you." By this time, I was shocked. I could not decide whether the Ferrari was a good thing or not, but he definitely had my attention. "Now, Todd, where I need you to drive is on the Ferrari racing circuit, with the other Ferraris; but if I put you on the racing circuit with only talent, you would be destroyed. It is only through skill merged with talent that a Ferrari driver can win championships on the racing circuit. That is where I need you to be; I need you to take your talent, the Ferrari, and hone it, add skill to it, do different things with it, and become so skilled that, when you exit the freeway to drive onto the track, you will terrify the other drivers. Your skill will be so advanced, it will scare them; and your talent will add winning fuel." So when I take the stage to deliver a presentation, I have worked on the skill needed to take my talent to the next level. What that means to you, the participant, is that I am more effective. My vision of helping you is made possible because I view myself as that Ferrari on the racetrack. And this is what I want you to now do for yourself. When you view yourself as a talented person with great ideas, that is only the start. You must then see yourself as needing to take your talent and adding to it with skill, but skill takes time and is risky to achieve. It is risky because to gain skill requires you to ask people to give you feedback. It requires you to embrace learning in a new way. You will be forced to see yourself as growing rather than as complete, and once you see yourself this way, as a Ferrari needing skill to become faster on a racetrack, your life starts to change. You become hungry for growth and expansion, both professionally and personally.

Coincidentally, this book feels very similar to my presentations and workshops, only bigger. I have taken you on this journey to present you with lessons, ideas, and tools to become a Disruptor in your own life. So, I feel that same overwhelming emotion. Have I given you, the reader, everything you need to go out and accomplish your visions and goals? When I look at the previous chapters and their content, I feel that I have provided you with everything I can, but the hardest part of this journey to a better life depends on you, the reader. I hope you devoted time and continue to push yourself to return to the lessons to work on the applications, practicing them, and making the concepts stick in your everyday life. But before we end this chapter and finish the book, I will highlight a few important pieces of connected lessons, as well as give you a few more tools to help you take bigger calculated risks during your time on this racing circuit called life. Let's start with something obvious.

LIFE OWES YOU NOTHING—
NOW TAKE A RISK AND GO GET EVERYTHING

Becoming a Disruptor, even if it seems so small to you, means you have chosen to never go back to who you were before. It's just not possible. You have expanded your mind with new possibilities, ways that may or may not work, or have created new ideas. Whatever you were before this book, if you have applied the concepts, then you are altered. For some, it will be as simple as finding a new passion to pursue. For others, it will be changing careers or starting a business. You may start a workout plan or a diet and stick to it; you may start to focus and find a path to something you want to do in your life; or you may find a hobby. For those of you who are already at the top of your career, it may be how you can retire feeling fulfilled. For others who are already successful, this may be going to a level or taking a risk you felt you should put off until "later." There are limitless possibilities, and all you have to do is go out there and find a way to get them. If you are ready to take life by the horns, there is something you have already learned. All Disruptors learn it: life owes you nothing! Life is not about luck; it's about vision, persistence, and motivation to go get what you want. To be a Disruptor as I define it means you are now seeking ways to *get* breakthrough results, not waiting for them.

Too often we get stuck in this mind-set: life owes me. Every day may seem like you're back to the grind and you feel that you'll never "get a break" or you're "unlucky." You may keep telling yourself you will try harder next time, or when you feel it's the right time, or when you are making "X" amount of money, or driving "Y" car. You may also feel that you have tried and tried, but nothing is working out, since life has not yet handed you all the good stuff. In these moments, you have to be fearless to think outside the box, to be brave and speak up in a meeting, to go and talk to someone you have been dying to talk to, to apply for that new position, or to just start talking to people who are where you want to be to see how they got there and if you will actually like it when you get to that place. So put an end to the victim story of me, me, me (or more accurately, boo, hoo, hoo), and use the lessons in this book to actually take ownership over your own fulfilling experiences in life. Because getting up, eating, going to work, leaving work, eating again, watching some useless entertainment, going to bed, and starting all over again the next day may not be your dream life. Sure, you may have many add-ons to this boring description of life, like kids, grandkids, a terrible boss, or the gym, but every day that you get up and just keep trucking along, you are wasting time. Life will end, most of the time unfulfilled. But all of that is in your hands—how you see it all, how you thrive within your experiences, and how you decide to see the world.

WATCH FOR NAYSAYERS

If you are like most people who read this or who attend my presentations, you are excited. That's a good thing. You will start to share this with others and begin to make changes. Just remember, on your journey to a better you, some of those around you will perhaps try to stop you from arriving at whatever destination you have envisioned. How far you go, with or without anyone's support, is up to you. When you decide that you are going to live your life the way I have outlined in this book, you will need to put on your big boy or big girl pants and get ready to approach life from a new perspective, because anyone who has not experienced the information in this book could be a source of "You can't" or "You shouldn't" language. You will need to approach the next phase of your life's achievements without excuses, without blaming others for your challenges, and, overall, in a way that makes you impervious to the negative opinions of others. Remember, you are in charge of you.

YOUR WHY

Now you may say, "But, Todd, I am happy where I am." If that's the case, here is my question to you: "Why are you reading this? Are you helping a friend?" Because if you have the amazing life you have always wanted and it is enough for you, you would not be here, turning these pages. You are craving something more from life. Something to fill that hole in you that makes you feel like you should do more, have more, or be somewhere else. There's a VERY specific reason you picked up the book. If you are still wondering what that reason is, you may need to go back to "Your 'Why'" (chapter 3). Your reasons for doing everything in your life must be defined. As I discussed in that chapter, you will either find a very Intentional Why that drives your decisions in each area of life, or you will continue to let the Habitual Why drive you.

THERE GOT ME HERE, AND HERE GETS ME THERE

Another important tool is to remember where you came from, *all* of it, because every past situation, perceived failure, risk taken, and decision made has gotten you where you are right now. It may be hard to believe, especially if you view your past as difficult, but every happy and every sad moment has guided you to where you are today. You are reading this book in this place—"Here"; and now you are preparing for a new place—"There." To add perspective, as I sit here typing, I take breaks and look up to see my amazing fiancée and the love of my life, Diana, sitting across the table. She is editing the last chapter I just finished: USE IT! I hear her laughing at some points, and then I see the beauty in her teary eyes as she reads an emotionally touching part. I take a moment, look around the house, and take in the coziness and beauty of our home; I hear the birds singing outside, and feel the cool Colorado breeze. These moments may seem unimportant or mundane, but to me they are priceless, because I feel a sense of connectedness to it all. I am happy and, most of all, fulfilled. It's the end of August, summer is ending and the current temperature is only seventy degrees. Our kids are coming home soon, and the week will be filled with laughter, fun, school, and work, as well as the many new exciting things that will present themselves throughout the upcoming days. It occurs to me that I am fulfilled, but certainly not finished. I enjoy the journey, but I still see the vision of more experiences.

I remember like it was yesterday, that drive to Chicago to become an entertainer. I remember the times on stage all over the world. My thoughts bounce to the many corporate successes and learning opportunities. I think about the decision to become a marijuana-industry leader and all the media attention that came with it. Then I look again at Diana, and I realize that all of it led me right here. I could not be exactly where I am right now if I had made different choices or had changed my mind about what I wanted to do in my life. I would not be here if I quit when things were hard, and I would not be here if I stopped when I finally reached one of my visions. In life, no matter how many experiences you have or how many goals you fulfill, you will never be completely done. If I had been content with reaching just one of my dreams, I would have missed out on all of the other experiences that make me who I am today. All those risks were required for me to grow and learn, and all of the mistakes colored my life. You must never forget that everything lies within you—your dreams, your aspirations, and your motivation to go for it. It is all sitting in you, waiting to spring forth. Go for whatever you want in your life. Look around the place you are in right now—do you love any of it? Do you love your career, your relationship, your education, your life, or any other situations or things that surround you? If you love even one of those things, then you must see the past as a series of disruptive moments that brought you here, where you are right now. Even more important, is there anything you don't love about your life? I have worked with and coached very successful leaders who are miserable in their personal lives because they haven't fulfilled a dream of theirs. It's called being human, and this is the moment to go in a new direction. Just as your past has guided you to this place and time that encompasses all of your experiences and tangible possessions, beginning right now you will start a new journey that will guide you to a place in the future. But now you have a conscious choice to make: what do you want in your future? You are free to create new positive disruptive risks taking you on a new journey that may take two months, five years, or an entire lifetime. The best part is that you can start right now; remember to respect the journey from here to there, because it moves your life in the direction you choose. The perspective that your past got you here, and that your here takes you there, is the focus you need to change any behaviors so that they drive you to a future of TOTAL fulfillment.

DON'T DO IT BECAUSE IT'S EASY; DO IT BECAUSE YOU CAN AND MUST

When I turned fifteen, all I could think about was driving. For an impatient teen like me, having a car and driving was the most critical task on my very short list of "must haves" in my life. At the time, money was tight, so I knew a *new* car was not going to happen. Nevertheless, I begged my dad for a car. I would ask him over and over again to help me get a car, but he would just shrug it off, knowing the cost was an issue. Finances weren't a picnic for my mother, either; she was busy rebuilding her life with a new husband and additional kids. She didn't have any money for a car. As my dream for a car grew and grew, I started to see the dire financial issues: on one side was my father and stepmom rebuilding their financial well-being, and on the other side was my mother and stepfather doing the same. This was the unintended consequence of having divorced parents: everyone, including me, had to rebuild their lives; and it took time. Unfortunately for me, an easy way to get a car in time for my sixteenth birthday was simply not presenting itself and, of course, I was panicked.

Then, one day, my father had a car brought to the house. It wasn't just any car; it was an old, white VW Bug with a black hardtop. The inside looked like a rabid squirrel had attacked it to find the last morsel of food, and the engine looked like it had run into an immovable object at about a hundred miles an hour. The wreck was completely nonfunctioning. I was surprised that we would buy a car that wasn't working—and I mean light-years away from ever working. Nevertheless, my dad paid around $125 to buy the car. It was for me. I know this will seem ungrateful, but I was not excited. I felt like, "Well, I guess I have something I could call a car", but the bigger problem was that I felt like it would forever sit in the driveway as a heap of junk. I failed in that brief moment to see the perspective and the point that my father was making, which was to take the journey into restoring it. He took a risk to give me an experience unlike any I had had up to that point in life and, being the teenager I was, I did not immediately grasp the importance. After I stared at it for a while and felt my driving experience being shattered, I finally looked up at my dad, who was patiently standing next to the garage and, with defeat in my voice, I asked, "Now what?" To which he replied, "Now we rebuild it." And that was all he said. I could only imagine the shock and confusion on my face when he said we were going to rebuild it. I was speechless. This car was dead, actually deader than dead; it was a murdered relic from the past for which resurrection seemed out of the realm of possibility. One light was falling out, the interior was seemingly beyond repair, and the sheer sight of the paint job made my panic worse. I almost said the words, "We can't." As I inhaled to get the phrase out, I opened and shut my mouth, because I remembered (as you should from my discussion on this earlier) that my father would have no part of any phrase with the word *can't* in it. So the only thing I could do was make a commitment to my father and to myself to rebuild and restore this heap of scrap metal. Isn't that a metaphor for all of us in our lives? Some situations seem hopeless, and we can feel like the only thing in front of us is a heap of junk. We see any restoration as impossible. Sadly, we can also see ourselves this way as we grow older, work longer, and go through more situations in life. It's easy for you to feel like I did that day: it's hopeless, I want to scrap it. And that's when you need to push forward using the lessons from this book.

We started working on the car the following day. We forged on, day in and day out, working on that beat-up car and dealing with all of the many challenges in our path. Because I am left-handed and my father is right-handed, we fought constantly about what was the right direction to properly turn bolts. The two of us—my father, who is first a thinker and then a doer, and me, a doer while thinking—created quite some disagreements and arguments about how to approach each task needed to repair and rebuild the car. Even though we had our differences, we kept pushing forward on the car's repairs and saw days turning into months. This wasn't a one-day or even a one-month task. The more we fixed and repaired systems or structures on the car, the more challenges seemed to arise. I had never experienced hard and tedious effort like I did with my dad while toiling away on that car. On weekends, we would spend the day and often go late into the night working on one small problem that turned out to be huge. On weekdays, I would come home from school to find myself jumping right into dismantling a seat or installing new wiring. Even after months of hard work, I still couldn't imagine how this car would ever become something drivable, let alone a vehicle I would want to pick up a date with! Each task seemed daunting.

Every day for a year, I would go to school with banged-up fingers, while my father would head to his job as a leader of his company with the same scratches and bruises. It seemed that every day we hit a new roadblock, from the simple broken bolt here and there, to the more challenging wiring situation that caused the lights to come on only when we turned on the radio. (That actually happened.) On this year-long journey, I learned quite a bit about my dad. He is a man of few words, and the lessons I gained came not by what he said but by how he approached and worked on the project. I learned that he could get frustrated with my lack of care for detail, so I strived to be more careful and specific with the task at hand. I realized that striving to meet his level of attention to detail was actually the best learning experience, especially when you take a little extra time to wire your accelerator cable. I watched my father take on parts of the car restoration that he literally had no idea how he would achieve, only to completely solve the challenge in a way that made it better. That year, he taught me about what you do when you hit an obstacle while you are working on a project. I had to reword his phrasing for the rest of my life's challenges and this book, but the message was the same: when life serves up a roadblock, you first throw a hammer at the wall, then you walk outside to "think," then you find a way to solve your challenge, and, most importantly, you don't ever quit. At least he never threw the hammer my way; well, okay, perhaps once, but I am told it was by accident.

Back then, I didn't realize we were rebuilding that car not because it was easy but because we could, and we needed to in order for me to have a car on my sixteenth birthday. When I think about the time, money, effort, and energy my father and I put into that car, I gain renewed respect for him as a father. He never gave up on the car, and especially on me, during that year. You should look at your life the same way. If you want to do something and find a way to live a more fulfilled life, then you will need to realize that sometimes you need to reset, reboot, and keep going no matter how hard it gets. If I had allowed the many challenges of the car to be more painful than the Intentional Why of having it, then I would have failed. If my father had not been so dedicated to rebuilding the car for me and helping me find my freedom as a teenager, we would have quit the first time his bare hand slipped off a bolt in the garage and slammed into a jagged edge of metal on the vehicle. It inspired in me the realization that when you have a strong vision and motivation, you keep going—no matter how many cuts and bruises you get—in order to reach the final goal.

So, you see, *You, Disrupted* was not about me at all. It was always about you. If you take on life the way we took on that challenge of a total car restoration, then you will get the same results we accomplished. My dad took the risk to buy it in the first place, knowing it would be a huge challenge. We refused to give up, were always led with a sense of urgency, had a strong vision, built a plan of execution, and kept our motivation to finish, no matter what. After a year, we had completely restored a destroyed, old vehicle that was on its way to a junkyard. Toward the end, everyone was cheering for the project's success; even my stepfather got involved in the restoration of the Bug. I see him now as a Disruptive Influencer because he knew how to paint vehicles professionally, and he was the one who finished the car with an amazing candy-apple red finish. On my sixteenth birthday, I passed my driver's exam, but I was more excited and proud that I got to drive a symbol of disruptive thinking that would stick with me forever. Like you, I wanted something. For me, at the time, it was a car, and even though I did not know how and when a way would present itself, I never lost hope that I would reach my vision. And, just like many times in my life and perhaps yours as well, we all have to have the help of a powerful Disruptive Influencer and Disruptor. For me, it was my father, and my stepfather.

WHAT'S YOUR CHOICE?

You will have a choice just like we did back then on that project. You can take an easy road and simply not do the most important work: work on your own self. You could ask others or look on the Internet for some quick fix to your current problem. You can avoid risks, either personal or professional. But what will you do when life gets diffi-cult? Will you quit and blame everyone and everything else because you failed? Or will you take ownership over your existence, apply the lessons from this book to your life, repeatedly, until you get what you want or where you want to go? As I stated earlier, when my dad and I set out to restore that old Volkswagen, we did not accomplish it all in a day. We had no idea how we would do it. We simply took one part that needed attention and worked on it until we figured it out. Was it hard? Yes, it was hard—and frustrating—but with time and each new step we took to get closer to our vision, it got easier, because we knew every challenge would be solved eventually. You will have to do the same. Take each chapter and apply the lessons to the smallest challenges in your life until you are comfortable with taking on larger ones. Soon, with all this practice, you will become the Disruptor you wanted to be when you picked up this book.

NOT WHAT YOU EXPECTED IS OFTEN JUST WHAT YOU NEED

When I joined the marijuana industry, it was not what I expected—as I have mentioned, the pace was faster than I had anticipated and the work and dedication required were on another level. The risks I had to take were terrifying. But that is the point. When you become more disruptive, you will encounter things you don't expect. The unknown and the unique are all expressions of a chance to improve yourself. The problem with resisting the unexpected and always playing it safe is often a lost chance to encounter the exact thing we need. Embrace the unexpected and see it as learning and growing toward your goal. I could never have guessed that I would be on major news outlets all over the world or that I would have taken that first company to the largest brand status in such a short time. I did not imagine that I would eventually go on to create a technology company, with a team of dedicated people, cofounders, and users of the product, which connected hundreds of thousands of people all over the world with a shared interest. But I did, and High There! became a reality. I promise you this, you will also do some amazing things in both huge and small ways.

At every stage, because I believed in disrupting so much, I kept pushing toward a fulfilling future. Over time, my fear was eclipsed by an overwhelming sense of purpose, my Intentional Why. My mother's past experiences and pain with cancer, as well as my own understanding that my life had an end point, drove me to push harder and faster than others, without apology. The way my mother not only survived that experience but found ways to thrive in it stays with me to this day. My sister continues to be a source of inspiration and love, as she is now in a new stage of her life, living with my mother, working, and seeking new experiences each day. I booted and rebooted my life constantly as the need arose, and I never lived in regret or doubt.

IMPACT

Everything you do, say, and become in your lifetime, no matter your profession or location in the world, will impact every person around you. And their interaction with the people around them will impact the world. You have a responsibility to everyone to be the best and most fulfilled person you can be so that you can help and inspire others. You also have the responsibility to be the best and most fulfilled person for yourself, so you can enjoy your life to the fullest. However, I will not be able to do this for you, to get you where you want to go—because this is your journey. The next step for you is a choice. Because your "Now what?" is actually: NOW! Right now. Right this minute. It's time. Time to take on the excuseless life and become something new. It's time for you NOW to implement the lessons from this book and go forward to success. And above all it's time to take a risk for yourself.

RISK

Throughout the book, it was my intention to constantly remind you about risk. If someone asked me to define the book with another word besides *Disruption*, I would definitely say *Risk*. Most of our lives are spent in a feeling of crisis that creates perpetual reactivity. As outlined in chapter 3, we jump from one bad decision to another in that time of crisis due to our Habitual Why. I'm asking you to redefine what crisis is in your life and how that relates to risk. If you redefine it to be a sense of urgency that arises from passion and intentional purpose so that you can live a Disruptor's life filled with more calculated risks, then I think you are on the right track.

We are taught to be afraid and to stress out about everything—sometimes even things that haven't even happened yet. Our fix for that? A default into nonsense ideas that have no action attached to them. For example, "Cheer up, everything will be great," or "Smile, you will be happy," have no action for you to take so that you can get out of the rut. Those platitudes are emotional fortune cookies designed to make you feel better without giving you the recipe for really *getting* better. We need to figure out our Intentional Why and then use it to disrupt our life by taking risk. We need more doing and less procrastination when it comes to something that's important to us. Every single one of us is running out of time to reach our dreams, and the more time that passes, when we don't even take one step in the right direction, the more we feel unfulfilled. So what do you do in those moments when you want to go for something big in your life or at work, but you don't know how or are scared to challenge yourself by taking a risk?

Imagine a bear named Crisis—not a cuddly fellow that will be nice to you, but an angry and hungry bear that sees you as his dinner. Now imagine that the bear is chasing you; that feeling is a feeling of a crisis. Your adrenaline is rushing through your body, your heartbeat is through the roof, and the only thing that you can do is run toward the cliff in front of you and jump, because this is your only chance of survival, your perpetual reactivity. You do this not out of fear but out of a sense of removing yourself from danger. As you approach the end of your path, you throw yourself off of the cliff and out of the paws of the bear. From another perspective, this is how true ideas begin to be born. Imagine if the cliff was the opportunity for you to take your life in a different direction, and the bear was the push to actually take that risk—the opportunity to grow. So what do you do when you fall? Well, you can find out what's at the bottom of the cliff, or maybe you will learn how to fly. When you feel the need to push yourself, imagine that your survival depends on reaching that goal or vision. Only then, when you feel like you are in the crisis mentality of your choosing, will you start to take bigger risks to come up with big and amazing ideas for how to reach your vision. You can now begin to create your own crisis feeling around your need to expand and elevate your life experience. If you lack motivation, think of the bear. That bear is your death chasing you, but that cliff is the freedom to be whatever you want to be.

Risk, to anyone who masters this teaching, is exciting. We love something that contains a degree of adrenaline, because it means we will also have an opportunity to learn. Risk is not scary to a Disruptor, which you hopefully have become by now. It is a necessary moment, to get us over the fear of doing and into the next phase of action and a thrilling experience. Don't avoid risk: find it, define it, remember the lessons to navigate it, and USE IT!

BEFORE I SAY GOOD-BYE . . .

Just last week, right before finishing this book, I was giving a workshop to a group of leaders and entrepreneurs. After the workshop, one of them sent me an e-mail that simply said, "Todd, this workshop was not what I expected, but it was just what I needed. Thank you." That's what I hope you take from this book. While it may not have been what you expected, I do hope it was exactly what you needed.

NOTES

CHAPTER 1: DISRUPTION IS NOT DESTRUCTION

1. E. D. Kantor, C. D. Rehm, J. S. Haas, A. T. Chan, and E. L. Giovannucci, "Trends in Prescription Drug Use among Adults in the United States from 1999–2012," *JAMA* 314, no. 17 (2015): 1818–31.

2. Insurance Institute for Highway Safety, Highway Loss Data Institute, "General Statistics," http://www.iihs.org/iihs/topics/t/general-statistics/fatality facts/state-by-state-overview (accessed January 20, 2017).

3. Centers for Disease Control and Prevention, "Accidents or Unintentional Injuries," last updated September 15, 2016, https://www.cdc.gov/nchs/fastats/accidental-injury.htm (accessed January 20, 2017).

CHAPTER 2: BEING A DISRUPTIVE INFLUENCER

1. *The Late Late Show with Craig Ferguson*, episode no. 1891, aired March 11, 2014.

2. Richard Stimson, "The Wright Brothers Plus One; The Influence of Their Sister," Wright Stories, http://wrightstories.com/the-wright-brothers-plus-one-the-influence-of-their-sister/ (accessed January 20, 2017).

3. Ibid.

CHAPTER 4: A BAG OR A BOX . . . TIME IS TICKING

1. Sanjay Gupta, "Dr. Sanjay Gupta: It's Time for Medical Marijuana Revolution," CNN, April 20, 2015, http://www.cnn.com/2015/04/16/opinions/medical-marijuana-revolution-sanjay-gupta/ (accessed January 22, 2017).

2. *The 11th Hour*, CNN, "Legal Marijuana Becoming Big, Profitable Business in Colorado," aired December 2, 2013; transcript available at http://edition.cnn.com/TRANSCRIPTS/1312/02/elhr.01.html (accessed January 22, 2017).

ABOUT THE AUTHOR

Todd Mitchem is the CEO of TMC; he and his team work with organizations and industries of all sizes, in every part of the world, bringing out hidden potential while teaching how to change the way we all think about business, government, working together for common goals, and—most important—positively disrupting risk. All of his teachings can be applied immediately and have a unique and powerful ability to reshape business and personal lives. For his expertise, Todd has delivered more than two thousand presentations globally, and he has been featured on every major news outlet in the world. Todd believes that everyone has a different learning style, and that's why he also hosts workshops and presentations, teaching people of all walks of life the core lessons from *You, Disrupted*. He has leveraged his unique ability to deliver a message in a way that inspires and changes lives. Todd is a captivating and electrifying speaker, transferring his knowledge and radically different views spanning many industries, by delivering motivational, bold, and edgy presentations, which not only inspire and enthuse the crowd but also provide them with tools and real-life examples to reach their goals. You can learn more about Todd and book him as a presenter in your area at www.toddmitchem.com.